Sustainable Development in Africa-EU Relations

The European Union has been one of the most vocal advocates of 'sustainable development', particularly in its dealings with developing countries. Even prior to the formulation of the UN Sustainable Development Goals (SDGs), the EU has insisted upon the need for sustainable approaches to poverty reduction and economic growth in the Global South. When examining EU relations with African countries as part of the African, Caribbean and Pacific (ACP) group, however, it becomes clear that the translation of Europe's sustainability discourse into practice is highly problematic. Notably, there are concerns that the EU's free market approach to development – embodied in its EPA trade deals – is incompatible with genuine, pro-poor forms of sustainable growth. Moreover, the EU is often seen as a hegemonic actor whose trade and aid interventions in Africa often do more to perpetuate poverty than to ameliorate it. This book casts a critical light on Africa-EU relations with regards to the EU's sustainability pledges. It does this through looking at an array of issues – not least trade, aid, the environment, and democratic institutions. In this vein, the book poses a challenge to EU trade and development discourse in the era of the UN SDGs.

The chapters in this book were originally published as a special issue of *Third World Thematics: A TWQ Journal.*

Mark Langan is senior lecturer in International Politics at Newcastle University, UK. His research examines the intersection of global trade and international development. He is particularly interested in EU trade and development co-operation with the African, Caribbean and Pacific states and studies of moral political economy.

Sophia Price is head of Politics and International Relations at Leeds Beckett University, UK. Her research focuses on feminist political economy, pro-poor development strategies and the external relations of the European Union, particularly its trade and aid relations with the Africa, Pacific and Caribbean Group of States.

ThirdWorlds

Edited by Shahid Qadir, *University of London, UK*

ThirdWorlds will focus on the political economy, development and cultures of those parts of the world that have experienced the most political, social, and economic upheaval, and which have faced the greatest challenges of the postcolonial world under globalisation: poverty, displacement and diaspora, environmental degradation, human and civil rights abuses, war, hunger, and disease.

ThirdWorlds serves as a signifier of oppositional emerging economies and cultures ranging from Africa, Asia, Latin America, Middle East, and even those 'Souths' within a larger perceived North, such as the U.S. South and Mediterranean Europe. The study of these otherwise disparate and discontinuous areas, known collectively as the Global South, demonstrates that as globalisation pervades the planet, the south, as a synonym for subalterity, also transcends geographical and ideological frontier.

Recent titles in the series include:

Corruption in the Aftermath of War
Edited by Jonas Lindberg and Camilla Orjuela

Everyday Energy Politics in Central Asia and the Caucasus
Citizens' Needs, Entitlements and Struggles for Access
Edited by David Gullette and Jeanne Féaux de la Croix

The UN and the Global South, 1945 and 2015
Edited by Thomas G. Weiss and Pallavi Roy

The Green Economy in the Global South
Edited by Stefano Ponte and Daniel Brockington

Food Sovereignty
Convergence and Contradictions, Condition and Challenges
Edited by Eric Holt-Giménez, Alberto Alonso-Fradejas, Todd Holmes and Martha Jane Robbins

The International Politics of Ebola
Edited by Anne Roemer-Mahler and Simon Rushton

Rising Powers and South-South Cooperation
Edited by Kevin Gray and Barry K. Gills

The 'Local Turn' in Peacebuilding
The Liberal Peace Challenged
Edited by Joakim Öjendal, Isabell Schierenbeck and Caroline Hughes

China's Contingencies and Globalization
Edited by Changgang Guo, Liu Debin and Jan Nederveen Pieterse

The Power of Human Rights/The Human Rights of Power
Edited by Louiza Odysseos and Anna Selmeczi

Class Dynamics of Development
Edited by Jonathan Pattenden, Liam Campling, Satoshi Miyamura and Benjamin Selwyn

Third World Approaches to International Law
Edited by Amar Bhatia, Usha Natarajan, John Reynolds and Sujith Xavier

Fragility, Aid, and State-building
Understanding Diverse Trajectories
Edited by Rachel M. Gisselquist

Rural Transformations and Agro-Food Systems
The BRICS and Agrarian Change in the Global South
Edited by Ben M. McKay, Ruth Hall and Juan Liu

Sustainable Development in Africa-EU Relations
Edited by Mark Langan and Sophia Price

New Mechanisms of Participation in Extractive Governance
Between Technologies of Governance and Resistance Work
Edited by Esben Leifsen, Maria-Therese Gustafsson, Maria A. Guzmán-Gallegos and Almut Schilling-Vacaflor

For more information about this series, please visit: https://www.routledge.com/series/TWQ

Sustainable Development in Africa-EU Relations

Edited by
Mark Langan and Sophia Price

Routledge
Taylor & Francis Group
LONDON AND NEW YORK

First published 2018
by Routledge
2 Park Square, Milton Park, Abingdon, Oxon, OX14 4RN, UK

and by Routledge
711 Third Avenue, New York, NY 10017, USA

Routledge is an imprint of the Taylor & Francis Group, an informa business

British Library Cataloguing in Publication Data
A catalogue record for this book is available from the British Library

ISBN 13: 978-0-8153-9649-9

Typeset in Myriad Pro
by RefineCatch Limited, Bungay, Suffolk

Publisher's Note
The publisher accepts responsibility for any inconsistencies that may have arisen during the conversion of this book from journal articles to book chapters, namely the possible inclusion of journal terminology.

Contents

Citation Information

The chapters in this book were originally published in *Third World Thematics: A TWQ Journal*, volume 1, issue 4 (2016). When citing this material, please use the original page numbering for each article, as follows:

Chapter 1

The EU and 'pro-poor' contributions to sustainable development in the post-2015 consensus
Mark Langan and Sophia Price
Third World Thematics: A TWQ Journal, volume 1, issue 4 (2016), pp. 431–436
https://doi.org/10.1080/23802014.2016.1327797

Chapter 2

Framing the climate-development nexus in the European Union
Frederik De Roeck, Sarah Delputte and Jan Orbie
Third World Thematics: A TWQ Journal, volume 1, issue 4 (2016), pp. 437–453
https://doi.org/10.1080/23802014.2016.1286947

Chapter 3

Managing neo-liberalisation through the Sustainable Development Agenda: the EU-ACP trade relationship and world market expansion
Sophia Price and Alex Nunn
Third World Thematics: A TWQ Journal, volume 1, issue 4 (2016), pp. 454–469
https://doi.org/10.1080/23802014.2016.1287528

Chapter 4

Regional encounters: explaining the divergent responses to the EU's support for regional integration in Africa, the Caribbean and Pacific
Tony Heron and Peg Murray-Evans
Third World Thematics: A TWQ Journal, volume 1, issue 4 (2016), pp. 470–489
https://doi.org/10.1080/23802014.2016.1281089

Chapter 5

Equal partnership between unequal regions? Assessing deliberative parliamentary debate in ACP-EU relations
Sarah Delputte and Yentyl Williams
Third World Thematics: A TWQ Journal, volume 1, issue 4 (2016), pp. 490–507
https://doi.org/10.1080/23802014.2016.1309257

Chapter 6

Feigned ambition. Analysing the emergence, evolution and performance of the ACP Group of States
Niels Keijzer
Third World Thematics: A TWQ Journal, volume 1, issue 4 (2016), pp. 508–525
https://doi.org/10.1080/23802014.2016.1309257

Chapter 7

Promoting sustainable development or legitimising free trade? Civil society mechanisms in EU trade agreements
Jan Orbie, Deborah Martens, Myriam Oehri and Lore Van den Putte
Third World Thematics: A TWQ Journal, volume 1, issue 4 (2016), pp. 526–546
https://doi.org/10.1080/23802014.2016.1294032

Chapter 8

The EU's Economic Partnership Agreements with Africa: 'Decent Work' and the challenge of trade union solidarity
Stephen R. Hurt
Third World Thematics: A TWQ Journal, volume 1, issue 4 (2016), pp. 547–562
https://doi.org/10.1080/23802014.2016.1305871

Chapter 9

Oil and cocoa in the political economy of Ghana-EU relations: whither sustainable development?
Mark Langan and Sophia Price
Third World Thematics: A TWQ Journal, volume 1, issue 4 (2016), pp. 563–580
https://doi.org/10.1080/23802014.2016.1314768

Notes on Contributors

Sarah Delputte is a postdoctoral assistant at the Centre for EU Studies, and a lecturer at the Department of Political Science at Ghent University, Belgium.

Frederik De Roeck is a PhD researcher at the Centre for EU Studies at Ghent University, Belgium, with a scholarship funded by the Research Foundation Flanders (FWO).

Tony Heron is professor of International Political Economy at the University of York, UK.

Stephen R. Hurt is senior lecturer in International Relations at Oxford Brookes University, UK.

Niels Keijzer is a researcher based at the German Development Institute/Deutsches Institut für Entwicklungspolitik (DIE), Bonn, Germany.

Mark Langan is senior lecturer in International Politics at Newcastle University, UK.

Deborah Martens is a PhD researcher at the CEUS (Centre for EU Studies, Belgium) since December 2014 with a grant from the Special Research Fund.

Peg Murray-Evans is a research associate in the Department of Politics at the University of York, UK.

Alex Nunn is professor of Global Political Economy at the University of Derby, UK.

Myriam Oehri is a postdoctoral researcher and lecturer at the Global Studies Institute and the Department of Political Science and International Relations, University of Geneva, Switzerland.

Jan Orbie is an associate professor at the Department of Political Science, and Director of the Centre for EU Studies at Ghent University, Belgium.

Sophia Price is head of Politics and International Relations at Leeds Beckett University, UK.

Lore Van den Putte obtained her PhD in September 2016 at the CEUS (Centre for EU Studies, Belgium). Her research concerns the promotion of labour norms in EU (as well as US) bilateral trade agreements.

Yentyl Williams is a PhD researcher on EU relations with Africa, the Caribbean and the Pacific (ACP) group of states at the Centre for EU Studies, University of Ghent, Belgium.

Notes on Contributors

INTRODUCTION

The EU and 'pro-poor' contributions to sustainable development in the post-2015 consensus

Mark Langan and Sophia Price

ABSTRACT
The EU has expressed a long-standing commitment to sustainable development, from the 1997 Treaty of Amsterdam through to the current Europe 2020 strategy for sustainable development and inclusive growth. Commitment at a regional level has been matched by the role the EU has played at a global level, particularly in relation to the UN Sustainable Development Goals (SDGs). This collection examines the EU's role in supporting the post-2015 consensus through a discussion of the EU's trade and development policy, with a particular focus on the African, Caribbean and Pacific (ACP) countries.

The European Union (EU) has expressed a long-standing commitment to sustainable development, from the 1997 Treaty of Amsterdam through to the current Europe 2020 strategy for sustainable development and inclusive growth. Commitment at a regional level has been matched by the role the EU has played at a global level, particularly in relation to the United Nations processes aimed at addressing climate change and the setting of the Millennium Development Goals (MDGs), and their successor Sustainable Development Goals (SDGs). The creation of the latter targets was viewed by the European Commission as validation of its long-standing approach:

> Sustainability is a European brand. The EU has a strong starting position and track record, with a high level of economic development, social cohesion, democratic societies and a commitment to sustainable development which is firmly anchored in the European Treaties.[1]

This collection examines the role the EU has played in addressing and supporting the post-2015 consensus on sustainable development – through a discussion of the EU's trade and development policy, with a particular focus on its relations with the Africa, Caribbean and Pacific (ACP) Group of States. The rationale for this focus is the longevity of the ACP–EU relationship, which has its roots in the 1957 Treaty of Rome, the founding Treaty of the European Economic Community. As such, it is the EU's longest standing development cooperation relationship, which has undergone continual reform and renegotiation, from the Lomé Conventions, first signed in 1975, through to the present Cotonou Partnership Agreement and its associated Economic Partnership Agreements (EPAs). The renegotiations and ongoing liberalisation of the relationship has placed pro-poor and poverty alleviation strategies at the centre of the ACP–EU partnership and, therefore, presents a useful lens through which to explore the contributions of the EU to sustainable development.

The UN Sustainable Development Goals (SDGs) have been warmly welcomed by donors, as well as major corporations involved in the UN Open Working Group (OWD), which helped devise the post-2015 agenda. In contrast to the preceding Millennium Goals, the SDGs are widely viewed as a pivot towards economic growth strategies tied to private sector development (PSD).[2] Goal 8 and Goal 9, for instance, put a firm focus upon the creation of decent jobs and a business 'enabling environment'. Accordingly, the SDGs are regarded as a vital step towards the building of the economic base for social development, the stimulation of global markets – through improvements to the trade and competitive potential of developing countries – and a shared prosperity conducive to poverty reduction.

In contrast, however, there are a number of critical questions that have emerged to counter such a positive endorsement of the SDGs. First, whether this turn to PSD and growth is in fact something 'novel' in donor relations with developing countries. Much of donor praise for the SDGs omits recognition of how PSD and free market policies have been embedded within long-standing development strategies, whether in the time of the Millennium Goals, or further back to structural adjustment programmes.[3] Second, whether the enhanced emphasis on growth strategies will lead to a further entrenchment of free market policies that can often be detrimental to the needs of the poor, and to producers and workers in developing countries. Third, in light of these concerns, whether a new and alternative model of development should be sought. Quintos[4] remarks that the SDGs have in fact mobilised civil society and progressive groups to push for a 'vision of a new development model to counter the neoliberal assault'.

Despite these concerns, the European Commission has been one of the most vocal supporters of the SDGs. In fact, the concept of sustainable development itself is said to be a European construct, one which demonstrates the EU's normative power in development agendas. It is in the context of the controversies surrounding the SDGs and their 'pro-poor' growth agenda, that this collection examines the contributions of the EU to sustainable development in ACP countries.

The eight contributions to this collection provide a holistic overview of EU sustainable development interventions across an array of thematic areas, including trade, climate change, civil society engagements, private sector development and Aid for Trade, joint parliamentary institutions, and regional integration. They bring together specialists on EU external relations, from a range of perspectives focused around political economy and development studies. Together they provide timely insight into EU trade and development policies in the context of the post-2015 consensus and critically analyse the relationship between EU policy objectives and the material impact of its interventions.

The climate-development nexus, in which policies to address climate change are integrated into broader sustainable development frameworks, is explored by De Roeck, Delputte and Orbie[5] through the analysis of climate adaption in the framing of EU development discourse. They identify three frames of adaption and find that the human security frame has a strong presence in the climate-development nexus within EU discourse, which translates to various notions of climate resilience. The growth frame presents climate change as a threat to sustainable development, provoking responses based on the creation of 'enabling environments' for investment and technologies, whilst the justice/equity frame emphasises inequitable distribution of climate-related impacts. Taken together De Roeck et al. find that there is a bias towards global, top-down framing of climate change adaption, with little role for the agency of developing countries, local actors and civil society. This in turn prompts conclusions about the EU as a global actor in international climate change and development by highlighting its normative aspirations with a distinctly neo-liberal flavour. Drawing on the Foucauldian concept of 'governmentality', De Roeck et al. argue the prevalence of the top-down human security and growth frames act as discursive strategies for donors and international institutions to develop a centralised way to deal with climate change in development. In doing so, the structure of the relationship between the Global North and South is embedded, as Northern donors become responsible for the 'resilience' of the passive Southern aid recipients. The concept of resilience thus, serves as a discursive tool for rolling out a neo-liberal governmentality vis-a-vis the Global South, focused on individualisation and the 'disciplining of states, governments and elites' into accepting a neo-liberal development paradigm.

From a historical materialist position, Price and Nunn[6] explore similar themes in the development of the ACP–EU relationship and argue that the concepts of sustainable development and poverty reduction are drawn on to legitimate the process of world market expansion. This, they argue, is a multi-scalar process that is further entrenched by the trade liberalisation underpinned by regionalisation projects. The ACP–EU relationship embeds a form of dependent development that is pro-market and that attempts to embed the world market in different national and regional ACP contexts. In developing their analysis of the ACP–EU relationship they position their own theoretical argument in contrast to the other major theoretical interpretations of the relationship: predominantly realist, constructivist, neo-Gramscian and Uneven and Combined Development (U&CD) perspectives. They conclude that reorganisation of the ACP–EU relationship into the EPA trade regime represents an attempt to ensure neo-liberalisation in the name of pro-poor and sustainable development. However, key to this analysis is a rebuttal of the idea that this will be a process of homogenisation and policy convergence, but rather one that produces 'variegated' responses that have been embraced and recognised by the EU.

Heron and Murray-Evans[7] also emphasise this variegation or 'uneveness' in the ACP responses to the EU's promotion of regional integration. They highlight the 'growing enthusiasm among EU policy-makers' for the promotion of regionalisation in the ACP as a response to the pressures for the liberalisation of the ACP–EU relationship. They argue that the variances in the ACP's national and regional responses are due to the degrees of congruence between the institutional development in existing regional projects with those prescribed by the EU. They develop an explanatory model based on the degrees of congruence in order to explain the variances in ACP responses to the EPAs, based on (i) coherence of the EPA group with existing regional institutions; (ii) compatibility of the EPA regional configurations with pre-existing customs union obligations; (iii) delegation of supranational negotiating authority; and (iv) the presence/absence of regional leadership. They conclude that the divergent ACP responses to the EU's attempts to promote regional integration will have consequences for both governance and development.

Delputte and Williams[8] further the analysis of institutional factors within the ACP–EU relationship, through a particular exploration of the ACP–EU Joint Parliamentary Assembly (JPA). They take a deliberative approach to explore the parliamentary debate on the trade-development nexus through the EPA negotiations, in order to assess whether the JPA approaches the ideal type of an equal partnership. Through a focus on five key areas (participation, openness, common good, constructive politics and power neutralising mechanisms) Delputte and Williams argue that real dialogue is not always guaranteed and that despite a rhetoric of 'equal partnership' the relationship remains asymmetrical. They conclude that ideas 'do not always travel in reciprocal directions' which questions the 'fundamentals of equal partnership between unequal regions'. For Delputte and Williams, it also raises questions about the power, impact and relevance of the JPA, and the broader rationale of the relationship that ostensibly seeks to 'discuss issues' and to 'facilitate greater understanding between the EU and the ACP'.

Keijzer[9] similarly expands this institutional focus via a broader analysis of the evolution and role of the ACP as a Group. The article, which draws on the literature on international organisation, independence and performance, reviews the organisational formations of the Group and the ACP secretariat's development cooperation mandate. He argues that the group has 'performed at a suboptimal level' and as such has failed to deliver on its supranational objectives. However, its member states have used their membership of the Group to access certain EU benefits, particularly important funding and patronage purposes. For Europe, meanwhile, the existence of the Group has allowed the EU to legimitise its differentiated treatment of its development cooperation partners. Keijzer concludes that the future of the ACP is 'more likely to be shaped by the outcome of the upcoming post-Cotonou negotiations with Europe than by its own independent actions'.

Orbie, Martens, Oehri and Van Den Putte[10] explore the involvement of civil society actors in the sustainable development chapters of EU trade agreements. They highlight how the inclusion of these chapters creates institutionalised mechanisms for civil society participation which constitute an 'original and distinctively European approach' to the promotion of labour rights, environmental principles and economic development through trade. This, they argue, not only presents certain institutional shortcomings but also underpins a more fundamental critique that the inclusion of civil society mechanisms may legitimise the underlying free-trade orientation of the agreement through the co-optation of critical actors. In the case of non-profit organisations, Orbie et al. argue that their approach to participation can be characterised as both constructive and critical. They are 'walking a tightrope' between legitimising free trade and obtaining results for the cause they represent, whilst being critical of the civil society mechanisms, their limited impact and lack of substantive dialogue. Their approach therefore, might not result in co-optation but possibly a more radical rejection of free-trade agreements. Moreover, this underlines a divergence between non-profit and business organisations, with the latter being more positive about civil society mechanisms. Orbie et al. posit that this might result in these mechanisms reinforcing the existing asymmetric power relations between business and non-profit organisations in trade policy influence, rather than balancing them in favour of sustainable development.

Questions of the legitimation of, and resistance to, trade liberalisation strategies are further explored by Hurt[11] in his analysis of the incorporation of the International Labour Organisation's Decent Work Agenda into the EU's trade and development policies. He highlights how the Decent Work Agenda has become an increasingly central feature of the global development orthodoxy which is reflected in turn in the EU's trade policy and the EPAs. In an approach that focuses on the material interests and core neo-liberal assumptions central to the EU's trade agenda, Hurt argues that this incorporation provides a rhetorical justification for a policy approach that reflects the interests of European capital. The negotiations of EPAs have, however, encountered significant resistance from African trade unions, which have taken a critical stance against the EU's liberalisation agenda. Hurt explores the prospects for transnational labour solidarity as a counter-hegemonic force. This, he argues, has been compromised in the past as the European Labour Movement has been more convinced by the inclusion of labour standards into the trade agreements. Hurt argues, however, that recently there has been more criticism of the EPAs by the European Labour Movement amidst more explicit solidarity with their African counterparts. As such trade unions play an important role within global sustainable development orthodoxy, either as legitimators of trade liberalisation or as counter-hegemonic actors resisting these forces and advancing a more transformative agenda.

Langan and Price[12] similarly point to the material gains for European corporate interests within the EU's pursuit of its sustainable development agenda. Their article focuses on the EU's pro-poor Private Sector Development (PSD) objectives within the context of EPAs. Specifically, the authors focus on the West Africa EPA, EU relations with Ghana, and the 'pro-poor' prospects of the Ghanaian oil and cocoa sectors. They assess the contribution of these sectors to Ghanaian development, particularly in terms of a shift from the production of raw commodities to higher levels of value-added activities. Moreover, they consider the likely impact of EU Aid for Trade provision for pro-poor PSD and socially equitable growth. The case studies reveal that despite the EU's discursive focus on poverty reduction, its material interventions do more to favour European headquartered corporations than to assist local businesses and citizens in Ghana. Whilst there have been some attempts to rebalance the economic gains, for example, through Fair Trade programmes, questions remain about the success of these strategies. Langan and Price therefore, raise fundamental questions about the EU's free market approach to sustainable development, and highlight how EU trade and aid interventions might in fact undermine pro-poor sustainable development goals.

Funding

This work was supported by International Political Economy Working Group of the British International Studies Association and University of Leicester.

Acknowledgements

The editors and contributors to this collection would like to thank the International Political Economy Working Group of the British International Studies Association for their part-funding of the initial workshop on *EU Contributions to Equitable Growth and Sustainable Development in the Post-2015 Consensus*. This workshop was held at, and supported by, the University of Leicester in April 2016. It provided opportunity for the development of ideas and papers that now make up this collection.

Notes

1. European Commission, "Sustainable Development."
2. Koehler, "Seven Decades of "Development" and Now What?"; Mawdsley, "DFID, The Private Sector and the Re-centering of an Economic Growth Agenda"; Scheyvens et al., "The Need to Move Beyond Business as Usual"; and UN Global Compact, *SDG Compass*.
3. Koehler, "Seven Decades of "Development" and Now What?"; and Mawdsley, "DFID, The Private Sector and the Re-centering of an Economic Growth Agenda."
4. Quintos, *The Post-2015 Corporate Development Agenda*, 14.
5. De Roeck et al., "Framing the Climate-development Nexus in the European Union."
6. Price and Nunn, "Managing Neo-liberalisation through the Sustainable Development Agenda."
7. Heron and Murray Evans, "Regional Encounters."
8. Delputte and Williams, "Equal Partnership Between Unequal Regions?"
9. Keijzer, "Feigned Ambition."
10. Orbie et al., "Promoting Sustainable Development or Legitimizing Free Trade?"
11. Hurt, "The EU's Economic Partnership Agreements with Africa."
12. Langan and Price, "Oil and Cocoa in the Political Economy of Ghana-EU Relations."

Bibliography

De Roeck, F., S. Delputte, and J. Orbie. "Framing the Climate-development Nexus in the European Union." *Third World Thematics* (2017): 1–17. doi:10.1080/23802014.2016.1286947.

Delputte, S., and Y. Williams. "Equal Partnership between Unequal Regions? Assessing Deliberative Parliamentary Diplomacy in ACP-EU Relations." *Third World Thematics* (2017): 1–18. doi:10.1080/23802014.2016.1309257.

European Commission. *Sustainable Development: EU Sets out Its Priorities*. Brussels: European Commission, 2016. Accessed March 6, 2017. http://europa.eu/rapid/press-release_IP-16-3883_en.htm

Heron, T., and P. Murray-Evans. "Regional Encounters: Explaining the Divergent Responses to the EU's Support for Regional Integration in Africa, the Caribbean and Pacific." *Third World Thematics* (2017): 1–20. doi:10.1080/23802014.2016.1281089.

Hurt, S. "The EU's Economic Partnership Agreements with Africa: 'Decent Work' and the Challenge of Trade Union Solidarity'." *Third World Thematics* (2017): 1–16. doi:10.1080/23802014.2016.1305871.

Keijzer, N. "Feigned Ambition. Analysing the Emergence, Evolution and Performance of the ACP Group of States." *Third World Thematics* (2017): 1–18. doi: 10.1080/23802014.2016.1296331.

Koehler, G. "Seven Decades of "Development", and Now What?" *Journal of International Development* 27, no. 6 (2015): 735–751.

Langan, M., and S. Price. "Oil and Cocoa in the Political Economy of Ghana-EU Relations: Whither Sustainable Development?" *Third World Thematics* (2017): 1–18. doi:10.1080/23802014.2016.1314768.

Mawdsley, E. "DFID, the Private Sector and the Re-centring of an Economic Growth Agenda in International Development." *Global Society* 29, no. 3 (2015): 1–20.

Orbie, J., D. Martens, M. Oehri, and L. Van den Putte. "Promoting Sustainable Development or Legitimizing Free Trade? Civil Society Mechanisms in EU Trade Agreements." *Third World Thematics* (2017): 1–21. doi:10.1080/23802014.2016.1294032.

Price, S., and A. Nunn. "Managing Neo-liberalisation through the Sustainable Development Agenda: The EU-ACP Trade Relationship and World Market Expansion." *Third World Thematics* (2017): 1–16. doi:10.1080/23802014.2016.1287528.

Quintos, P. *The Post-2015 Corporate Development Agenda: Expanding Corporate Power in the Name of Sustainable Development*. Quezon City: IBON, 2015.

Scheyvens, R., G. Banks, and E. Hughes. "The Need to Move beyond Business as Usual." *Sustainable Development* 24, no. 6 (2016): 371–382.

UN Global Compact. *SDG Compass: UN Executive Summary*. New York: United Nations Global Compact, 2015.

Framing the climate-development nexus in the European Union

Frederik De Roeck, Sarah Delputte and Jan Orbie

ABSTRACT
This paper aims to assess the framing of adaptation in the development discourse of the European Union (EU). Theoretically, three frames (security, growth and justice/equity) are constructed. Overall, we find clear traces of the EU's normative aspirations as a global actor. Instead of framing climate change as a national or global security threat, human security implications of climate change are emphasised, representing it as a threat to individual livelihoods. Justice/equity considerations are also voiced, acknowledging the disproportionate impact of climate change on developing countries. In terms of agency, we find mostly a global, top-down framing of adaptation in developing countries.

Introduction

In recent years, the international development community has increasingly emphasised the importance of integrating climate change in international development. This is due to its multidimensional nature, meaning it can potentially impact a wide range of development activities.[1] The broad spectrum of affected sectors creates many linkages with development policies, especially when it comes to climate change adaptation.[2] This was recently reconfirmed by the adoption of the Sustainable Development Goals, which include in their mandate the need for international climate action to promote mitigation and adaptation in the Global South.

The emergence of the climate-development nexus has given leeway to a growing body of literature on the integration of adaptation in the aid architecture of donors.[3] However, these studies tend to approach the nexus in a technical manner, by listing a range of procedural and organisational adjustments that allow donors to take climate change into account.[4] In contrast, some emerging studies use a more critical perspective by introducing a broader conceptualisation of adaptation as a complex political and social process influenced by power relations, rather than a linear and neutral response to change.[5]

This paper situates itself within these critical approaches. It aims to analyse the different *frames* that are used to represent adaptation in development discourse. A frame can be defined as an 'organising principle that transforms fragmentary or incidental information into a structured and meaningful problem, in which a solution is implicitly or explicitly included' and the act of framing as 'the process of constructing, adapting and negotiating frames'.[6] Frame analysis allows these discursive constructions to be examined. *Critical* variants often start from a Foucauldian interpretation of discourse, labelling it as a power mechanism which favours dominant frames while excluding alternative ones.[7] Therefore, we will look for different framings of adaptation, while also incorporating the power dimension behind these frames. Existing research has already addressed the discursive dimension of global climate governance,[8] and different frames regarding climate adaptation in particular.[9] A critical inquiry into its discursive linkage with development cooperation is, however, largely absent.

This paper assesses the framing of climate adaptation within the development discourse of the European Union (EU).[10] Although the EU combines its leadership role within the international climate change regime[11] with its status as the largest aid donor in the world, virtually no attention has hitherto been given to the nexus within EU studies. Moreover, the fact that the EU combines its normative aspirations towards developing countries with 'superpower temptations' rooted in its security and market interests,[12] creates a particularly interesting case to see how potential tensions between different role conceptions influence the framing of adaptation in its development discourse.

The next section will first introduce the concept of framing and frame analysis, as well as addressing its value for assessing the climate-development nexus. Subsequently, we will distinguish between three frames which have been identified in relation to climate change: security, growth and justice/equity. Each of these frames will be discussed separately, including insights on how to recognise them in discourse and differentiations between top-down and bottom-up variants in terms of the agency of actors involved. In light of these frames, an assessment of 36 EU policy documents and speeches was made using NVivo software. We will conclude by discussing the implications of our findings, as well as providing directions for further research.

Critical frame analysis

Frame analysis has so far been used mainly in social movement theory and gender studies.[13] However, its basic underpinnings stretch beyond these topics and can be used for other areas as well. Within EU studies, frame analysis has proven to be a valuable technique to analyse the discourse surrounding a wide array of policy domains.[14] It has also been introduced in studies concerning EU development cooperation, assessing gender mainstreaming, for example.[15]

Framing studies start from the social-constructivist assumption that meaning is never a given, but is always socially constructed by actors. Different interpretations can be attributed to the same issue, and actors can steer debates and policies through the act of framing by providing and reproducing a problem definition (diagnosis) and a set of possible solutions (prognosis).[16] Critical frame analysis adds to these insights by assessing power (im)balances between different actors, paying specific attention to discursive biases and inconsistencies within frames, as well as processes of exclusion through which certain ideas, solutions and actors are silenced and thus marginalised.[17]

This paper also argues that the framing of climate change in development cooperation will influence the way it is integrated in development activities. Therefore, this process can only be fully grasped by also engaging with the discursive struggle that shapes it. Examining the frames that are being used to represent the climate-development nexus in discourse is thus necessary, as 'each framing influences the questions asked, the knowledge produced and the adaptation policies and responses that are prioritized'.[18] Some authors have rightfully argued that concepts that are used extensively in the discourse surrounding the nexus – 'improving climate resilience', 'achieving sustainable development'– are essentially empty shells, deriving meaning from the context in which they operate.[19] Therefore, instead of treating these concepts in discourse as a given, research should try to uncover the frames in which they are represented, in order to truly grasp what they represent.

The existing literature on climate governance has already touched upon some controversial issues in this context. First of all, studies have focused on the securitisation of climate change, pointing out possible implications of a dominant climate security framing.[20] Other authors have identified a 'neoliberal' framing of climate change, which renders tackling climate change compatible with pursuing growth.[21] Third, a justice/equity-centered frame has been advocated in existing literature, focusing on the unfair distribution of climate impacts and how to achieve equity in this regard, both internationally as well as between different societal groups.[22] Finally, a distinction can be made between global/top-down and local/bottom-up framings of adaptation. While frames within the former category highlight the importance of the global climate change regime, including its scientific underpinnings and policies, the latter type of frames assign an active role to local actors and also incorporate notions of local knowledge regarding adaptation.[23] In the following paragraphs, we will link these frames to the nexus, while distinguishing between top-down and bottom-up variants within every frame.

Security framing

A constructivist conception of security was introduced by Barry Buzan and Ole Waever (the 'Copenhagen School'). Their concept of securitisation was a departure from the narrow notion of security that focuses exclusively on the military dimension. Instead, they proposed a broader conceptualisation of security issues. Their central argument is that security policy cannot be seen as a mere reaction to an objective threat. Instead, it is socially constructed by speech acts by political actors and communities.[24] Securitisation therefore deals with the discursive strategy of representing issues as existential security threats in order to justify extraordinary measures.[25]

According to Buzan,[26] the shift towards securitising the environment was a result of an increased awareness of the impact of humankind's industrial expansion into ecosystems and its potential security implications. Therefore, it was seen by many as a force for the good, as it catapulted environmental issues into the realm of 'high' politics, introducing sustainability to the security debate.[27] However, it was also problematised by the Copenhagen School and a range of other authors,[28] who raised concerns about the danger of 'militarizing the environment and the rise of nationalistic attitudes in order to protect the national environment'.[29] This is also the case for climate change, which rejuvenated this debate after it was sidelined in the early 2000s, mostly due to the war on terror and the fact that the link between environmental degradation and conflict was no longer seen as credible in academic circles.[30] The issue regained political salience after climate security was put on the international political agendas of the EU and the UN by the end of the 2000s.[31]

Some conceptions of the link between climate change and security are still rooted in this environmental conflict discourse, as they advocate a narrow, state-centric version in both the diagnosis and the prognosis.[32] Within this 'realist' security framing, climate change is seen as a factor that could negatively influence already poor environmental conditions in many developing countries, increasing security risks.[33] Climate change is thus portrayed as a threat to the security of the state or the international system as a whole, through the potential destabilisation of regions and upsurge in climate refugees (i.e. 'diagnosis').[34] Climate adaptation should engage in identifying hotspots of environmental insecurity with the highest risk of conflict, and military capacity should be built in case such conflicts would come about (i.e. 'prognosis').[35]

In contrast, a human security framing advocates a different conception of security within the nexus. This frame highlights the vulnerability of individuals and local communities in the wake of climate change.[36] Apart from this overarching emphasis on the individual, there is a variety of frames that can be linked to human security. First, a *narrow human security* framing engages with the potentially catastrophic consequences of climate-related disasters, and the threats they pose to individual livelihoods.[37] The prognosis is therefore mostly related to mitigating these consequences.[38] It can be situated within a techno-scientific approach to climate change, aimed at reducing the exposure of livelihoods to climate-induced disasters, which can be pursued by installing insurance strategies and scientific monitoring systems.[39] Second, *contextual human security* links the climate vulnerability of local actors to a broader range of conditions, like socio-economic well-being and cultural and political conditions.[40] Contrary to the narrow human security framing, it introduces a social component to climate change in development, allowing for policy responses beyond techno-scientific interventions.

In relation to the agency of the actors involved, some diversification is possible in both the realist and human security frames. Regarding the former, the main referent object is the state, whereas individual actors are only relevant as their exposure to environmental degradation can trigger violent conflict. However, a realist security framing can differ in the extent that an active role is prescribed to the state in dealing with these issues. Developing countries can be labelled as 'fragile' or 'under severe stress' of climate change, while denying the possibility that they may be capable of determining their own adaptation policy in order to minimise the risk of conflict.[41] Moreover, the capacity of states can be bypassed by elevating the climate vulnerabilities of states and regions to the global level, labelling them as international security concerns requiring top-down intervention.[42]

When considering agency in the context of a human security framing, reducing the vulnerability of local entities still does not guarantee their actual emancipation.[43] Defining vulnerability could still be a top-down process, in which the local level is treated as a passive victim of forces beyond its control. In contrast, a bottom-up security frames starts from the notion of agency and empowerment, either from the national or the local level. It highlights the national or local implications of climate change and the capacity of the state or local actors to identify and tackle vulnerabilities that could lead to climate-related insecurities.[44]

Growth framing

The discursive construction of climate change has been labelled in the literature as ecological modernisation, in order to be compatible with growth thinking.[45] Central to this frame is the argument that capitalism can modernise itself, evolving towards a climate-neutral state.[46] As a result, ecological degradation is decoupled from the current growth model which can be made more climate friendly.[47] This is combined with a sense of optimism towards technological, economic and political systems and their ability to handle the problem.[48] In international climate governance, ecological modernisation has given leeway to a number of market-based mechanisms in order to facilitate emission reductions. Well-known examples are carbon trading, like the EU's emission trading system, and carbon offsetting, in which actors can compensate for their own emissions by investing in projects aimed at reducing emissions elsewhere.[49]

The growth paradigm has profoundly influenced development cooperation over recent decades. In the 1980s, a widespread belief in growth through deregulation and marketisation culminated in the Washington Consensus, which ended up being heavily criticised by developing countries themselves.[50] The subsequent Post-Washington Consensus marked a shift in development thinking, revolving around pro-poor growth and poverty reduction.[51] In addition, a 'human development' approach started to gain ground, expanding development to include (among others) gender inequality, environmental degradation and climate change.[52] Although this is generally seen as a departure from the neoliberal, market-centered development paradigm of the 1980s, some authors argue that – rather than losing relevance – free market thinking still dominates current development practices. In their view, issues like climate change were merely absorbed in order to fit this paradigm. [53]

Within this frame, the impact of climate change on developing countries is seen as a threat to economic growth and poverty reduction efforts. Adaptation in development cooperation becomes a matter of economising ecology in order to safeguard growth.[54] In terms of prognosis, a win-win relationship between growth and adaptation is instated, as an increase in the welfare of local livelihoods is seen as a major component of adaptation.[55] This frame therefore re-legitimises the classic notion of development as the pursuit of growth and favors market recipes like increased flexibility, cost-effectiveness and deregulation.

A strong belief in ecological modernisation can once again lead to a top-down framing of adaptation, preaching the dissemination of adaptation technologies through global markets. McMichael[56] labels this as the 'marketisation of development adaptation' and argues that the agency of developing countries and local actors is denounced by promoting the top-down introduction of technologies from global markets over local adaptation strategies. In the agricultural sector for example, this framing could eventually undermine local agricultural practices, which become overruled by gene patenting from global biotechnological firms.[57] A bottom-up frame that links adaptation to marketisation and technological optimism would include an element of local agency, acknowledging local knowledge on adaptation as a valuable source of innovation and entrepreneurship.[58]

Justice/equity framing

A third frame highlights equity and social justice issues in relation to climate adaptation. Discussions on historical responsibility for climate change and its disproportionate impact on developing countries have dominated international negotiations ever since their inception in 1992.[59] This frame acknowledges the inequity of climate change impacts. It starts from the diagnosis that climate change will hit developing countries the hardest, especially considering the fact that their populations are still heavily dependent on natural resources in order to generate a living.[60] At the national and local levels, climate change can aggravate inequality as it impacts differently on different sectors in society.[61] Therefore, adaptation in development becomes a matter of ensuring that its effects do not widen inequality in combination with aid activities. In contrast, the adaptation capacity of local actors can be built by addressing issues of equity and inequality through development cooperation.[62]

Once again, a distinction can be made between top-down and bottom-up forms of equity framing, which relates to the distinction between distributive and procedural justice.[63] Distributive justice framing is solely preoccupied with the distribution of climate impacts across countries, groups of people within countries, and across time. The only thing that matters is how development policy balances the uneven distribution of climate impacts. In other words, only the outcome of development cooperation in terms of improving climate equity is important, which corresponds with a consequentialist and utilitarian approach to climate justice.[64] This again allows for top-down adaptation in development, in which equity in terms of mitigating climate impacts is defined on the international level or by donors themselves. In contrast, procedural justice highlights the importance of stakeholder participation. Within this framing, an adaptation strategy can only improve equity 'if mechanisms are in place to ensure that that those impacted at the sub-national level have their interests considered'.[65] In this sense, achieving climate justice entails a bottom-up approach towards adaptation in development in which all stakeholders affected by adaptation policies are included in the policy design.[66] For example, donors could support community-led natural resource management systems for sectors in which they are active, in order to generate locally embedded and sustainable policy options (Table 1).[67]

Analysis of framing in EU discourse

We will now use our typology to delve into the representation of the climate-development nexus in the discourse of the EU. The EU makes for a unique case in this regard, as it combines its self-proclaimed role as largest development aid donor in the world with international leadership in the international climate change regime.[68] Moreover, its 'eternal struggle' as a global actor between its identity as a normative power and its realist interests[69] creates an interesting dynamic which could influence the use of frames. Regarding its role as a donor, there is already a considerable literature on Policy Coherence for Development, which points out the tensions between normative aspirations in development and other agendas like trade interests and security issues.[70] In addition, the literature on EU climate leadership has also labelled it a strong advocate of ecological modernisation and a top-down, centralised form of climate governance within the global climate regime.[71] Therefore, it is interesting to see whether and how the three identified frames are represented and interact at the intersection of these two policy domains.

In order to conduct this research, phases of data gathering were alternated with data analysis until saturation was reached. In total, 36 documents issued by the European Commission have been assessed (for the full list, please consult Appendix 1). NVivo 11 software was used for systematically coding the data. It proved to be a useful tool in determining the prevalence and representation of the frames in EU discourse. Analysed documents include transcripts of speeches by the current and previous Commissioners in charge of climate change and development, and a range of policy documents and press releases elaborating on the link between both. These span multiple topics within the nexus in EU aid

Table 1. Summary of three frames.

	Agency of actors			
	Top-down		Bottom-up	
Frame	*Realist*	*Human*	*Realist*	*Human*
Security	• National or regional climate insecurity framed as global threats • Adaptation to avoid conflict + military capacity building • Passive framing of developing countries in dealing with climate-related insecurities	• Individual insecurity in the wake of climate-disasters (narrow)/broader vulnerability to potential climate impacts (contextual) • Adaptation to reduce exposure to disaster (narrow)/reduce climate vulnerability (contextual) • Active framing of local actors in reducing exposure/ overall vulnerability	• National and regional insecurity due to climate change • Adaptation to avoid conflict + military capacity building • Active framing of developing countries, state can deal with climate-related insecurities	• Individual insecurity in the wake of climate-disasters (narrow)/broader vulnerability to potential climate impacts (contextual) • Adaptation to reduce exposure to disaster/ reduce climate vulnerability • Active framing of local actors in reducing exposure/ overall vulnerability
Growth	• Climate change threatens growth and poverty reduction efforts in developing countries • Adaptation through the implementation of market recipes. Win-win relationship between economic growth and climate resilience • Importance of international markets in providing technologies for adaptation		• Climate change as a threat to economic growth and poverty reduction efforts in developing countries • Adaptation through the implementation market recipes. Win-win relationship between economic growth and climate resilience • Importance of local knowledge as driver of climate-related innovation and entrepreneurship	
Justice/equity	• Climate change as a driver of inequity in terms of its impact, both on the international and national level • Adaptation in development needs to address inequity and injustice to avoid maladaptation • Distributive justice: equitable distribution of climate-related impacts		• Climate change as a driver of inequity in terms of its impact, both on the international as well as the national level • Adaptation in development needs to address inequity and injustice to avoid maladaptation • Procedural justice: equitable distribution of climate-related impacts and participation of stakeholders	

policies, ranging from climate financing in the Global South to disaster risk reduction in the wake of climate change and climate mainstreaming. The time period covered ranged from the early 2000s to the 2015 Paris summit.

Findings

First of all, ever since the first communications on the nexus, EU discourse has been closely related to the human security frame. Climate change is conceived as a problem of the increasing prevalence of natural disasters (e.g. floods, droughts, soil erosion etc.), thereby posing a real threat to developing countries and livelihoods. This human security frame is often used as an introduction and accompanied by a range of alarmist adjectives emphasising the gravity of the situation (e.g. *deadly* disasters,[72] *severe* and *irreversible* impacts,[73] *intense* storms[74]). In contrast, a realist security frame is only rarely present in the analysed documents. National and international security implications of climate change are sometimes mentioned, usually in relation to conflict as a result of resource scarcity and an expected increase in climate refugees.[75] However, this is nowhere near as prominent in EU discourse as the human security framing.

In line with this prevalence of human security in the diagnosis, the concept of climate resilience has entered EU discourse in recent years, becoming heavily emphasised in recent EU documents. This discursive representation is in line with the 'empty shell' argument mentioned earlier. It is included routinely in EU discourse as the overarching objective to achieve 'sustainable, climate-resilient' development, but this is a blank construction provided with a different content depending on the context in which it operates. Hence, its meaning fluctuates between a strong techno-scientific interpretation of adaptation and a more contextualised one. The following two quotes illustrate the difference between the two:

> [...] boost local, national and regional capacities and resilience in ways that link sustainable development, risk management and adaptation in a "win-win-win" situation. It will thus improve regional capacities for climate monitoring, modelling, and vulnerability assessments.[76]

> Adaptation is about building resilience within communities and economies to the increased risks resulting from climate change. It is a vast and cross-cutting development challenge.[77]

As apparent in the two quotes, the former type of climate resilience in EU discourse is used more in the context of disaster risk reduction and is therefore strongly preoccupied with scientific monitoring, disaster risk reduction and risk management. In contrast, contextualised notions of resilience also include socio-economic factors that could potentially aggravate the impact of climate change. Much in line with contextual human security, resilience in this regard goes beyond the mere threat of climate-induced disasters and the ability of individuals and communities to withstand such events. Besides the framing of climate adaptation as a 'vast and cross-cutting challenge' for development, other noted examples in EU discourse are the formulated need to 'mainstream climate resilience in development cooperation'[78] and the aim to also 'reduce underlying risk factors'[79] to potential climate disasters, which is linked to rapid urbanisation, inadequate natural resource management, poor health etc. This seems to indicate that a multi-sectoral approach is favored as a policy response within the nexus.

Through the constant emphasis on the potentially disastrous impact of climate change for developing countries in the diagnosis, the human security frame also includes an element of geographical differentiation, which can be linked to a justice/equity frame. Almost all EU speech acts recognise the differentiation of climate change impacts – emphasising the fact that developing countries are the least responsible, but the most affected by climate change[80] – and climate change responsibilities – mentioning the need to cooperate based on respective capabilities and specific circumstances of developing countries.[81] In contrast, there is a clear tendency to frame the prognosis in global terms. This is constantly re-emphasised by referring to a global or universal partnership in fighting climate change:

> The overall objective of this strategy is to assist EU partner countries in meeting the challenges posed by climate change, in particular by supporting them in the implementation of the UNFCCC and the Kyoto Protocol.[82]

> The Paris conference should agree to assist those countries that need assistance to set up emission inventories, monitoring, reporting and verification systems, and to develop low emission and climate resilient development strategies with the right incentive structures.[83]

Going back to the differentiation between distributive and procedural justice, the former thus seems dominant in EU discourse, as climate change as a development challenge is consistently framed in relation to the climate change regime and the global level. Despite the strong emphasis on the unequal impact of climate change on developing countries, there is very little evidence of framing that recognises the capacity within developing countries to cope with climate change. We find a similar silence regarding the inclusion of NGOs. Only two references were found mentioning the inclusion of non-governmental stakeholders such as civil society organisations, social institutions, academia, etc. Alternatively, the EU stresses its own importance by emphasising its 'natural alliance'[84] with the developing world, mostly based on values again related to the multilateral level:

> The EU and the Pacific Small Island States are longstanding allies. We share a lot of common ground – respect for science, equity, and the multilateral rules based approach.[85]

Therefore, although the prognosis to a certain extent recognises the broader socio-economic context in fighting climate change, we find no evidence that this is matched by an active framing of local actors.

Not only are the described impacts of climate change linked to natural disasters that could lead to calamities in developing countries, there is also almost always the direct threat that climate change poses to sustainable development, achieving the MDGs and more recently the SDGs. In comes the growth frame, as development outcomes are often mentioned in terms of – or even equated with – economic growth. This takes the form of emphasising the 'costly impact'[86] of climate change that could 'hamper economic development' of developing countries.[87] In this sense, adaptation in development thus becomes a matter of ensuring that the pursuit of economic growth can continue unabated.

There is also a strong element of opportunity with regards to the prognosis, which is aimed at starting a transition towards a greener and more sustainable economy, thereby leap-frogging the high-carbon phase of development. In relation to adaptation, there is a strong emphasis on the necessity of developing countries to create 'enabling environments'[88] in order to attract international investments, private climate finance and technologies. Considering the agency of actors involved, the main sources of innovation and entrepreneurship for climate adaptation are thus placed outside developing countries themselves throughout EU discourse. The overarching mantra is that help is needed in facilitating these enabling environments to attract investments and technologies from the outside, whereas very few accounts mention the potential of innovation from the bottom-up. Therefore, it is safe to say that a top-down growth frame also dominates in relation to adaptation.

Discussion and conclusion

This article aimed to unravel the framing of the climate-development nexus within EU discourse. First, we found a strong presence of the human security frame, emphasising the threat climate change poses to individual livelihoods as a result of an expected increase in natural disasters (i.e. diagnosis). This translates to different notions of climate resilience, ranging from techno-scientific policies to deal with such disasters to more contextualised forms of the concept, focusing on the socio-economic vulnerabilities of communities (i.e. prognosis). Second, the growth frame is represented by diagnoses of climate change as a threat to growth and 'sustainable development'. For adaptation, this relates to striving towards 'enabling environments' in developing countries in order to attract climate-friendly investments, finance and technologies. Third, the justice/equity frame is represented through emphasis of the inequitable distribution of climate-related impacts to developing countries and the role of development cooperation in tackling this inequity. There is a bias towards a global, top-down framing of adaptation, with very little attention given to the agency of developing countries, local actors and civil society.

If we interpret our findings in the context of the EU as a global actor in both the international climate change regime and in international development, echoes of its normative aspirations can clearly be detected, albeit with a distinct (neo)liberal flavour. Although we find strong evidence of the EU framing of climate change as an 'existential threat' to developing countries, this is never used to justify extraordinary military measures. Instead, the human security implications of climate change in developing countries are emphasised, which Manners[89] argues is compatible with a normative agenda targeting 'sustainable peace'. The fact that the EU stresses the inequity in terms of climate change impacts in the Global South further adds to this point. However, despite the absence of 'hard' securitisation in EU discourse, a number of critical comments can be formulated which could be the subject of further research.

Firstly, the policy implications of linking security and climate change in the context of development cooperation could be evaluated more thoroughly. Similar research by Trombetta[90] concerning the climate-migration nexus highlighted the securitising potential of 'subtle' linkages with security in discourse, which can be situated within a human security framing. In her view, the absence of a discursive link towards exceptional measures does not rule out 'hard' securitisation in policy practices. In light of the argument made by Manners, which renders human security compatible with the EU's international normative aspirations, future research could engage more with this debate.

Secondly, the strong prevalence of a top-down framing of adaptation in development is problematic in different ways. Assuming the EU's leadership role within the global climate change regime, it is logical that it would echo many of the globalist frames advocated within this regime in its relationship with developing countries. Only now can we mark a shift in international climate governance in which emerging economies and developing countries are also becoming more emancipated actors. It is becoming clear that the international climate change regime is evolving towards a hybrid system of voluntary, country-led cooperation in which Southern actors claim a larger role. This is forcing the EU to invest more in diplomatic alliances with the Global South,[91] which could influence its discourse regarding the climate-development nexus in the years to come. Since our period of analysis does not include the post-Paris period, the overall representation of the frames within the nexus remained fairly consistent over time. Further research should examine to what extent this evolving context is influencing EU discourse.

Third, the prevalence of a top-down human security and growth frame can be linked to the Foucauldian concept of 'governmentality'.[92] These frames are considered discursive strategies for donors and international institutions to develop a centralised way of dealing with climate change in development. Implicitly, a geopolitical reality of the 'developed' Global North and the 'underdeveloped' Global South is installed, in which Northern donors are responsible for the 'resilience' of the passive Southern aid recipients by installing technologies like centralised risk management schemes and scientific monitoring systems.[93] The dominance of resilience thinking is also apparent in EU discourse, with the concept becoming omnipresent in more recent communications surrounding the nexus. Notable examples are the new EU Global Strategy and the updated European Consensus for Development. Authors such as Joseph have attributed the concept's popularity to the fact that it that lacks any deeper meaning and serves as a discursive tool for rolling out a neoliberal governmentality vis-à-vis the Global South, focused on individualisation and 'the disciplining of states, governments and elites' into accepting a neoliberal development paradigm.[94] This fits with our findings regarding the overall prevalence of the three identified frames and with the fact that the meaning of resilience in EU discourse surrounding the nexus also changes depending on the context. Therefore, the governmentality approach could be promising for future research into this topic.

Disclosure statement

No potential conflict of interest was reported by the authors.

Funding

This work was supported by the Fonds Wetenschappelijk Onderzoek [grant number 11ZU217N].

Acknowledgments

Earlier versions of this paper were presented at the 'EU and the SDGs' workshop at the University of Leicester on 20 April 2016 and the UACES conference in London on 6 September 2016. We would like to thank all participants for commenting on these draft versions.

Notes

1. Persson and Klein, "Mainstreaming Climate Adaptation into ODA," 2, 3; and Kok et al., "Integrating Development and Climate Policies," 104, 105.
2. Huq and Reid, "Mainstreaming Adaptation in Development," 16, 17.
3. Agrawala and Van Aalst, "Adapting Development Cooperation," 183–193; Ayers and Huq, "Supporting Adaptation," 675–692; and Fankhauser and Schmidt-Traub, "Climate Resilient Development," 1–26.
4. Klein et al., "Portfolio Screening," 23–44; and Agrawala et al., "Incorporating Climate Change," 1–38.
5. Eriksen et al., "Reframing Adaptation," 523.
6. Verloo, "Mainstreaming Gender Equality," 20.
7. Ibid., 19.

8. Bäckstrand and Lövbrandt, "Planting Trees to Mitigate Climate Change," 50–75; and Bäckstrand and Lövbrandt, "Climate Governance Beyond 2012," 123–147.
9. Dewulf, "Contrasting Frames," 321–330; McEvoy et al., "Resilience and adaptation," 280–293; and McGray et al., "Weathering the Storm," 17–25.
10. For a general introduction to the EU's environmental and climate policies, please consult Delreux and Happaerts, *Environmental Policy and Politics.*
11. Bäckstrand and Ëlgstrom, "The EU's role in Climate Negotiations," 1369–1386.
12. Orbie, "The EU's Role in Development," 17–36.
13. Johnston and Klandermans, "The Cultural Analysis of Social Movements," 217–247; Snow and Benford, "Ideology, frame resonance," 197–217; Lombardo and Meier, "Framing Gender Equality," 101–129; and Verloo and Lombardo, "Contested Gender Equality," 21–49.
14. Daviter, "Policy Framing in the EU," 654–666.
15. Debusscher, "Mainstreaming Gender," 39–49.
16. Lombardo and Meier, "Framing Gender Equality," 105.
17. Verloo and Lombardo, "Contested Gender Equality," 27.
18. Dewulf, "Contrasting Frames," 325.
19. Joseph, "Resilience as Embedded Neoliberalism," 38–52; and Methman, "'Climate Protection' as Empty Signifier," 1–28.
20. Oels, "From Securitisation of Climate Change," 185–207; and Grove, "Insuring 'Our Common Future,'" 536–563.
21. Bäckstrandt and Lövbrandt, "Planting Trees," 52, 53; and Oels, "Rendering Climate Change Governable," 195–197.
22. Thomas and Twyman, "Equity and Justice," 115–124.
23. Cannon and Müller-Mahn, "Vulnerability, Resilience and Development Discourses," 621–635.
24. Trombetta, "Environmental Security and Climate Change," 585–602.
25. Waever, *Securitisation and Desecuritisation*, 1–31; and McDonald, "Securitisation and the Construction of Security," 563–587.
26. Buzan, *Rethinking Security,* 7.
27. Dyer, "Environmental Security," 441–450.
28. See Buzan et al., *Security: A New Framework For Analysis,* 71–95; and Graeger, "Environmental Security?" 109–116.
29. Deudney cited in Trombetta, "Environmental Security," 586.
30. Trombetta, "Environmental Security," 589, 590.
31. Oels, "From Securitisation of Climate Change," 189.
32. Barnett, *Security and Climate Change*, 4, 5.
33. Ibid., 6.
34. Trombetta, "Environmental Security," 596; and Oels, "From Securitisation of Climate Change," 186, 187.
35. Detraz and Betsill, "Climate Change and Environmental Security," 314 and Barnett, "Security and Climate Change," 1–17.
36. Duffield and Waddel, "Securing Humans in a Dangerous World," 1–23.
37. Dewulf, "Contrasting Frames," 326.
38. See O'Brien et al., "Climate Change and Disaster Management," 64–80.
39. Dewulf, "Contrasting Frames," 324, 325.
40. Ibid., 325, 326.
41. Chandler, "Resilience and Human Security," 213–229.
42. Stern and Öjendal, "Mapping the Security-Development Nexus," 16, 17.
43. Cannon and Müller-Mahn, "Vulnerability, Resilience and Development Discourses," 621–635; and Thomas and Twyman, "Equity and Justice," 115–124.
44. In the context of human security, see for example Allen, "Community-Based Disaster Preparedness," 81–101.
45. See Mol, "Ecological Modernisation," 138–149; and Spaargaren and Mol, "Sociology, Environment and Modernity," 323–344.

46. Buttel, "Ecological Modernisation as a Social Theory," 57–65; and Mol, "Ecological Modernisation," 138–149.
47. Bäckstrand and Lövbrand, "Planting Trees," 52, 53.
48. Baker, "Sustainable Development as a Symbolic Commitment," 297–317.
49. Liverman, "Conventions of Climate Change," 293; and Hyams and Fawcett, "The Ethics of Carbon Ofsetting," 91–98.
50. Sheppard and Leitner, "Quo Vadis Neoliberalism?" 186, 187.
51. Ibid., 187.
52. Doidge and Holland, "A Chronology of EU Development Policy," 68–75.
53. Methman, "Climate Protection," 1–28; and McMichael, "Contemporary Contradictions," 247–262.
54. Newll, "Climate Change And Development," 120–126.
55. Ibid., 120–126; and Cannon and Müller-Mahn, "Vulnerability, Resilience and Development Discourses," 621–635.
56. McMichael, "Contemporary Contradictions," 252.
57. Ibid., 252.
58. See Aubert, "Promoting Innovation," 1–38.
59. Okereke, "Climate Justice," 462.
60. Thomas and Twyman, "Equity and Justice," 115, 116.
61. Ibid., 117, 118.
62. Thomas and Twyman, "Equity and Justice," 115–124; and Smit and Pilifosova, "Adaptation to Climate Change," 879–906.
63. Paavola and Adger, "Justice and Adaptation," 1–19.
64. Ibid., 7.
65. Klinsky and Dowlatabadi, "Conceptualisations of Justice," 93.
66. Ibid., 93, 94; and Paavola and Adger, "Justice and Adaptation," 1–19.
67. Thomas and Twyman, "Equity and Justice," 119.
68. Gupta and Grubb, *Climate Change and European Leadership*, 3–83; and Schreurs and Tiberghien, "Multi-Level Reinforcement," 19–46.
69. Orbie, "The EU's Role in Development," 17–36.
70. See Carbone, "Mission Impossible," 323–342; Carbone and Keijzer, "The EU and Policy Coherence for Development," 30–43.
71. Bäckstrandt and Lövbrandt, "Climate Governance Beyond 2012," 123–147.
72. European Commission, "Commission Proposes a Global Alliance," 2.
73. European Commission, "The Paris Protocol," 3.
74. Piebalgs, "Climate Change: Don't Forget the Pacific," 2.
75. See Barroso, "Climate and Environment," 2.
76. Piebals, "Working Together," 3.
77. European Commission, "EU Climate Funding for Developing Countries," 7.
78. Piebalgs, "Engaging With Vulnerable Countries," 2.
79. European Commission, "EU Strategy for Supporting Disaster Risk Reduction," 8.
80. E.g. European Commission, "Commission Proposes a Global Alliance," 1; and European Commission, "Africa Climate Briefing," ii.
81. European Commission, "EU Climate Funding for Developing Countries," 4.
82. European Commission, "Climate Change in the Context of Development," par. 11.
83. European Commission, "The Paris Protocol," 4.
84. E.g. European Commission, "Africa Climate Briefing," ii.
85. European Commission, "Speech by Commissioner Miguel Arias Canete," 1.
86. European Commission, "Q&A on the White Paper," 4.
87. European Commission, "Pacific Islands and Climate Change," 1.
88. E.g. European Commission, "The Paris Protocol," 5.
89. Manners, "Normative Power Europe Reconsidered," 182–199.
90. Trombetta, "Linking Climate-induced Migration and Security," 131–147.
91. Bäckstrandt and Ëlgstrom, "The EU's role in Climate Negotiations," 1369–1386.

92. Grove, "Insuring Our Common Future?" 536–563; and Bäckstrandt and Lövbrandt, "Planting Trees to Mitigate Climate Change," 50–75.
93. Grove, "Insuring Our Common Future?" 553.
94. Joseph, "Resilience as Embedded Neoliberalism," 51.

Bibliography

Agrawala, Shardul, and Maarten Van Aalst. "Adapting Development Cooperation to Adapt to Climate Change." *Climate Policy* 8, no. 2 (2008): 183–193.

Agrawala, Shardul, Arnoldo Matus Kramer, Guillaume Prudent-Richard, Marcus Sainsbury, and Victoria Schreitter. "Incorporating Climate Change Impacts and Adaptation in Environmental Impact Assesssments: Opportunities and Challenges." *Climate and Development* 4, no. 1 (2012): 26–39.

Allen, Katrina M. "Community-based Disaster Preparedness and Climate Adaptation." *Disasters* 30, no. 1 (2006): 81–101.

Aubert, Jean-Eric. *Promoting Innovation in Developing Countries: A Conceptual Framework*. World Bank Policy Research Working Paper No. 3554. Washington, DC: World Bank, 2005.

Ayers, Jessica-M., and Saleemul Huq. "Supporting Adaptation to Climate Change: What Role for Official Development Assistance?" *Development Policy Review* 27, no. 6 (2009): 675–692.

Bäckstrand, Karin, and Ole Elgström. "The EU's Role in Climate Change Negotiations: From Leader to 'Leadiator'." *Journal of European Public Policy* 20, no. 10 (2013): 1369–1386.

Bäckstrand, Karin, and Eva Lövbrand. "Planting Trees to Mitigate Climate Change: Contested Discourses of Ecological Modernisation, Green Governmentality and Civic Environmentalism." *Global Environmental Politics* 6, no. 1 (2006): 50–75.

Bäckstrand, Karin, and Eva Lövbrand. "Climate Governance beyond 2012: Competing Discourses of Green Governmentality, Ecological Modernisation and Civic Environmentalism." In *The Social Construction of Climate Change: Power, Knowledge, Norms, Discourses*, edited by Mary E. Pettenger, 123–147. Hampshire: Ashgate, 2007.

Baker, Susan. "Sustainable Development as Symbolic Commitment: Declaratory Politics and the Seductive Appeal of Ecological Modernisation in the European Union." *Environmental Politics* 16, no. 2 (2007): 297–317.

Barnett, Jon. "Security and Climate Change." *Global Environmental Change* 13, no. 1 (2003): 7–17.

Buttel, Frederick H. "Ecological Modernisation as Social Theory." *Geoforum* 31, no. 1 (2000): 57–65.

Buzan, Barry, Ole Wæver, and Jaap De Wilde. *Security: A New Framework for Analysis*. London: Lynne Rienner Publishers, 1998.

Cannon, Terry, and Detlef Müller-Mahn. "Vulnerability, Resilience and Development Discourses in Context of Climate Change." *Natural Hazards* 55, no. 3 (2010): 621–635.

Carbone, Maurizio. "Mission Impossible: The European Union and Policy Coherence for Development." *European Integration* 30, no. 3 (2008): 323–342.

Carbone, Maurizio, and Niels Keijzer. "The European Union and Policy Coherence for Development." *The European Journal of Development Research* 28, no. 1 (2016): 30–43.

Chandler, David. "Resilience and Human Security: The Post-interventionist Paradigm." *Security Dialogue* 43, no. 3 (2012): 213–229.

Daviter, Falk. "Policy Framing in the European Union." *Journal of European Public Policy* 14, no. 4 (2007): 654–666.

Debusscher, Petra. "Mainstreaming Gender in European Commission Development Policy: Conservative Europeanness?" *Women Studies International Forum* 34, no. 1 (2011): 39–49.

Delreux, Tom, and Sander Happaerts. *Environmental Policy and Politics in the European Union*. London: Palgrave Macmillan, 2016.

Detraz, Nicole, and Michele M. Betsill. "Climate Change and Environmental Security: For Whom the Discourse Shifts." *International Studies Perspectives* 10, no. 3 (2009): 303–320.

Dewulf, Art. "Contrasting Frames in Policy Debates on Climate Change Adaptation." *Wiley Interdisciplinary Reviews: Climate Change* 4, no. 4 (2013): 321–330.

Doidge, Mathew, and Martin Holland. "A Chronology of European Union Development Policy: Theory and Change." *Korea Review of International Studies* 17, no. 1 (2015): 59–80.

Duffield, Mark, and Nicholas Waddell. "Securing Humans in a Dangerous World." *International Politics* 43, no. 1 (2006): 1–23.

Dyer, Hugh. "Environmental Security and International Relations." *Review of International Studies* 27, no. 3 (2001): 441–450.

Eriksen, Siri H., Andrea J. Nightingale, and Hallie Eakin. "Reframing Adaptation: The Political Nature of Climate Change Adaptation." *Global Environmental Change* 35 (2015): 523–533.

Fankhauser, Samuel, and Guido Schmidt-Traub. "From Adaptation to Climate-resilient Development." *Climate and Development* 3, no. 2 (2011): 94–113.

Graeger, Nina. "Environmental Security?" *Journal of Peace Research* 33, no. 1 (1996): 109–116.

Grove, Kevin J. "Insuring "Our Common Future?" Dangerous Climate Change and the Biopolitics of Environmental Security." *Geopolitics* 15, no. 3 (2010): 536–563.

Huq, Saleemul, and Hannah Reid. "Mainstreaming Adaptation in Development." *IDS Bulletin* 35, no. 3 (2004): 15–21.

Johnston, Hank, and Bert Klandermans. "The Cultural Analysis of Social Movements." *Social Movements and Culture* 4 (1995): 3–24.

Joseph, Jonathan. "Resilience as Embedded Neoliberalism: A Governmentality Approach." *Resilience* 1, no. 1 (2013): 38–52.

Klein, Richard J. T., and Siri E. H. Eriksen, Lars Otto Næss, Anne Hammill, Thomas M. Tanner, Carmenza Robledo, and Karen L. O'Brien. "Portfolio Screening to Support the Mainstreaming of Adaptation to Climate Change into Development Assistance." *Climatic Change* 84, no. 1 (2007): 23–44.

Klinsky, Sonja, and Hadi Dowlatabadi. "Conceptualisations of Justice in Climate Policy." *Climate Policy* 9, no. 1 (2009): 88–108.

Kok, Marcel, Bert Metz, Jan Verhagen, and Sascha Van Rooijen. "Integrating Development and Climate Policies: National and International Benefits." *Climate Policy* 8, no. 2 (2008): 103–118.

Lombardo, Emanuela, and Petra Meier. "Framing Gender Equality in the European Union Political Discourse." *Social Politics: International Studies in Gender, State & Society* 15, no. 1 (2008): 101–129.

Manners, Ian. "Normative Power Europe Reconsidered." Paper presented at the CIDEL Workshop, CiteseerX: Oslo, 2004.

McDonald, Matt. "Securitisation and the Construction of Security." *European Journal of International Relations* 14, no. 4 (2008): 563–587.

McEvoy, Darryn, Hartmut Fünfgeld, and Karyn Bosomworth. "Resilience and Climate Change Adaptation: The Importance of Framing." *Planning Practice & Research* 28, no. 3 (2013): 280–293.

McGray, Heather, Anne Hammill, Rob Bradley, E. Lisa Schipper, and Jo-Ellen Parry. "Weathering the Storm: Options for Framing Adaptation and Development." *World Resources Institute, Washington, DC* 57 (2007): 1–57.

McMichael, Philip. "Contemporary Contradictions of the Global Development Project: Geopolitics, Global Ecology and the 'Development Climate'." *Third World Quarterly* 30, no. 1 (2009): 247–262.

Methmann, Chris Paul. "'Climate Protection' as Empty Signifier: A Discourse Theoretical Perspective on Climate Mainstreaming in World Politics." *Millennium-Journal of International Studies* 39, no. 2 (2010): 345–372.

Mol, Arthur P. J. "Ecological Modernisation: Industrial Transformations and Environmental Reform." *The International Handbook of Environmental Sociology* (1997): 138–149.

Newll, Peter. "Climate Change and Development: A Tale of Two Crises." *IDS Bulletin* 35, no. 3 (2004): 120–126.

O'Brien, Geoff, Phil O'Keefe, Joanne Rose, and Ben Wisner. "Climate Change and Disaster Management." *Disasters* 30, no. 1 (2006): 64–80.

Oels, Angela. "Rendering Climate Change Governable: From Biopower to Advanced Liberal Government?" *Journal of Environmental Policy & Planning* 7, no. 3 (2005): 185–207.

Oels, Angela. "From 'Securitisation' of Climate Change to 'Climatisation' of the Security Field: Comparing Three Theoretical Perspectives." In *Climate Change, Human Security and Violent Conflict*, edited by Jurgen Scheffran, Michael Brzoska, Hans Günter Brauch, Peter Michael Link, and Janpeter Schilling, 185–205. Berlin: Springer, 2012.

Okereke, Chukwumerije. "Climate Justice and the International Regime." *Wiley Interdisciplinary Reviews: Climate Change* 1, no. 3 (2010): 462–474.

Orbie, Jan. "The EU's Role in Development: A Full-fledged Development Actor or Eclipsed by Superpower Temptations?" In *The EU and Global Development*, edited by Stefan Gänzle, Sven Grimm, and Davina Makhan, 462. London: Palgrave Macmillan, 2012.

Paavola, Jouni, and Neil Adger. "Justice and Adaptation to Climate Change." *Tyndall Centre Working Paper* 23 (2002): 1–24.

Persson, Åsa, and Richard J. T. Klein. "Mainstreaming Adaptation to Climate Change into Official Development Assistance." Paper presented at the Proceedings of the Berlin conference on the human dimensions of global environmental change, Berlin, 2008.

Schreurs, Miranda A., and Yves Tiberghien. "Multi-level Reinforcement: Explaining European Union Leadership in Climate Change Mitigation." *Global Environmental Politics* 7, no. 4 (2007): 19–46.

Sheppard, Eric, and Helga Leitner. "Quo Vadis Neoliberalism? The Remaking of Global Capitalist Governance after the Washington Consensus." *Geoforum* 41, no. 2 (2010): 185–194.

Smit, Barry, and Olga Pilifosova. "Adaptation to Climate Change in the Context of Sustainable Development and Equity." *Sustainable Development* 8, no. 9 (2003): 879–912.

Snow, David A., and Robert D. Benford. "Ideology, Frame Resonance, and Participant Mobilization." *International Social Movement Research* 1, no. 1 (1988): 197–217.

Spaargaren, Gert, and Arthur P. J. Mol. "Sociology, Environment, and Modernity: Ecological Modernisation as a Theory of Social Change." *Society & Natural Resources* 5, no. 4 (1992): 323–344.

Stern, Maria, and Joakim Öjendal. "Mapping the Security—Development Nexus: Conflict, Complexity, Cacophony, Convergence?" *Security Dialogue* 41, no. 1 (2010): 5–29.

Thomas, David S. G., and Chasca Twyman. "Equity and Justice in Climate Change Adaptation amongst Natural-Resource-Dependent Societies." *Global Environmental Change* 15, no. 2 (2005): 115–124.

Trombetta, Maria Julia. "Environmental Security and Climate Change." *Cambridge Review of International Affairs* 21, no. 4 (2008): 585–602.

Trombetta, Maria Julia. "Linking Climate-induced Migration and Security within the EU." *Critical Studies on Security* 2, no. 2 (2014): 131–147.

Verloo, Mieke. "Mainstreaming Gender Equality in Europe. A Critical Frame Analysis Approach." *The Greek Review of Social Research* 117, no. B (2005): 11–34.

Verloo, Mieke, and Emanuela Lombardo. "Contested Gender Equality and Policy Variety in Europe." In *Multiple Meanings of Gender Equality. A Critical Frame Analysis of Gender Policies in Europe*, edited by Mieke Verloo, 21–49. Budapest: CEU Press, 2007.

Wæver, Ole. *Securitisation and Desecuritisation*. Copenhagen: Center for Freds-og Konfliktforskning, 1993.

Appendix 1. List of analysed texts

Policy documents

(1) Council of the European Union. '2215th Council Meeting: Development. 1999.
(2) European Commission. 'Africa Climate Briefing.' 2014.
(3) European Commission. 'COM(2003) 85 – Climate change in the context of development cooperation.' 2003.
(4) European Commission. 'COM(2007) 540 – Building a global climate change alliance between the European Union and poor developing countries most vulnerable to climate change.' 2007.
(5) European Commission. 'COM(2009) 84 – EU strategy for supporting disaster risk reduction in developing countries.' 2009.
(6) European Commission. 'COM(2015) 44 – A Global Partnership for Poverty Eradication and Sustainable Development after 2015.' 2015.
(7) European Commission. 'COM(2015) 81 – The Paris Protocol – A blueprint for tackling global climate change beyond 2020.' 2015.
(8) European Commission. 'European Union climate funding for developing countries in 2013.' 2013.
(9) European Commission. 'European Union climate funding for developing countries in 2014.' 2014.

(10) European Commission. 'European Union climate funding for developing countries in 2015.' 2015.
(11) European Commission. 'European Union fast start funding for developing countries: 2010–2012 Report.' 2012.
(12) European Commission. 'Frequently Asked Questions on EU Development policy.' 2010.
(13) European Commission. 'Global Climate Change Alliance: From integrated climate strategies to climate finance effectiveness.' 2013.
(14) European Commission. 'Global Climate Change Alliance: Using Innovative and Effective Approaches to Deliver Climate Change Support to Developing Countries.' 2011.
(15) European Commission. 'Guidelines on the Integration of Environment and Climate Change in Development Cooperation.' 2010.
(16) European Commission. 'Pacific Islands – EU relations: Focus on Climate Change.' 2012.
(17) European Commission. 'Questions and Answers on the White paper on climate change adaptation.' 2015.
(18) European Parliament. 'Answers to the European Parliament: Questionnaire to the Commissioner- Designate Neven Mimica. 2014.

Speeches/press releases

(1) Barosso, José Manuel. 'Climate and Environment – factors of peace and development in the XXI century.' 2007.
(2) Cañete, Miguel Arias. 'Speech by Commissioner Miguel Arias Cañete at the 46th Pacific Islands Forum Plenary Session.' 2015.
(3) European Commission. 'Ahead of Rio+20: Climate change and sustainable development to be discussed at the EU-Pacific Islands Forum meeting.' 2012.
(4) European Commission. 'Commission Proposes a Global Alliance to Help Developing Countries Most Affected by Climate Change.' 2007.
(5) European Commission. 'Climate Action: Helping the Pacific fight against climate change.' 2013.
(6) European Commission. 'EU and 79 African, Caribbean and Pacific countries join forces for ambitious global climate deal.' 2015.
(7) European Commission. 'Global Climate Change Alliance + Launch: EU's contribution to tackle climate change in developing countries.' 2015.
(8) European Commission. 'Pacific Islands and Climate change: Commission takes the lead to help with adaptation and fight poverty.' 2011.
(9) Hedegaard, Connie. 'Europe's view on International Climate Policy.' 2010.
(10) Hedegaard, Connie. 'Science is crucial in supporting the low carbon transition'. 2012.
(11) Hedegaard, Connie. 'Rio Must Get It Right.' (2012). Published electronically 15/06/2012. https://www.euractiv.com/section/sustainable-dev/opinion/rio-must-get-it-right/.
(12) Hedegaard, Connie. 'Climate Change: our common challenge, our common opportunity'. 2012.
(13) Hedegaard, Connie. 'Acceptance speech for CSR Honor Award'. 2012.
(14) Piebalgs, Andris. 'Climate change and access to Energy: a priority for EU development policy.' 2012.
(15) Piebalgs, Andris. 'Climate change: don't forget the Pacific. For a stronger EU-Pacific joint action.' 2011.
(16) Piebalgs, Andris. 'Engaging with vulnerable countries through better adaptation and resilience action.' 2014.
(17) Piebalgs, Andris. 'How to make EU Development policy supportive of inclusive growth and sustainable development.' 2010.
(18) Piebalgs, Andris. 'Working together to deliver progress in the fight against climate change in Latin America & the Caribbean.' 2013.

Managing neo-liberalisation through the Sustainable Development Agenda: the EU-ACP trade relationship and world market expansion

Sophia Price and Alex Nunn

ABSTRACT
The EU suggests that it is committed to 'sustainable development' including through its institutionalised relationship with the states of the African, Caribbean and Pacific group in the Cotonou Partnership Agreement. This paper reviews this relationship with a view to outlining the way in which concepts like 'sustainable development' and 'poverty reduction' act as legitimation for processes of world market expansion. The paper reviews a range of interpretations of this relationship which view it either from a constructivist or material – Uneven and Combined Development – perspective. We critique these interpretations and provide an alternative materialist reading.

Introduction

This paper seeks to locate the EU's Sustainable Development Agenda, and its position within the 'post-2015 Consensus' within an analysis of neoliberalisation of EU external relations. We argue that a specific focus on the EU's relationship with the African, Caribbean and Pacific (ACP) group exemplifies a multi-scalar project of neoliberalisation, in which the discourse of sustainability is married to mechanisms that seek to manage the process of world market expansion within state–society complexes throughout the Global South and, simultaneously, the EU. In doing so, we explore the range of alternative readings of the EU–ACP relationships and the wider literature on EU external trade.

The contribution of the paper is twofold. We seek to place the EU–ACP relationship in a wider analysis of 'sustainable development', in line with the theme of this special issue, where sustainable development is located in a wider critical analysis of its relation to neoliberalisation. Second, we offer a novel interpretation of EU–ACP trade liberalisation which acknowledges the contributions of the major interpretations of the relationship from realist, constructivist, neo-Gramscian and Uneven and Combined Development (U&CD) perspectives. However, by contrast, our interpretation rests on the location of these contributions in a wider understanding of world market expansion, and the politics of generalised competitiveness that is associated with this. The originality of our approach is to suggest in relation to realists, neo-Gramscians and promoters of U&CD, that the EU–ACP trade relationship should not be read merely as the EU securing competitiveness relative to the ACP. Our contribution relative to constructivists is to acknowledge the role of ideas but to suggest that these are important only in as much as they arise from material processes and have material affects, in this case, principally world market expansion and *generalised* competitiveness. The significant implications of this are wide ranging and discussed briefly in the conclusion, but are of importance to those wanting to contest what they see as the damaging social, political and economic effects of trade liberalisation in *both* ACP and EU societies. The discussion is therefore based on an interpretation of policy documents and a critique of the relevant secondary literature.

The paper proceeds in four main parts. The first explores the EU's Sustainable Development Agenda and the centrality afforded to market-led strategies and in particular trade liberalisation. The second documents the evolution of the EU–ACP relationship in the form of the Cotonou Partnership Agreement (CPA). The third explores the links between sustainable development and the CPA and the fourth examines a range of explanations for this relationship, identifying their weaknesses and advancing our own interpretation.

The EU's sustainability agenda

The EU has a long-standing policy commitment to 'sustainable development' running as far back as the 1997 Treaty of Amsterdam, Article 1 of which committed the EU and its member states to 'promote economic and social progress ... taking account of the principle of sustainable development and within the context of the accomplishment of the internal market and of reinforced cohesion and environmental protection and ... ensuring that advances in economic integration are accompanied by parallel progress in other fields'. It was also central to the much vaunted, if failed, Lisbon Strategy[1] and the current Europe 2020 strategy for sustainable and inclusive growth,[2] and, more recently still to the EU's engagement with the UN's renegotiation of the Millennium Development Goals into the Sustainable Development Goals.[3] A full review of these strategies is neither possible or necessary here; we offer instead just a brief identification of the six key features of the EU's engagement with sustainable development as a general objective throughout this period, and which, we argue, are broadly reflected in its relationship with the ACP. Beyond the long-standing nature of this commitment, the further five features are:

(1) The commitment to securing sustainable development has long been seen as central to the *EU's external relations* with other states, and in particular with developing countries.[4]

(2) The commitment to sustainable development is pursued *in partnership with a range of inter-connected international organisations*, including the Bretton Woods organisations, the WTO, the OECD and the UN.[5] The EU's institutional relations with the ACP group; partly a legacy product of formal imperialism, offers the EU an important strategic role in this partnership.

(3) Through these external relations with ACP states and partnerships with international organisations, as well as its own internal reform processes, the EU's commitment to sustainable development is *universal*; being applicable to all societies at all development levels, characterised by 'shared responsibility, mutual accountability

and engagement by all'. Such universality is then inherently multi-scalar, linking local communities to the national, macro-regional and global levels.

(4) The approach taken to *sustainable development is market based* and predicated on 'Private Sector Development'. The central thrust of sustainable development is to create and secure the conditions for increased trade, investment and economic growth.[6]

(5) Sustainable development then is about the *promotion of world market expansion*, both intensively (market deepening) and extensively (market broadening), and within both the EU and the wider world. The promotion of world market expansion then requires trade liberalisation externally and internally, and domestic policy reform to secure generalised conditions of competitiveness and to cope with the domestic effects of this.

As other authors point out, this way of framing of 'sustainable development' as a continuation of pre-existing economic growth strategies is contradictory[7] or a wholly neoliberal construct.[8] As Wanner[9] notes, when arguing in similar terms about the current popularity of 'green growth' as an extension of sustainable development, what is actually being sustained is a process of neoliberalisation. Of course this sort of analysis might easily be seen to support the notion that politically mobilised concepts such as sustainable development – and add to that 'inclusive growth', 'poverty reduction' – are powerful in and of themselves. Through showing the connection between the sustainable development understanding of EU external relations and the EU–ACP relationship we wish to show that ideas like this are significant, but only in as much as they are located in, and shape, material processes. As such, we argue that sustainable development as carried through the EU–ACP relationship, should be read as a component of the material process of world market expansion. The need to frame such a material project in more amenable terms – such as sustainable development – may always be present but is particularly acute at a time when the risks to world market expansion, from environmental degradation, natural disasters and socio-political tensions associated with poverty and inequality, are most apparent.[10] It is in this context that the EU–ACP relationship can be viewed. It represents the longest – standing development cooperation between the EU and countries in the Global South and has come under continual pressure for liberalisation, particularly from the 1990s onwards. Those pressures are now framed as being in line with broader 'sustainable development' commitments.

Attempts to engender 'sustainable development' and secure trade liberalisation, however, are often not successful as blanket policies or through one-size-fits-all institutions. Classic examples here are the substantively stalled WTO world trade negotiations or the failure of structural adjustment policies in the 1980s/1990s. Rather, policy frameworks to secure world market expansion and the consequent neoliberalisation require sensitivity to localised institutional, political, social and economic forms. Without this, reform might easily cause economic collapse or political backlash, as in the case of the structural reforms promoted under the 'Washington Consensus' of the 1980s/early 1990s. As such, agents promoting world market expansion are required to both cut across scales and to pursue reform in ways that recognise the need for localised and path dependent change. It is this that causes scholars such as Peck and Brenner to focus on the ways in which neoliberalisation operates differently at multiple scales[11] (ie as a multi-scalar process) and in ways that cuts across scales through institutional mechanisms (ie as both inter-scalar and trans-scalar, in the latter case where it jumps over an intervening scale, such as where international organisations bypass the domestic state and engage directly with sub-state actors). They also call attention to the ways that neoliberal*isation*, as a process, is an ongoing and variegated political programme.[12] It is in this context that we explore and understand the evolution of the CPA.

The evolution of the CPA since 2004

The EU has maintained an institutionalised relationship with the states of the African, Pacific and Caribbean group of states since the 1960s in the form of the Yaoundé and Lomé agreements. The Lomé relationship was reflective of a post-independence and paternalistic relationship between the EU and ACP, characterised by a broadly Keynesian approach to managed development. The Lomé conventions provided non-reciprocal trade, preferential access for ACP goods to the EU market, commodity stabilisation measures to offset market volatility and development aid based initially on grants. Essentially, Lomé embodied some elements of the collective demands of newly independent developing countries in the 1970s, as expressed, for instance, in the demands for, and declaration of, a New International Economic Order. By contrast Lomé's replacement; the CPA – which was negotiated in the latter half of the 1990s – represented a clear attempt to ensure that the EU–ACP trade relationship became WTO compliant and in line with broader neoliberal reforms.[13]

The CPA, incorporating the expanded membership of the EU and the now 79 ACP member states, provided a framework for the relationship for the new millennium. The geographical expansion of the range of the partnership means that taken together this represents a majority of states within the United Nations and a total population of some 1.5 billion people,[14] including most developing countries.[15] The explicit aim of the CPA is to tackle poverty, create economic growth and develop governance, via 3 pillars of cooperation on (1) development, (2) political and economic reform; and (3) trade. It is funded by the European Development Fund (EDF), with ACP countries also receiving funds directly from the EU budget. The 11th EDF for the period 2014–2020 is €30.5 billion. The CPA entered into force in April 2003 and was revised in 2005 and 2010.[16] In 2010, it was extended to incorporate new areas of climate change, food security, regional integration, state fragility, aid effectiveness and importantly migration.

Much focus has been placed on the prioritisation of increased reliance on the private sector, and encouragement for ACP states to create enabling environments and conditions for private sector growth. As a corollary, the discourse of sustainability, codified in the 2015 Sustainable Development Goals, has been reframed as 'inclusive and sustainable growth' through private sector development and regional integration.[17] The provision of PSD funds which accompany the EPAs are regarded as a catalyst to unlock private finance, although the Commission does envision the private sector operating in tandem with 'social, traditional and cooperative forms of economy'.[18]

The prioritisation of private sector development reflects ongoing attempts to embed global market integration in path-dependent ways and increasingly sophisticated inter-scalar linkages between the EU and sub-regional, national and sub-national interests in the ACP. Through this there is a common tendency toward the creation of an attractive investment climate for capital, the provision of an infrastructure to valorise that capital and sufficient protections in the rule of law to ensure that surpluses can be realised:

> Private financial flows, like remittances, foreign investments and finance from institutional investors, are already larger than all public resources combined. To fully capitalise on the potential of the private sector it is necessary to create enabling conditions for private initiative, trade and finance, for sustainable investments and decent employment creation, and to bring informal activities into the formal sector. It also requires a strong commitment by companies to catalyse private sector investment in areas where market gaps exist and to engage in responsible practices as part of their core business strategies.[19]

Central to this has been the substantive shift from Lomé's non-reciprocal preferential trade regime between the EU and the ACP as a block of countries to a series of reciprocal, WTO compliant Economic Partnership Agreements (EPAs), based on regional groupings. The EPA negotiations began in 2002, and were due to be concluded by December 2007, however, the process proved to be more difficult and lengthy than expected. Only the Caribbean region was able to meet the deadline, while, as we predicted in 2004[20] the negotiations with other regional groupings proved difficult. Moreover, a coalition of resistance emerged (encompassing EU and ACP member states, civil society activists and NGOs) that challenged the liberalisation agenda on the basis of the potential threat it posed to the development of ACP economies, though the Commission continues to downplay these concerns.[21]

In the face of a lack of progress, inertia and dissent, 'Interim Agreements' were proposed and in some cases agreed. In 2011, the EU was able to leverage its position by threatening to withdraw preferential market access to the EU for any state that had not concluded and ratified an interim EPA. While trade with ACP countries represents only a small proportion of EU imports and exports, the EU is a major trading partner for ACP countries, being the main destination for its agricultural and manufactured products. The deadline of October 2014 was set for countries to either sign an EPA, fall under one of the new Generalised System of Preferences (GSP) schemes, or have no trade preferences at all. By the end of 2014, full or interim EPAs had been concluded with all seven regions: West Africa, Central Africa, Eastern and Southern Africa, Eastern African Community, Southern African Development Community (SADC), the Caribbean and the Pacific. The negotiations were concluded in the face of stalled multi-lateral trade liberalisation via the Doha Round, and at a time when the central role that the EU plays in ACP has been challenged by Brazil, China and India which are 'strategically positioning themselves in these regions with an increased presence, growing investment and trade relations, and a growing cooperation portfolio'.[22]

Through the reformulation of the relationship the EU has been able to fashion new trade relations with the ACP that are fully WTO-compliant, covering 'substantially all trade' (approx. 80%) in goods and services, investment and trade-related rules. The current agreements fall into three categories: Comprehensive Agreements that cover trade in goods and in services, and agreement on other trade-related measures; Goods Only EPAs that cover only the trade in goods but with 'rendezvous' clauses to extend the remit of the agreement; and interim Goods Only EPAs that cover only goods at present while ongoing negotiations for Comprehensive EPAs continue. The trade pillar of the EU–ACP relationship has been fundamentally transformed into a multi-pronged relationship with a variety of sub-regional groupings, better able to deal with variation in regional, sub-regional and national conditions. The rationale that underpins these reforms is explicitly framed in terms of 'sustainable development', based on regional integration to foster gradual integration into the world economy and the diversification from primary production to manufacturing.

While these relationships provide for reciprocal free trade and fully liberalised access to EU markets, they also allow for a transition period for the ACP states to adjust to liberalisation via protection of sensitive sectors. This enables legacy social and institutional structures to adapt to the pressures of competition in the world market and helps to offset (in theory at least) the scope for opposition. The Commission therefore rebuts claims about the coercive nature of EU–ACP relations by arguing that 'EPAs respect national sovereignty – instead of imposing development strategies, EPAs ask countries to determine their own development strategies and the pace and sequence of reforms'.[23] Similarly, it points to the collaborative nature of the associated aid programmes, which it argues are created through dialogue with the recipient countries, allowing them to be tailored 'to local needs and circumstances'.[24]

Reciprocal but asymmetric arrangements are fully compatible with rules of the World Trade Organisation and allow for differentiation by taking into account the socio-economic circumstances of the partners. The concept of differentiation, including the targeting of both resources and particular trade provisions at the poorest and most fragile states, is one of four key principles of *Agenda for Change* that underpin the EU's poverty reduction and sustainable development strategies. This requirement reflects the heterogeneity of the ACP Group whose membership ranges from middle-income countries to least developed and fragile states. Differentiation therefore is designed to cope with such variety, with the EU advocating 'graduation' from bilateral development for the more developed states.[25] The EU therefore not only advocates EPAs as inter-scalar institutional connections to secure differentiated pathways towards liberalisation, but also recognises this requires variegated institutional arrangements too.

The need to accommodate ACP LDCs within these new arrangements might appear unnecessary, as the EPAs seem to add little to the existing trade arrangements that they have with the EU. All LDCs already have duty free access to the EU via the 'Everything But Arms' scheme, however, the Commission argues that their inclusion in the EPAs offer additional benefits. These include more flexible rules of origin; cooperation on trade-related issues such as technical barriers to trade and improved infrastructure; enhanced regional markets and rules via integration projects; the safeguarding of local economies and prevention of trade disruption via gradual liberalisation and the embedding of relations within a 'partnership of equals' that cannot be altered without mutual agreement (in contrast to the EBA which is 'granted' by the EU).

Alongside differentiation, the principles of coordination, concentration and coherence are key elements in the alignment of the EU's poverty eradication and sustainable development strategies with the broader liberalisation agenda. This is further evidenced via the negotiation and conclusion of a variety of agreements that both complement and extend each other. For example, the EPA negotiations, have been accompanied by the development of broader strategic partnerships, such as the Africa–EU strategic partnership, the Joint Caribbean – EU Partnership Strategy, and the strategy for a strengthened partnership with Pacific Islands. The Africa–EU Partnership integrates those African sub-Saharan countries that have been part of the Lomé/Cotonou relationship with Northern African countries, which are not part of CPA. The Cotonou and EPA processes then offer overlapping and inter-scalar mechanisms for tying varying trade liberalisation and sustainable development projects together; not in a neat and hierarchically ordered fashion but in a complex network of agreements and financing projects.

Heron and Murray-Evans[26] argue that the outcomes of the EPA negotiations so far are 'sub-optimal' in terms of the EU Commission achieving its original aims and subsequent attempts to expand the remit to of the agenda to include Trade in Services and 'Singapore

Issues' such as 'behind the border' regulations in product markets and other public service provisions. Moreover, they point to the numbers of ACP states that have not signed the EPAs, and are instead linked to the EU via the 'Everything But Arms' Initiative or the GSPs. They attribute this the Commission's failure to operationalise its 'market power' in the face of challenges and contestation from a coalition of support for the ACP.

However, this assessment underplays the achievements of the process so far. The seven EPA agreements that have been negotiated provide a framework for a 35 year process of gradual liberalisation which allows for the slow social, institutional, economic, political adjustment to full integration into the world market. While some of the agreements are not yet 'comprehensive', they contain provisions for the ongoing negotiation of the depth and range of the agreements. As such, the current agreements will be subject to ongoing reform and change rather than being an end point. Furthermore, the provisions that allow for differentiation provide for the sequencing of these reforms and timescales, and agency for the ACP states within these decisions. Those ACP states that are not currently signatories are included in these ongoing negotiations, whilst having their relations with the EU secured via other institutional provisions and regional arrangements, such as the Africa–EU Partnership. Finally, while the constitution of the regional EPA associations are still under construction, the EPA process has provided a mechanism for the sub-division of the ACP into smaller, and more manageable negotiating partners.

In these ways, the EPAs establish pathways of future reform for world market expansion, taking account of the need for this to respond to scalar differentiation. While the EU's development policies, like other aspects of EU meta-governance[27] frequently fail, this then provides the self-reflective logic for further policy experimentation and reform. In that sense, attempts at inter-scalar neoliberalisation 'fail forward'.[28] Within this process, the EU has demonstrated some degree of relative autonomy, through its leadership and preferences for wide scale liberalisation and the expansion of the negotiating agenda, despite the expressed opposition by certain member states. Its aims reflect a wider institutional agenda, in line with other institutions of global governance.

Interpreting the ACP–EU relationship

There is a growing body of literature on the EU–ACP relationship. A range of debates are present, for instance, about whether the CPA marked an essential break[29] or continuity[30] in the EU–ACP relationship, around the generally unequal nature of the partnership,[31] about the overall effectiveness of the relationship in generating economic growth and poverty reduction [32]. There are four main rival critical interpretations of the relationship. The first sees the EU–ACP as predominantly a social construction, where key concepts such as 'partnership', poverty reduction, democratisation, and now, we might add; sustainable development, are infused with power relations to lock in the ACP to a dependent form of development.[33] The second, third and fourth perspectives proceed from shared materialist foundations either in the quite different Gramscian,[34] U&CD,[35] or realist[36] traditions – which nevertheless see the ACP as subject to an unequal power relationship with the EU in which they are once again locked in to an ongoing relationship of inequality.

The basic unevenness in the EU–ACP relationship is featured in a range of analytical accounts. Carbone argues that 10 years on from the beginning of the Cotonou agreement 'despite its emphasis on partnership, the patterns of asymmetrical relations of the previous century have been reinforced'[37]. Hurt drew on an explicitly Gramscian analysis of material coercion and consent which undermined the idea of partnership and pointed to the manner in which the EU sought to 'externalise' responsibility for reciprocity by pointing to the pressures from the WTO.[38] Carbone concurs, arguing the ACP's capacity to shape policy outcomes has been limited.

> The negotiations of the EPAs, of course, show that the ACP has somehow managed to resist the EU's agenda. But in general, the objective conditions in which ACP states find themselves place them in a weaker position. Moreover, the asymmetrical relationship has been strengthened by the EU's actions deconstructing the ACP Group and undermining ACP Group solidarity.[39]

He argues that the promotion of norms appears paternalistic, with a gap between rhetoric and reality.

The constructivist line of argument associates EU trade policy with a broader projection of normative liberal goals in shaping world politics and the global economy.[40] While some constructivists share the liberal institutionalist perspective on the expansion of European ideas as benign, more critical constructivists identify the way liberal ideas are used to pursue and veil particular interests.[41] They identify multiple competing liberal goals which result from internal interests shaping EU external policy. These partly contradictory liberal objectives then locate the site of social struggle in the construction of the idea of Europe, and European external policy.[42] Critical constructivists emphasise a 'new trade politics'[43] where the EU seeks 'deep' trade agenda of domestic reform in developing countries, often locking them in – through reciprocal free trade agreements to patterns of development likely to promote European 'values'.[44] Indeed, Langan[45] shows how these normative European values in trade/aid partnerships with developing countries are often loudly trumpeted but subordinated to the goals of competitiveness at the point of implementation.

Many of these constructivist accounts of the EU–ACP trade relationship closely resemble our own depiction. For example, Storey locates our earlier analysis[46] within his analysis of a normative Europe and its diffusion of 'a particular and controversial "norm" of economic governance'.[47] Langan too shows how EU external trade – including with the ACP – is used to drive a particular 'moral economy' in the ACP which suits the interests of EU capital, and is only thinly veiled by legitimating norms of rights, democratisation and poverty reduction.[48] Constructivist accounts, however, reject a materialist analysis due to its prior analytical focus on material as opposed to ideational processes.[49]

By contrast, Andreas Bieler[50] argues that the EU–ACP relationship should be seen through a primarily materialist lens. He argues that EU external trade should be understood within the *Global Europe* strategy whose objective is to ensure the unequal competitiveness of EU produced commodities relative to those produced elsewhere. So the EU intends to lock ACP states into an uneven but combined trading relationship whereby dependence on EU markets for primary commodities is matched with imports of EU services and manufactured goods. This relationship also helps to offset claims for transnational working class solidarity on the grounds that workers and trade unions in the EU are placed in a contrasting material position to those in the global south. This approach partly speaks to the demands set out by Will Brown for an understanding of the relationship between 'western' and African states that simultaneously asserts the unevenness of bargaining relationships between different states and looks for the uneven and combined nature of societal differences and connections between very different forms of state/society relationship.[51] Brown therefore advises caution in relation to big picture analyses which suggest an internally coherent and universal tendency among international actors seeking reform in African states or, the universal application of reform in these states without considering the specific difficulties of this process inside very different state–society relationships. It is necessary therefore to give space for different non-market and pre-capitalist forms of power within African states which have often frustrated the liberal reform efforts of international organisations.[52] For Brown, this critique extended to our own earlier analysis of Cotonou,[53] which he suggested that had overstated the coherence of the locking-in process.[54]

From a more Gramscian underpinning, a number of authors[55] argue that the CPA represents a system to encourage greater competitiveness and has a more general significance in ensuring wider compliance with multilateral liberalisation. They argue that EU material and ideational interests within the historical context of EU–ACP relations, are represented in EU efforts to 'lock-in' neoliberalisation via EPAs, reducing their 'policy space' and undermining regional integration.

We have much sympathy with these materialist and critical constructivist accounts but we seek to differentiate our understanding somewhat. There is much to commend in Bieler/Brown/Hurt/Langan's analysis. We share the analysis of the inherent tendency of capitalist social relations toward expanded reproduction. Following Neil Smith,[56] we also see this process of intensive and extensive expansion resulting in uneven patterns of development. However, we contend that development may *be* both uneven and combined, but that does not mean that U&CD explains this as a predictive law. Further, one consequence of Bieler's analysis is that there is very little difference in his interpretation of the European Commission's objectives in trade negotiations from a realist/mercantilist understanding[57] of the Commission pursuing its comparative advantage in services trade. We see it as important to once again assert the importance of seeing EU trade with the ACP, or developing and emerging market economies more generally, in the context of wider developments in trade liberalisation and world market expansion, leading to generalised competitiveness as opposed to merely the competitiveness of one state/regional bloc relative to others.

The EU promotes extensive world market expansion, through EU enlargement, external trade liberalisation and development cooperation and the broadening and deepening of the internal market. The outcome of this is that both labour and capital in the EU and its development 'partners' are exposed to increased generalised competitiveness. Within that more global objective the EU may also try to secure a greater proportion of the surplus value produced globally, through advantageous external trade deals, but this is a secondary objective to world market expansion. It is precisely this that explains why the EU seeks trade liberalisation with both developed (as in, for example, the various other liberalisation processes eg Trans-Atlantic Trade and Investment Partnership) and developing countries at the same time as it also seeks internal liberalisation. New sectors (eg digital, legal and public services) are targeted for both internal and external liberalisation in the full knowledge of the effects of competition in product and labour markets which have already experienced liberalisation and a resulting labour market polarisation. The Commission itself targets this polarisation as a high level policy problem (segmented labour markets, absolute and in-work poverty etc.) and acknowledges their cause as increased (including international) competition in these markets,[58] yet it continues to pursue liberalisation in sectors currently protected.[59] The parallel here with pursuing trade liberalisation, private sector development and openness to MNCs in the global south, under the banner of 'sustainable development' and 'inclusive growth' is notable.

Concerns with relative comparative advantage may shape the pace of liberalisation and the relative enthusiasm of different member states, lobby and interest groups to support the Commission's stance. However, the Commission itself remains implacably in favour of expanding and deepening the trade regime across and within sectors, internally, and externally with both developed and developing economies. Some sectional interests may hope to reap the benefits of U&CD but this is within an overall preference for the promotion of intensively and extensively expanded capitalist reproduction. As further support for our argument, the Commission continues to pursue trade liberalisation with countries which have been remarkably successful in recent years at catch-up industrialisation and trade competition vis-à-vis the EU, such as China. At the same time, the competitive threat posed by China, India and other emerging economies is used now as the logic for efforts to increase the competitiveness of EU societies, in the same way as the US and Japan were a generation earlier.[60] It is also a motivation to ensure that trade liberalisation progresses with some ACP states (eg Angola and South Africa) in the context of trade competition in these countries from China.[61] In sum, we argue that U&CD may *describe* the result of trade liberalisation (and more broadly the combination of domestic social relations and international competition) in some sectors and between some places (including sub-nationally[62]) but it does not necessarily *explain* it.[63]

For an explanation we need to locate the EU–ACP trade relationship within a multi-scalar process of world market expansion, driven by the twin systemic pressures of competition, and class struggle.[64] Accordingly, while we attach importance to the universal force of competitiveness as a systemic property of an expanding world market, the consequences of this are socially and historically embedded and path dependent; resulting in myriad different hybrid institutional forms. Here what Brenner/Peck et al.[65] refer to as 'variegated neo-liberalisation' does not lead to simple convergence, but is characterised by the co-evolutionary variation in the institutional, ideological and material forms that Brown identifies, or what might be *described* as U&CD. World market expansion must take this path dependent form for a variety of reasons, including the specificities of domestic class and other struggles; inter-capitalist competition; the ways in which these struggles are permeated with international alliances and divergences; and the particulars of production and pre-existing trade relationships. Rather than convergence, complex processes of inter-scalar policy borrowing and experimentation[66] occur through social struggles which sometimes seek to shape processes with tendentially universal characteristics – such as trade liberalisation, democratisation, environmental regulation – to best suit localised conditions. National and sub-national elites seek to promote their own interests, sometimes with, and sometimes against transnational capital. As Bieler[67] shows, this may produce elite coalitions with capital and organised labour, but at other times there will be more scope for transnational solidarism from below.

Trade liberalisation has been fully subject to these complex and dynamic struggles, unfolding within the context of a world market expansion that has altered the geo-politics of multi-lateral cooperation. As this has led to stalling multi-lateral trade liberalisation, elites and those with much to gain from further liberalisation, have sought other means, and regional and sub-regional arrangements have proliferated as a result. In that sense, and others, policy reform for neoliberalisation is not universally successful and frequently results in failure. Far from halting the momentum behind neoliberalisation though, failure is often used as a justification for further reform. In times of growth, it makes sense to use neoliberalisation to 'fix the roof while the sun shines'; in times of economic crisis neoliberalisation is justified on the grounds that reform is then more urgently needed. When policy reform fails, it typically 'fails forward'[68] with failure being the logic for renewed efforts to overcome barriers and opposition and to engage in more policy experimentation.

The ongoing changes to the EU–ACP relationship represents an inter-scalar reform process which is likely to exhibit different path-dependent social struggles at the sub-regional, state and sub-state scales, within pressures for trade liberalisation and market oriented reform. Ideas are significant here but only inasmuch as they emerge from material processes of social struggle and have material consequences, primarily in this case in relation to world market expansion. As Marx and Engels[69] famously argued in the 1840s, to assume that ideas have some life outside of material social struggles is a somewhat bizarre conclusion – and as we read it this is not what 'constructivists' argue; rather constructivism appears as the assertion that within processes of policy reform, ideas and the institutions that are shaped by them, matter. That much we concede. However, rhetorical principles and concepts such as sustainable development must be located within an understanding of world market expansion and the contradictory processes that this realises.

Conclusion

The evolution of the EPA trade regime between the EU and ACP remains characteristic of an attempt to ensure neoliberalisation in the name of pro-poor and sustainable development. This is a multi-scalar process that is further entrenched via the regionalisaion of the trade agenda on which the Cotonou reforms rest. The form of dependent development promoted by the 'partnership' is pro-market in orientation and attempts to secure and deepen the embedding of the world market in different national ACP contexts. This is not a simple process of homogenisation and policy convergence but embedding the world market in the domestic political economy – a process that even when subject to universal processes, most notably competitiveness, is always nationally specific and path dependent by necessity. Variegation in the extent to which trade is liberalised between countries, between sectors and the way in which liberalisation or even protectionism is justified and achieved are to be expected. As it has evolved the EU–ACP relationship has embraced and recognised this variegation.

The variegated reform that results from the EU–ACP relationship is much more expansive than mere trade liberalisation. It extends to social protection and other aspects of social policy and is veiled in the language of poverty reduction and sustainable development. Spreading the ideology of market freedom at the same time as enmeshing domestic society in the web of the world market is part of a proletarianising strategy which is common – even in its different policy experiments and institutionalised forms across the different EPAs and states. If this is about securing compliance with EU authored ideational frameworks for sustainable development, those ideas both spring from the material expansion of the world market and its contradictions, and have material effects – whether successful or not – in the forms of development that arise from them.

While policy reform is not always successful, this does not mean that alternative paths to development open up. Rather, restless policy experimentation is tried – in different funding arrangements and in different negotiating approaches between EPAs. That trade liberalisation and policy reform sometimes – *often* even – fail or stall is merely the invitation for further evolution. In the end, the EU's attempt at sustainable development is to sustain both world market expansion and the processes of variegated reform that it entails by establishing the multi-scalar governance mechanisms, that this can operate through. These include establishing alliances with major international organisations around key framing concepts such as sustainable development and poverty reduction, the long-term institutionalised EU–ACP relationship as in the CPA, sub-regional cooperation in the EPAs and 'deep' domestic reform processes too.

Disclosure statement

No potential conflict of interest was reported by the authors.

Acknowledgments

The authors would like to thank the editor Mark Langan and two anonymous reviewers for their helpful comments which have helped to clarify and improve the quality of the argument in the paper considerably. They would also like to thank participants at a discussion on EU–ACP relations at the ISA in 2016, especially Nicole Lindstrom, Elitsa Garnizova and Jamie Scalera for helpful discussion and comments. Remaining errors or omissions are, of course, our own.

ORCID

Alex Nunn http://orcid.org/0000-0002-1362-2170

Notes

1. EC, "A Sustainable Europe for a Better World"; "Towards a Global Partnership."
2. Nunn and Beeckmans, "The Political Economy of Competitiveness and Continuous."
3. Council of the European Union, "Council Conclusions on a Transformative Post-2015 Agenda"; Council of the European Union, "A New Global Partnership for Poverty Eradication and Sustainable Development After 2015"; EC, "A Decent Life for All"; "A Decent Life for All"; "A Global Partnership for Poverty Eradication and Sustainable Development."
4. EC, "Towards a Global Partnership."
5. EC, "A Sustainable Europe for a Better World," 9.
6. EC, "A Global Partnership for Poverty Eradication and Sustainable Development," 12, 10, 9; "A Decent Life for All"; "A Decent Life for All," 1.
7. Sachs, *Planet Dialectics*.
8. Wanner, "The New 'Passive Revolution'."
9. Ibid.

10. Nunn, "Saving World Market Society from Itself?"
11. Peck, "Political Economies of Scale."
12. Brenner, Peck, and Theodore, "Variegated Neoliberalization," 209.
13. Nunn and Price, "Managing Development"; Hurt, "Co-Operation and Coercion?"; and Brown, "Restructuring North-South Relations."
14. EC, *Towards a New Partnership*.
15. Gomes, "Reshaping an Asymmetrical Partnership."
16. Carbone, "Rethinking ACP-EU Relations After Cotonou."
17. EC, "Increasing the Impact of EU Development Policy."
18. EC, "Joint Consultation Paper," 6.
19. Ibid.
20. Anonymised for review.
21. Pape, "An Old Partnership in a New Setting."
22. EC, "A Global Partnership for Poverty Eradication and Sustainable Development."
23. EC, "Economic Partnership Agreements."
24. EC, *ACP Funding Programmes*.
25. Ibid.
26. Heron and Murray-Evans, "Limits to Market Power."
27. Nunn and Beeckmans, "The Political Economy of Competitiveness and Continuous."
28. Brenner, Peck, and Theodore, "Variegated Neoliberalization."
29. Carbone, "Rethinking ACP-EU Relations After Cotonou," 745.
30. Brown, "Restructuring North-South Relations."
31. Farrell, "A Triumph of Realism Over Idealism?"; Gomes, "Reshaping an Asymmetrical Partnership"; Hurt, "Co-operation and Coercion?"; "The EU–SADC Economic Partnership Agreement Negotiations."
32. Hurt, "The EU–SADC Economic Partnership Agreement Negotiations"; and Langan, "Decent Work and Indecent Trade Agendas."
33. Langan, "ACP–EU Normative Concessions from Stabex to Private Sector Development"; "A Moral Economy Approach to Africa-EU Ties"; "Decent Work and Indecent Trade Agendas."
34. Hurt, "Co-operation and Coercion?"; "The EU–SADC Economic Partnership Agreement Negotiations."
35. Bieler, "The EU, Global Europe, and Processes of Uneven and Combined Development"; Brown, "The World Bank, Africa and Politics"; "Debating the Year of Africa"; "Reconsidering the Aid Relationship."
36. Farrell, "A Triumph of Realism over Idealism?"
37. Carbone, "Rethinking ACP-EU Relations After Cotonou."
38. Langan, "Normative Power Europe and the Moral Economy of Africa–EU Ties."
39. Carbone, "Rethinking ACP-EU Relations After Cotonou."
40. Manners, "Normative Power Europe: A Contradiction in Terms?"
41. Storey, "Normative Power Europe?"
42. Rosamond, "Three Ways of Speaking Europe to the World."
43. Peterson and Young, *The European Union and the New Trade Politics*; Young and Peterson, "The EU and the New Trade Politics."
44. Carbone, "Rethinking ACP-EU Relations After Cotonou"; and Storey, "Normative Power Europe?"
45. Langan, "Decent Work and Indecent Trade Agendas."
46. Anonymised for review.
47. Storey, "Normative Power Europe?"
48. Langan, "Normative Power Europe and the Moral Economy of Africa–EU Ties"; "A Moral Economy Approach to Africa-EU Ties."
49. Langan, "A Moral Economy Approach to Africa-EU Ties."
50. Bieler, "The EU, Global Europe, and Processes of Uneven and Combined Development."
51. Brown, "Reconsidering the Aid Relationship."
52. Brown, "The World Bank, Africa and Politics."
53. Anonymised for review.

54. Brown, "Debating the Year of Africa," 17.
55. Hurt, "Co-operation and Coercion?"; "The EU–SADC Economic Partnership Agreement Negotiations"; Nunn and Price, "Managing Development."
56. Smith, *Uneven Development*.
57. eg Farrell, "A Triumph of Realism over Idealism?"
58. European Commission, "Employment and Social Developments in Europe 2011."
59. Nunn and Beeckmans, "The Political Economy of Competitiveness and Continuous."
60. Ibid.
61. Hurt, "The EU–SADC Economic Partnership Agreement Negotiations."
62. Charnock, Purcell, and Ribera-Fumaz, "New International Division of Labour and Differentiated Integration in Europe"; and Starosta, "Revisiting the New International Division."
63. Rioux, "Mind the (Theoretical) Gap."
64. Cammack, "Poverty Reduction and Universal Competitiveness"; "The UNDP and the End of Human Development"; Nunn and Beeckmans, "The Political Economy of Competitiveness and Continuous."
65. Brenner, Peck, and Theodore, "Variegated Neoliberalization"; and Peck, Theodore, and Brenner, "Neoliberalism Resurgent?"
66. Peck, "Political Economies of Scale."
67. Bieler, "The EU, Global Europe, and Processes of Uneven and Combined Development."
68. Brenner, Peck, and Theodore, "Variegated Neoliberalization," 209.
69. Marx and Engels, *The German Ideology (1845)*.

Bibliography

Bieler, A. "The EU, Global Europe, and Processes of Uneven and Combined Development: The Problem of Transnational Labour Solidarity." *Review of International Studies* 39, no. 1 (2013): 161–183.

Brenner, N., J. Peck, and N. Theodore. "Variegated Neoliberalization: Geographies, Modalities, Pathways." *Global Networks* 10, no. 2 (2010): 182–222.

Brown, William. "Debating the Year of Africa." *Review of African Political Economy* 34, no. 111 (2007): 11–27.

Brown, William. "Reconsidering the Aid Relationship: International Relations and Social Development." *The Round Table* 98, no. 402 (2009): 285–299.

Brown, William. "Restructuring North-South Relations: ACP-EU Development Co-operation in a Liberal International Order." *Review of African Political Economy* 27, no. 85 (2000): 367–383.

Brown, William. "The World Bank, Africa and Politics: A Comment on Paul Cammack's Analysis." *Historical Materialism* 11, no. 2 (2003): 61–74.

Cammack, P. "Poverty Reduction and Universal Competitiveness." *Labour, Capital and Society* 42 (2009): 1–2.

Cammack, P. "The UNDP and the End of Human Development: A Critique of the Human Development Report 2013." *The Multilateral Development Banks and the Global Financial Crisis* 6 (2014): 32–54.

Carbone, M. "Rethinking ACP-EU Relations After Cotonou: Tensions, Contradictions, Prospects." *Journal of International Development* 25, no. 5 (2013): 742–756.

Charnock, G, T. F. Purcell, and R. Ribera-Fumaz. "New International Division of Labour and Differentiated Integration in Europe: The Case of Spain." In *The New International Division of Labour: Global Transformation and Uneven Development*, edited by G Charnock and G Starosta, 157–180. London: Palgrave Macmillan, 2016.

Council of the European Union. "A New Global Partnership for Poverty Eradication and Sustainable Development After 2015 – Council Conclusions (9241/15)." EC, 2015.

Council of the European Union. "Council Conclusions on a Transformative Post-2015 Agenda." EC, 2014.

EC. *ACP Funding Programmes*. Brussels: EC, 2016.

EC. "A Decent Life for All: Ending Poverty and Giving the World a Sustainable Future (COM (2013) 092 Final)." EC, 2013.

EC. "A Decent Life for All: From Vision to Collective Action (COM(2014) 335 Final)." EC, 2014.

EC. "Economic Partnership Agreements." EC, n.d.

EC. "Employment and Social Developments in Europe 2011." EC, 2011.

EC. "Increasing the Impact of EU Development Policy: An Agenda for Change" COM 2011 637. EC, 2011.

EC. "A Global Partnership for Poverty Eradication and Sustainable Development after 2015 (COM(2015) 44 Final)." EC, 2015.

EC. "Joint Consultation Paper: Towards a New Partnership between the European Union and the African, Caribbean and Pacific Countries after 2020 (JOIN(2015) 33 Final)." EC, 2015.

EC. "Overview of EPA Negotiations." EC, 2016.

EC. "A Sustainable Europe for a Better World: A European Union Strategy for Sustainable Development (COM(2001) 264 Final)." EC, 2001.

EC. "Towards a Global Partnership for Sustainable Development (Com2002 82 Final)." EC, 2002.

EC. *Towards a New Partnership between the European Union and the African, Caribbean and Pacific Countries after 2020*. Brussels: EC, 2015.

Farrell, M. "A Triumph of Realism Over Idealism? Cooperation Between the European Union and Africa." *Journal of European Integration* 27, no. 3 (2005): 263–283.

Gomes, P. I. "Reshaping an Asymmetrical Partnership: ACP-EU Relations from an ACP Perspective." *Journal of International Development* 25, no. 5 (2013): 714–726.

Heron, T., and P. Murray-Evans. "Limits to Market Power: Strategic Discourse and Institutional Path Dependence in the European Union–African, Caribbean and Pacific Economic Partnership Agreements." *European Journal of International Relations*, April 13, (2016). Accessed April 2016. http://journals.sagepub.com/doi/full/10.1177/1354066116639359

Heron, T., and G. Siles-Brügge. "Competitive Liberalization and the 'Global Europe' Services and Investment Agenda: Locating the Commercial Drivers of the EU-ACP Economic Partnership Agreements." *Journal of Common Market Studies* 50, no. 2 (2012): 250–266.

Hurt, S. "Co-operation and Coercion? The Cotonou Agreement between the European Union and ACP States and the End of the Lomé Convention." *Third World Quarterly* 1 (2003): 161–176.

Hurt, S. "The EU–SADC Economic Partnership Agreement Negotiations: 'locking In' the Neoliberal Development Model in Southern Africa?" *Third World Quarterly* 33, no. 3 (2012): 495–510.

Langan, M. "ACP–EU Normative Concessions from Stabex to Private Sector Development: Why the European Union's Moralised Pursuit of a 'Deep' Trade Agenda is Nothing 'New' in ACP–EU Relations." *Perspectives on European Politics and Society* 10, no. 3 (2009): 416–440.

Langan, M. "Decent Work and Indecent Trade Agendas: The European Union and ACP Countries." *Contemporary Politics* 20, no. 1 (2014): 23–35.

Langan, M. "A Moral Economy Approach to Africa-EU Ties: The Case of the European Investment Bank." *Review of International Studies* 40, no. 3 (2014): 465–485.

Langan, M. "Normative Power Europe and the Moral Economy of Africa–EU Ties: A Conceptual Reorientation of 'Normative Power'." *New Political Economy* 17, no. 3 (2012): 243–270.

Manners, I. "Normative Power Europe: A Contradiction in Terms?" *JCMS. Journal of Common Market Studies* 40, no. 2 (2002): 235–258.

Marx, K., and F. Engels. *The German Ideology (1845)*. Moscow: Progress Publishers, 1968.

Nunn, A. "Saving World Market Society from Itself? The New Global Politics of Inequality and the Agents of Global Capitalism." *Spectrum: Journal of Global Studies* 7, no. 2 (2015).

Nunn, A., and P. Beeckmans. "The Political Economy of Competitiveness and Continuous Adjustment in EU Meta-governance." *International Journal of Public Administration* 38, no. 12 (2015): 926–939.

Nunn, A., and S. Price. "Managing Development: EU and African Relations through the Evolution of the Lomé and Cotonou Agreements." *Historical Materialism* 12, no. 4 (2004): 203–230.

Pape, E. "An Old Partnership in a New Setting: ACP-EU Relations from a European Perspective." *Journal of International Development* 25, no. 5 (2013): 727–741.

Peck, J. "Political Economies of Scale: Fast Policy, Interscalar Relations, and Neoliberal Workfare." *Economic Geography* 78, no. 3 (2002): 331–360.

Peck, J., N. Theodore, and N. Brenner. "Neoliberalism Resurgent? Market Rule after the Great Recession." *South Atlantic Quarterly* 111, no. 2 (2012): 265–288.

Peterson, J., and A. Young *The European Union and the New Trade Politics*. Abingdon, Oxon: Routledge, 2013.

Rioux, S. "Mind the (Theoretical) Gap: On the Poverty of International Relations Theorising of Uneven and Combined Development." *Global Society* 29, no. 4 (2015): 481–509.

Rosamond, B. "Three Ways of Speaking Europe to the World: Markets, Peace, Cosmopolitan Duty and the EU's Normative Power." *The British Journal of Politics & International Relations* 16, no. 1 (2014): 133–148.

Sachs, W. *Planet Dialectics. Explorations in Environment and Development*. London: Zed, 1999.

Smith, N. *Uneven Development: Nature, Capital, and the Production of Space*. London: University of Georgia Press, 2008.

Starosta, G. "Revisiting the New International Division of Labour Thesis." In *The New International Division of Labour: Global Transformation and Uneven Development*, edited by G. Charnock and G. Starosta, 79–103. London: Palgrave Macmillan, 2016.

Storey, A. "Normative Power Europe? Economic Partnership Agreements and Africa." *Journal of Contemporary African Studies* 24, no. 3 (2006): 331–346.

Wanner, T. "The New 'Passive Revolution' of the Green Economy and Growth Discourse: Maintaining the 'Sustainable Development' of Neoliberal Capitalism." *New Political Economy* 20, no. 1 (2015): 21–41.

Young, Alasdair R., and John Peterson. "The EU and the New Trade Politics." *Journal of European Public Policy* 13, no. 6 (2006): 795–814.

Regional encounters: explaining the divergent responses to the EU's support for regional integration in Africa, the Caribbean and Pacific

Tony Heron and Peg Murray-Evans

ABSTRACT

In this article, we map and explain the unevenness of African, Caribbean and Pacific (ACP) responses to the EU's external promotion of regional integration in the context of the Economic Partnership Agreements (EPAs). Although the controversies associated with the EPAs are typically attributed to a common set of problems, what remains to be fully explained is why these manifested themselves to a greater or lesser extent in different national and regional contexts. We account for this variance as a product of the degree of congruence between the institutional trajectory of individual regional projects and the model of economic integration prescribed by the EU in its post-Lomé prospectus for the ACP. We describe this congruence as either 'high', 'medium' or 'low' and use this explanatory model to account for variances in ACP responses to the EPAs, which would otherwise provide an untidy fit with accounts preoccupied with the economic determinants of bargaining outcomes.

Introduction

In this article, we map and explain the unevenness of African, Caribbean and Pacific (ACP) responses to the EU's external promotion of regional integration in the context of the Economic Partnership Agreements (EPAs). Although the controversies associated with the EPAs are typically attributed to a common set of problems, what remains to be fully explained is why these were manifest to a greater or lesser extent in different national and regional contexts. The predominant explanation of this puzzle focuses on the unevenness of trade dependences – i.e. the greater or lesser degree of enthusiasm shown for the EPAs by individual states is a direct correlate of their reliance on EU trade preferences – but this is only part of the story and in fact leads to a rather misleading account. It is, for instance, among the countries and regions least sensitive to the removal of EU trade preferences – e.g. CARIFORUM, Papua New Guinea, Lesotho and Mozambique – that we find the most enthusiasm for the EPAs. States such as Namibia and Ghana, in contrast, were publicly critical of the EPAs and even refused to sign agreements, in spite of heavy dependence on EU preferences.[1]

This anomaly, we suggest, exposes a crucial oversight in much of the critical commentary that the EPAs have generated.[2] That is to say, this commentary is preoccupied with the *economic* dimension of the EPAs – i.e. the introduction of the principle of reciprocity to trade in goods and the extension of this to services, alongside the so-called 'Singapore issues'.[3] This preoccupation leads to an underestimation of the *political* dimension of the EPAs – i.e. the EU's insistence on intraregional cooperation and the requirement that EPAs be concluded on a regional as opposed to bilateral basis – as a determinant of the outcome of the negotiations. This political dimension has its immediate origins in the Cotonou Partnership Agreement of 2000, which provided the blueprint for the EPAs and linked their successful conclusion to the creation, promotion and consolidation of regional institutions to be identified during the process of the negotiations. The general vagueness of Cotonou meant that, at the time, the precise means by which the economic and political dimensions of the agreements would be linked remained unspecified. But even at this early stage it was easy to detect a tension between the need to conclude the EPAs before the expiry of a World Trade Organisation (WTO) waiver on 31 December 2007 and the logically prior necessity of creating viable regional institutions on which to base the agreements. On the one hand, the impending expiry of the waiver, coupled with the EU's implied threat to downgrade ACP countries to the Generalised System of Preferences (GSP), provided the former with an obvious source of political leverage over the latter in its aim of securing reciprocal free trade. On the other hand, the desire to conclude these agreements on an interregional basis meant that in practice this leverage was immediately dissipated because of the vastly differing levels of trade dependence – in other words, sensitivity to the removal of unilateral preferences that the EPAs were designed to replace – within each ACP region. This was especially so in the case of Least Developed Countries (LDCs), which had little incentive to sign EPAs following the granting of one-way trade preferences under the separate Everything but Arms (EBA) initiative. In sum, from the outset the economic and political components of the EPAs appeared to be pulling in different directions.

In the article, we trace the interaction of the economic and political dimensions of the EPAs, and use this to explain the divergent responses within the ACP to the EU's promotion of regional integration. We suggest that, while differences in trade dependence – and consequently the ability of the EU to use this as bargaining leverage – cannot be ignored, the uptake of the EPAs also depended on the congruence between the institutional trajectory of individual regional projects and the model of economic integration prescribed by the EU in its post-Lomé prospectus. We describe this congruence as either 'high', 'moderate' or 'low', which, we suggest, was determined by: (i) coherence of the EPA group with existing regional institutions; (ii) compatibility of the EPA regional configurations with pre-existing customs union obligations; (iii) delegation of supranational negotiating authority; and (iv) the presence/absence of regional leadership. We then use this explanatory model to account for variances in ACP responses to the EPAs, which would otherwise provide an untidy fit with accounts preoccupied with the economic determinants of bargaining outcomes. In particular, we show that the EU's regional EPA prospectus was most fully realised in CARIFORUM, where there was a 'high' level of congruence between existing regional institutions and the model of economic integration on which the EPAs were premised. In cases of 'moderate' congruence, regions with a reasonable level of institutional coherence – but which had not fully internalised or implemented the model of neoliberal economic integration that underpinned the EPAs – were able to generate some collective bargaining leverage vis-à-vis the

EU in order to eventually arrive at watered-down region-based EPAs. In contrast, regions with 'low' levels of congruity tended to fall back on narrow economic calculations to secure the best (bilateral) market access deal available.

The EU's promotion of regional integration in the context of the EPAs

There is now an extensive literature chronicling the momentous changes in EU-ACP trade and development cooperation that followed the publication of the Commission's *Green Paper on Relations between the European Union and the ACP Countries* in 1996.[4] As we suggested in the introduction, there is a general preoccupation in the EU-ACP literature with the economic dimension of the EPAs – especially the shift to reciprocity – and underestimation of the importance of the political dimension in the form of intraregional trade liberalisation and cooperation. With the benefit of hindsight, we can now observe that it is the latter dimension that has done most to expose the problems and contradictions at the heart of the EPA prospectus.

The ostensible driver of the EU's decision to reform its long-standing preferential trade relationship with the ACP under the 1975 Lomé Convention was a series of legal challenges under the General Agreement on Tariffs and Trade (GATT) and WTO in the 1990s. Making Lomé WTO-compatible, however, did not require a region-based solution; indeed, a single ACP free trade agreement or a series of bilateral agreements between the EU and individual ACP countries might have been both legally and politically more straightforward.[5] There were, of course, practical reasons behind the Commission's decision to opt for region-based EPAs, given the heterogeneity and complexity of the ACP group that, by this point, numbered more than 70 countries.[6] It is difficult, however, to ignore the fact that this blueprint coincided with a growing enthusiasm among EU policy-makers for the external promotion of regionalism. Following the completion of the Single Market in January 1993, the EU had begun to place more emphasis on interregional cooperation as a stepping stone to multilateral trade liberalisation.[7] For the first time, the EU adopted the external promotion of regional integration as an explicit policy aim in its relations with its Mediterranean neighbours, the Common Market of the South (MERCOSUR) and the Association of Southeast Asian Nations (ASEAN). Its enthusiasm for the promotion of regionalism rested on the belief that the EU's own unique experience meant that it had a comparative advantage in offering this type of development assistance. The EU thus promised to 'add value' to the efforts of other donors,[8] in cementing the idea that South–South regionalism would foster integration into the global economy, produce economies of scale, stimulate investment and lock in trade reforms.[9] Where the 1996 Green Paper had asserted that a region-based approach would help to address the practical difficulties of uniform reciprocity, by the time the Cotonou Agreement had been signed and the EPA negotiations were under way, the EU had come to see collective negotiations as a way of developing the capacity of ACP regions. Further, the EPAs ultimately went beyond the modalities of the EU's support for regional integration in other regions – which had relied on trade cooperation, political dialogue, technical support and financial assistance – by making free circulation within ACP regions an explicit condition of market access via a 'regional preference clause'.[10]

The Cotonou Agreement was vague about how the twin trade principles of reciprocity and special and differential treatment for LDCs – both of which the EU argued needed to be implemented in line with multilateral trade disciplines – would be causally linked to the promotion of regional integration through the EPAs. The EU's implied threat to downgrade those ACP countries that failed to sign an EPA to the less generous GSP created a clear material incentive to accept the offer that the EU was proposing. This leverage was cemented by the existence of a clear deadline for the negotiations in the form of the expiry of the WTO waiver, which allowed the temporary continuation of Lomé preferences until 31 December 2007. What was unclear was how this leverage would be reconciled with the EU's desire to conclude these agreements on an interregional basis – a plan that required the prior creation of viable regional institutions on which to base the agreements. Furthermore, the regional dynamics of the negotiations meant that the leverage created by the threat of downgrade to GSP was immediately dissipated as a result of significant national variations in preference dependence within regions. The EU's unilateral offer of duty-free market access under EBA served only to heighten these intraregional tensions by creating very different sets of material incentives for states that would have to bargain for an EPA collectively.[11]

The key problem for the EPAs, then, was created by the EU's attempt to reconcile its drive for reciprocity and special and differential treatment (and its commitment to executing these in line with WTO rules) with its political agenda for the promotion of regional integration. In fact, the EPAs lacked any organising principle around which region-wide reciprocal agreements could incorporate these two competing principles. Although the EU originally depicted the Lomé Convention as a series of 'free trade areas' in accordance with Article XXIV of the GATT, there is little evidence (apart from a small proportion of European Development Fund (EDF) aid allocated to regional projects) that the promotion of regional integration was given much priority – certainly in comparison with the status it was accorded under the Cotonou Agreement and the EPAs. This is not to suggest that regionalism itself did not flourish under Lomé; indeed, it was during the 'second wave' of regionalism in the late 1960s and 1970s that many of the blocs that would eventually form the basis of the EPAs were first conceived.[12] However, the prevailing orthodoxy of 'ideological neutrality' held by EU policy-makers at this point in time meant that the promotion of regional integration was, like other things, largely a matter for the ACP to decide upon.

Most of the regional projects around which the EPAs are based have their origins in the state-led and inward-looking regional projects founded during this second wave of regionalism.[13] While some regional initiatives targeted the integration of regional markets, others were focused on political cooperation and solidarity while others promoted cooperation in a particular sector or issue.[14] During the 1990s, many of these regional initiatives were relaunched with a new market integration agenda leading to the creation of free trade agreements with (in some cases) the ultimate aim of forming customs and even monetary unions. This model explicitly followed the EU example, albeit based on an understanding that was somewhat abstracted from the actual historical experience of European integration. What is striking about this conversion to market integration in the ACP – Africa especially – is the fact that regions made commitments to the formation of customs unions while continuing to allow overlapping memberships with other regions with similar market integration aims. This is problematic since, by definition, customs unions should have a common external tariff (CET) and therefore overlapping customs unions are a logical impossibility. Furthermore, despite public commitments to this market integration agenda, states proved unwilling to pool sovereignty while the implementation of economic liberalisation has been highly uneven.

During the EPA negotiations, the disconnection between the EU's model of market integration and the (more or less independent) internal drivers of regional politics in the ACP was soon revealed.[15] The EPA negotiations were scheduled to take place in two separate phases – the first between the EU and the ACP group as a whole and the second between the EU and the subregions that would form the basis of the final agreements – but the first phase lasted little more than a year and achieved little of substance. The main reason for this is that the European Commission was anxious to proceed to the second phase of the negotiations, even though the precise configuration of the subregions was still to be determined. Although the Cotonou Agreement stipulated that this would be a matter for the ACP, the evidence suggests that by this point the EU already had a firm idea of the final configurations it had in mind. In 2001, for example, the European Commission released a communication stating that the configurations were 'not entirely at the discretion of the ACP'.[16] In setting out the criteria by which groups would qualify to take part in the negotiations, the document went on to declare, among other things, that each region must be 'effectively engaged in an economic integration process', that negotiations must take place in a single setting, lead to a single agreement and that participating countries would be prohibited from belonging to more than one subregion.[17] Further, the Commission considered existing customs unions – with an established CET – the preferred basis for an EPA group.[18]

Although the configuration of the Caribbean and Pacific regions was relatively straightforward given their geographical separation from the rest of the ACP (which is not to say that these cases were unproblematic), the situation was more complicated in Africa, because of the plethora of overlapping regional organisations with conflicting mandates.[19] There were five regional economic communities in Africa that contained mostly ACP countries and had economic integration as a central aim and that were therefore potential bases for an EPA negotiating group. These groups were: The Common Market for Eastern and Southern Africa (COMESA), The Southern African Development Community (SADC), The East African Community (EAC), The Economic Community of Central African States (ECCAS) and the Economic Community of West African States (ECOWAS).[20] While the eventual form of the negotiating regions was ostensibly a choice for the ACP countries, officials sought to persuade ACP countries to form configurations that were deemed viable in terms of their ability to negotiate and implement an EPA before the deadline at the end of 2007.[21] This created numerous problems. For one, in no case other than the EAC – whose EPA group membership originally straddled the East and Southern and SADC-minus configurations before it broke away in 2007 to form a fifth African subregion – did the EPA configuration match the contours of an existing regional project. In some cases (e.g. Mauritania), ACP countries were not part of any eligible existing regional integration process and were therefore made to fit into the nearest regional negotiating configuration without being a part of the underlying regional institution. In other cases, existing regional groups contained non-ACP countries that were excluded from the EPA negotiations. These included Egypt and Libya, which are members of COMESA, and South Africa, which was only allowed to join the SADC EPA group at a late stage in the negotiations. In eastern and southern Africa, existing regions were split into as many as three (and later four) negotiating groups.[22] The reality of the configurations, then, was far from the ideal set out by the EU that the EPA groups should all constitute regions 'effectively engaged' in economic integration.[23]

Divergent responses to regional EPAs

By 2007, relatively little progress had been made towards regional agreements in the majority of the EPA regions. On the eve of the expiry of the WTO waiver, the European Commission decided to permit individual countries and subregions to initial 'goods only' interim EPAs with a view to the completion of 'full' region-wide EPAs at a later date. In order to facilitate this, a new trade regime – Market Access Regulation (MAR) 1528 – was introduced to provide temporary duty-free market access for those countries that initialled an interim EPA. The enforced rush to sign full or interim EPAs to preserve preferential access to the EU market at the end of 2007 proved to be the point at which regional responses to the EPAs began to diverge. The CARIFORUM group became the only region to sign a full EPA in early 2008. The only other group to sign a regional EPA at this point – in this case a goods-only deal – was the EAC. In each of the other EPA regions – West Africa, the SADC EPA group, Central Africa, eastern and southern Africa (ESA) and the Pacific – the deadline proved to be highly divisive, with some countries initialling interim agreements while others refused to do so.

After the rush provoked by the WTO deadline negotiations slowed considerably. CARIFORUM began implementation of its EPA in this period. Elsewhere, some countries that had initialled interim deals at the end of 2007 went on to sign these agreements in 2008 and 2009 and a very small number – Madagascar, Mauritius and Seychelles (ESA) and Papua New Guinea (Pacific) – ratified and began implementation of their interim deals. Otherwise, little progress was made towards the ratification of existing agreements, their extension to include countries that had not initialled an EPA in 2007, or their conversion into comprehensive EPAs. In response, the EU attempted to recapture some of the leverage that had been created by the expiry of the WTO waiver by announcing that those countries that failed to ratify the interim agreements by 1 January 2014 (later extended to 1 October 2014) would cease to benefit from duty-free access to the EU market.[24]

Again, ACP responses to this new imperative diverged. The EAC, along with two regional groups previously divided over the interim EPAs – West Africa and the SADC EPA Group – came together to agree regional deals just before or (in the case of EAC) just after the October 2014 deadline.[25] Elsewhere, regional agreements have not been reached and the situation remains much the same as it was after the 2007 interim EPAs. In Central Africa, Cameroon is implementing its interim EPA, while the rest of the region trades with the EU under EBA, GSP or the EU's most-favoured nation tariff. In eastern and southern Africa, the EPA signed by Madagascar, Mauritius, Seychelles and Zimbabwe is being provisionally applied while the rest of the region (composed entirely of LDCs) trades with the EU under EBA. Likewise in the Pacific, Fiji and Papua New Guinea began applying their interim EPAs while the region's other members traded under EBA or GSP.

Table 1 presents data on ACP export dependence on the EU market and the proportion of exports to the EU that would face a tariff increase under GSP (applicable to non-LDCs only) against details of which countries concluded EPAs in 2007 and 2014. This data suggest that the market access incentives associated with the EPAs were important in shaping the outcome of the agreements. Yet this does not tell the full story. Of the two regions that signed or initialled full or interim EPAs in 2007/08 – CARIFORUM and EAC – in neither case were the constituent countries uniformly exposed to a loss of Lomé preferences. In the case of CARIFORUM, the region was almost entirely composed of non-LDCs (with the exception of

Table 1. ACP preference dependence and EPA signatories by region.

		Members of EPA group	Proportion of total exports to EU, 2004–2014 (%)*	Proportion of exports to EU subject to tariff increase under GSP (%)	EPA Concluded, 2007	EPA Concluded, 2014
CARIFORUM	Non-LDCs	Belize	30.2	75.1	✓	✓
		Guyana	24	72.3	✓	✓
		Grenada	23.1	9.1	✓	✓
		Jamaica	22.9	47.6	✓	✓
		St Lucia	20.9	27.4	✓	✓
		Dominica	20.6	42	✓	✓
		Suriname	15.4	44.8	✓	✓
		Antigua and Barbuda	15.1	1.4	✓	✓
		Bahamas	13.1	3.4	✓	✓
		Saint Vincent	12.7	3.9	✓	✓
		Barbados	11.6	21.7	✓	✓
		Trinidad and Tobago	11.4	17.4	✓	✓
		Dominican Republic	8.8	30.9	✓	✓
		Saint Kitts and Nevis	5.1	71.5	✓	✓
	LDCs	Haiti	4.4	–	✓	✓
West Africa	Non-LDCs	Côte D'Ivoire	41.7	31.5	✓	✓
		Nigeria	29.9	1.7		✓
		Ghana	28.3	16.3	✓	✓
	LDCs	Cape Verde	62.6	–		✓
		Liberia	52.1	–		✓
		Niger	37.7	–		✓
		Mauritania	33.1	–		✓
		Senegal	18.1	–		✓
		Gambia	16.8	–		✓
		Togo	11.1	–		✓
		Burkina Faso	9.5	–		✓
		Benin	9.2	–		✓
		Mali	5.2	–		✓
		Sierra Leone	4.5	–		✓
		Guinea-Bissau	0.5	–		✓
EAC	Non-LDCs	Kenya	24.8	56.5	✓	✓
	LDCs	Uganda	22.4	–	✓	✓
		Rwanda	16.0	–	✓	✓
		Tanzania	15.7	–	✓	✓
		Burundi	14.3	–	✓	✓

(Continued)

Table 1. (*Continued*).

		Members of EPA group	Proportion of total exports to EU, 2004–2014 (%)*	Proportion of exports to EU subject to tariff increase under GSP (%)	EPA Concluded, 2007	EPA Concluded, 2014
SADC EPA Group	Non-LDCs	Botswana	60.9	1.5	✓	✓
		Namibia	30.9	30.5	✓	✓
		South Africa	24.8	–		✓
		Swaziland	8.7	86.6	✓	✓
	LDCs	Mozambique	42.9	–	✓	✓
		Angola (e)	25.1	–		
		Lesotho	2.7	–	✓	✓
Central Africa	Non-LDCs	Cameroon	59.0	14.0	✓	✓
		Congo	21.0	3.3		
		Gabon	14.8	4.1		
	LDCs	Sao Tome & Principe	71.1	–		
		Central African Rep	56.0	–		
		Equatorial Guinea	34.9	–		
		DR Congo	21.8	–		
		Chad	4.4	–		
ESA	Non-LDCs	Mauritius	60.5	61.5	✓	✓
		Seychelles*	58.1	69.1	✓	✓
		Zimbabwe	12.8	35.6	✓	✓
	LDCs	Madagascar	53.6	–	✓	✓
		Comoros	37.9	–	✓	
		Malawi	34.9	–		
		Ethiopia	28.6	–		
		Djibouti	20.6	–		
		Zambia	5.6	–	✓	
		Sudan (N+S)	1.9	–		
		Somalia	1.3	–		
		Eritrea	no data			
Pacific	Non-LDCs	Marshall Islands	60.9	0.01		
		Papua New Guinea	17.4	28.1	✓	✓
		Timor Leste	15.6	6.8		
		Fiji	11.1	92.6	✓	✓
		Cook Islands	6.2	28		
		Nauru	5.3	52.2		

	Niue	1.7	8.1
	Palau	0.3	36
	Tonga	0.3	52.7
	Micronesia	0	29.5
LDCs	Solomon Islands	13.6	–
	Vanuatu	9.3	–
	Kiribati	0.3	–
	Samoa	0.3	–
	Tuvalu	No Data	–

*In some cases, data is only available for a limited part of the 2004–2014 period; Sources: International Trade Centre, Trade Map; Overseas Development Institute, The Costs to the ACP.

Haiti) facing a downgrade to GSP, but the extent to which their exports would be affected by this downgrade varied considerably – from Guyana facing a tariff rise on 72.3% of its exports to the EU, to Antigua and Barbuda facing a rise on only 1.4% of exports to the EU. In EAC, Kenya faced a tariff rise on 56.5% of its exports to the EU, but the rest of the region (all LDCs) faced no such threat. The two groups to conclude new regional EPAs in 2014 – West Africa and the SADC EPA group – also contained a mixture of LDCs and non-LDCs and varying levels of export dependence on the EU. Outside of these regions, patterns of acceptance and rejection of the EPAs reflected market access incentives more closely. All non-LDCs that faced tariff increases on a moderate or large proportion of their exports initialled EPAs to preserve preferential market access in 2007 and had signed and begun application of these agreements by 2014. LDCs were significantly less likely to initial an EPA, although some – Lesotho, Mozambique, Madagascar, Zambia and Comoros – did.[26]

Explaining regional EPA outcomes: institutional and ideational congruence

In order to explain the divergent ACP responses to the EU's attempts to promote regional integration through the EPAs we suggest that, while differences in preference dependence cannot be ignored, uptake of the agreements was also crucially dependent upon the political dimension of the negotiations – i.e. the congruence between individual ACP regions and the vision of liberal economic integration at the heart of the EU's prospectus. Building on the EU's own statements about the institutional prerequisites for a successful EPA,[27] we identify three initial criteria for assessing this congruence: (i) geographic coherence of the EPA group with existing regional institutions; (ii) compatibility of the EPA regional configurations with pre-existing customs union obligations; and (iii) delegation of supranational negotiating authority. To these criteria, we add a fourth that was not raised by the EU in its discussion of the institutional prerequisites for an EPA – (iv) the presence/absence of regional leadership. Our analysis suggests that while the various dominant regional actors played different roles and took different attitudes towards the negotiations, they were nonetheless crucial in compensating for other institutional weaknesses in several of the ACP regions. Using this model, we describe the congruence between the EPA groups and the EU's model of economic integration as 'high', 'moderate' or 'low' and argue that these differences account for the divergent regional outcomes in individual EPA negotiating groups (see Table 2).[28] Specifically we suggest that the region with 'high' congruence – CARIFORUM – was the one in which the EU's vision for regional economic integration was most fully realised.[29] Those with 'moderate' congruence – West Africa, EAC and the SADC EPA group – displayed a reasonable level of institutional coherence but only partial uptake of the specific regional institutional forms – as well as the broader ideological prospectus – that underpinned the EPAs. This institutional coherence gave these regions a degree of collective leverage that enabled them to challenge (albeit in limited ways) key aspects of the EPA prospectus in order to reach compromise regional agreements that better reflected their own regional priorities. Finally, those regions with 'low' congruence – Central Africa, ESA and the Pacific – were unable to formulate coherent regional negotiating positions and were more likely to fall back on narrow economic calculations to secure access to the EU market on a bilateral or subregional basis.

Table 2. Congruence between ACP groups and institutional prerequisites for EPA negotiations.

		(i) coherence of EPA group with existing regional institution	(ii) compatibility of EPA group with existing customs union obligations	(iii) delegation of supranational negotiating authority	(iv) presence of dominant regional actor
'High' congruence	CARIFORUM	*High.* CARIFORUM existed since 1992 and had an FTA since 2001	*High.* CARICOM CET applied from 2001; CARIFORUM CET implemented alongside EPA negotiation	*High.* CRNM led negotiations	*No*
'Moderate' congruence	West Africa	*Moderate.* ECOWAS plus 1	*Moderate.* West African Economic and Monetary Union has a CET that includes 8 of 16 EPA group members	*Moderate.* ECOWAS Commission at apex of three-tiered negotiating structure	*Yes.* Nigeria (77% of group GDP)
	East African Community (EAC)	*High.* EAC	*High.* EAC CET launched 2004	*Low.* Regional technical working groups establish regional positions but subject to approval by national ministries	*Yes.* Kenya (43.5% of group GDP)
	SADC EPA Group	*Low.* SADC minus 8 /SACU plus two	*Moderate.* SACU CET includes 5 of 7 members	*Low.* Negotiations conducted by national ministries of trade, led by Botswana	*Yes.* South Africa (67.7% of group GDP)
'Low' congruence	Central Africa	*Low.* CEMAC plus 2	*Low.* Plans to introduce a CEMAC CET not yet implemented	*Moderate.* Three tier negotiating structure with negotiations led by CEMAC Executive Secretary	*No*
	Eastern and Southern Africa (ESA)	*Low.* COMESA minus 8	*Low.* COMESA customs union launched 2009 but not yet implemented	*Moderate.* Regional Negotiating Forum shares competence with ministerial and ambassadorial staff	*No*
	Pacific	*Low.* Pacific Islands Forum minus 2, plus 1	*Low.* No CET	*Low.* Regional Negotiating Team led by national ministers; PIF provides administrative support	*Yes.* Papua New Guinea (52% of group GDP)

High congruence

Only one region – CARIFORUM – possessed a high (although not entirely unproblematic) level of congruence with the institutional preconditions of the model of economic integration at the heart of the EPAs. All but one of the Caribbean ACP countries – the Dominican Republic – were members of the Caribbean Community (CARICOM), a region that has achieved an advanced level of economic integration and institutional capacity, having applied a CET since 1991 and established the CARICOM Single Market and Economy (CSME) in 2006. To include Dominican Republic, the EPA group was based on the broader Caribbean Forum (CARIFORUM) region, which had been created in 1992 for the purpose of coordinating EDF assistance to the region.[30] Although less advanced than CARICOM, CARIFORUM had an active regional economic integration agenda, an FTA having been concluded between CARICOM and the Dominican Republic in 2001 with a CET being implemented simultaneously with the EPA negotiations.[31] Furthermore, during their preparations for the EPA talks, the CARIFORUM members agreed a negotiating structure that granted supranational authority to a quasi-autonomous body – the Caribbean Regional Negotiating Machinery (CRNM)[32] – the like of which did not exist in other ACP regions.[33]

Although not a perfect fit, the institutional trajectory of the CARIFORUM region was, by far, the closest of any of the EPA groups to matching the conditions that the European Commission had originally stipulated would be necessary to negotiate a regional EPA. Furthermore, the region's existing successes in implementing a process of economic integration modelled on the EU example reflected a measure of ideological convergence between Caribbean elites and their EU counterparts. Indeed, Bishop, Heron and Payne suggest that the CRNM – which was endowed with 'a forceful personality of its own' and 'considerable intellectual capacity, drive and confidence' – played an important role in stressing the claimed synergies between a full regional EPA and the Caribbean's existing efforts to pursue a neoliberal model of regional economic development.[34] Similarly, Elijah Nyaga Munyi presents survey evidence that Caribbean negotiators expressed a far stronger 'neoliberal bias' – in the sense that they were likely to believe that a reciprocal EPA would 'generally promote exports, export diversification and competition [...] better than the preferential Cotonou Agreement' – than those of other ACP regions.[35] CRNM officials also evidently subscribed to the EU narrative that the region would derive 'dynamic benefits' from the proposed inclusion of a services and investment component in a 'comprehensive' EPA.[36] In other words, what was important in the early realisation of a comprehensive regional EPA in the Caribbean was both the region's institutional capacity and the way in which this helped to foster a coherent ideological position compatible with that of the EU.

Moderate congruence

Outside of the Caribbean, ACP regions demonstrated a poorer fit with the institutional prerequisites of the EPAs. This was not simply a technical question of institutional capacity. It also reflected a weaker political and ideological commitment to the model of regional economic development at the heart of both the European project in general, and the EU's external promotion of regional integration through the EPAs more specifically.[37] Yet some regions outside of the Caribbean approximated the institutional forms on which the EPAs were predicated better than others (see Table 2). In particular, the West Africa group mapped closely onto the membership of ECOWAS (with only the addition of Mauritania required), while the EAC EPA group matched the EAC organisation exactly. Both of these regions had economic integration as their original aim and had made progress towards the creation of a customs union (in West Africa this has been implemented in the West African Economic and Monetary Union subregion while the EAC has been implementing a CET since 2004). Of all the African regions, ECOWAS is one of the more inclined towards supranationalism, as evidenced by the prominent role played by the ECOWAS Commission at the apex of the region's EPA negotiating structure.[38] Furthermore, the dominant regional actor, Nigeria, worked closely with the ECOWAS Commission to secure a unified regional approach to the negotiations – for example by placing pressure on Ghana and Côte D'Ivoire to refuse to go ahead with the implementation of interim EPAs without the agreement of the rest of the group.[39] The EAC's late conversion into an EPA negotiating group meant that its collective negotiating structures were less sophisticated that those of ECOWAS and the negotiations remained primarily in the hands of national ministries.[40] Here Kenya played a key leadership role in fostering regional negotiating positions.

While the SADC EPA group is included in the 'moderate' congruence category, its case is different. Here, it was to all intents and purposes impossible to establish an EPA group that matched the contours of existing regional projects, given the plethora of overlapping regional institutions in southern and eastern Africa. The SADC EPA group included only eight (seven, once Tanzania had defected to EAC) of the SADC regional economic community's members. The members of the SADC region were particularly suspicious of surrendering sovereignty to supranational institutions, which is why the EPA negotiations were led by national trade ministers on the basis intergovernmental consensus.[41] South Africa, however, wielded the considerable leverage that it enjoyed through the smaller Southern African Customs Union to bring the negotiating positions of the other four members of this group – Botswana, Lesotho, Namibia and Swaziland – into line with its own preferences.[42] In this way, South Africa's dominance to some extent compensated for the institutional shortcomings of the SADC EPA group by (belatedly) fostering a unified regional negotiating position. It is worth noting, however, that this position was arrived at largely through regional power play as opposed to institutionalised dialogue and cooperation.[43]

In each of these three regions, the formation and pursuit of a coherent regional agenda proved intensely challenging, as evidenced by the divisions within West Africa and the SADC EPA group in 2007 and the fact the EAC never signed the deal that it struck at this time. In the lead up to the later 2014 deadline, however, each of these groups was able (partially, at least) to pull together to negotiate collectively with the EU. Unlike in CARIFORUM, this did not mean accepting the EU's political and economic model in its entirety. Indeed, each of these three regions was able to coalesce around key objections to the agreements proposed by the EU. A degree of institutional coherence, then, provided these groups with a source of leverage vis-a-vis the EU. In other words, these groups were able to invoke the sanctity of existing regional institutions – to which the EU repeatedly professed its commitment – to extract concessions on a range of negotiating issues, including the extent of reciprocal tariff liberalisation, the inclusion of services and the Singapore issues as well as various technical clauses.[44] All told, these regions displayed sufficient institutional capacity to conclude agreements in 2014 – and thereby avoid the regional disruption that had been evident in other ACP groups – that to some extent subordinated the EPAs to local regional integration projects.

Low congruence

A final set of EPA negotiating groups offered a particularly low level of congruence with the institutional parameters on which the EPAs were premised. In Central Africa and ESA, regional organisations with a reasonable degree of institutional capacity – CEMAC and COMESA, respectively – existed. In both cases, however, the mismatch between the scope of these organisations and the geographic configuration of the negotiating group proved to be a significant stumbling block. For Central Africa, this problem emerged when the Democratic Republic of Congo – which was not a member of CEMAC but was a member of both SADC and COMESA – joined the group in 2005.[45] For ESA, this was evident from the start, with the COMESA region divided between two and later three, and then four, EPA negotiating groups. Both CEMAC and COMESA had plans to introduce customs unions at the time of the EPA negotiations, but had encountered considerable implementation problems.[46] This signalled just how difficult it would be to arrive at and implement a collective market access offer in relation to the EU. While both regions delegated some negotiating authority to regional bodies, the coherence of their negotiating structures was disrupted by their changing regional configurations – in particular after the EAC had formed a separate negotiating group in the case of the ESA configuration.[47] It is worth noting that both of these regions lacked any individual country with the resources and leadership capabilities to overcome collective action problems by articulating a regional negotiating position – something that had been important to a greater or lesser extent in each of the regions with 'moderate' congruence. The final 'low' congruence EPA group was the Pacific.[48] The only organisation on which the EPA could be built in this region was the Pacific Islands Forum (PIF), which included 13 of the 14 Pacific ACP countries but also Australia and New Zealand, the latter of which were involved in their own process of trade reform in relation to the Pacific island states. While the PIF Secretariat played a coordinating role in the negotiations, its capacity and legitimacy to do so was frequently questioned by both of the main players in the region – Fiji and Papua New Guinea.[49] Furthermore, there was little in the way of a record of successful economic integration in the Pacific – the only progress in this regard having been made by the Melanesian Spearhead Group (Fiji, Papua New Guinea, the Solomon Islands and Vanuatu).[50]

Each of these regions, then, was divided over whether to sign an interim EPA in 2007, and continued to be so in the face of the EU's new EPA deadline in 2014. Furthermore, the outcomes in these regions tended to closely reflect the immediate and easily traceable effects of a possible loss of EU market access. In short, preference-dependent non-LDCs signed EPAs while LDCs and those without significant preference dependence did not (see Table 1). This was not because countries in these regions were motivated by straightforward material interests to any greater extent than countries in the 'high' and 'moderate' congruence regions. Rather, countries acting in regions with low institutional capacity had relatively little opportunity or leverage to seek concessions from the EU in line with their perception of the type of EPA that would suit their political and economic preferences. Whether or not they felt that the EPA as a whole was aligned with their national or regional economic and political trajectory, these countries tended to fall back on narrow economic calculations about how best to secure access to the EU market. Indeed, even where some countries in these regions were sympathetic to the ideological prospectus of the EPAs – as was the case, for example, in Mauritius[51] – they were effectively prevented from concluding comprehensive EPAs because the EU wished only to pursue this more ambitious agenda on a regional basis. While the regions with 'moderate' congruence went on to negotiate compromise deals with the EU in 2014, the countries in 'low' congruence regions either signed and implemented the interim EPAs that they had concluded at the end of 2007 or reverted to one of the EU's alternative preference schemes.

Conclusion

The aim of this article was to map and explain the divergent responses of ACP regions to the EU's attempts to promote regional economic integration through the EPAs. In one region – CARIFORUM – the EPA resulted in the early and relatively complete adoption of the EU's regional economic prospectus. Elsewhere, in Africa and the Pacific, this regional model was adopted late and partially or not at all. While existing accounts of the EPAs identify a common set of controversies and roadblocks that marred the negotiations, they do not systematically account for the uneven regional trajectories of the EPAs. We acknowledge the importance of varying levels of ACP trade dependence – and the way in which these were underscored by the EU's efforts to secure both reciprocity and special and differential treatment through the EPAs – in explaining different countries' enthusiasm or otherwise for the agreements. Yet we have shown that such an account cannot on its own explain why some regions were able to overcome these divergent national-level incentives, why some were able to do so only belatedly and others still were not able to do so at all. We therefore turned our attention to the less discussed political dimension of the EPAs – i.e. the EU's decision to place a particular model of liberal economic integration and cooperation at the heart of the EPAs and the congruence (or lack thereof) between this model and the regional integration projects that existed on the ground in ACP regions.

Our key finding is that the level of congruence between the institutional trajectories of individual regional projects mattered in determining the regional coherence of the ACP response to the EPA in each individual negotiating group. We measured this congruence in terms of geographic coherence between the EPA group and existing regional institutions, the compatibility of the EPA with existing customs union obligations, the delegation of supranational negotiating authority and regional leadership. The varying levels of congruence of the EPA groups maps onto their responses to the regional dimension of the EPAs. CARIFORUM – the only EPA group with a high level of institutional congruence according to our criteria, and a region in which there was considerable ideological sympathy for the EU's favoured model of economic integration – was the region where the EPA model was most fully realised. Three regions in Africa displayed a 'moderate' level of congruence with the institutional requirements of the EPAs. Here, ideas also mattered in the sense that regions with reasonable institutional capacity and coherence – but which did not fully buy into the model of economic integration at the heart of the EU's EPA model – were able to generate some leverage in order to negotiate concessions from the EU and ultimately (and belatedly) arrive at compromise regional solutions. Finally, three regions with 'low' institutional congruence were unable to formulate coherent regional negotiating positions and – in the absence of opportunities to challenge the EU's approach to the negotiations – their constituent countries tended to make narrow strategic calculations about how best to maximise their access to the EU market at the lowest economic short-term cost.

The divergent ACP responses to the promotion of regional integration through the EPAs clearly have consequences for longer term governance and development in the ACP. In those groups where some countries have signed an EPA while others have not, the legacy of the agreements may serve to heighten intraregional barriers as non-signatories seek to avoid transhipment of EU goods that have entered the region on the basis of lower tariffs via an EPA member. This does not necessarily mean to say that the inverse is true and where an EPA group has signed a joint agreement, that this will support the aims of regional integration in that region. Here, much is dependent on questions such as whether the EPA region matches the contours of the underlying regional project; whether the terms of the EPA are compatible with the region's integration plans; and whether a long and sometimes acrimonious negotiating process has strengthened or weakened regional institutions and political ties. Measuring the precise institutional legacies of the EPAs in ACP regions is therefore an important avenue for future research.

Disclosure statement

No potential conflict of interest was reported by the authors.

Acknowledgement

The authors would like to thank the participants in the 'EU Contributions to Equitable Growth and Sustainable Development in the post-2015 Consensus' workshop, University of Leicester, 20 April 2016, at which a draft version of this paper was first presented. They would also like to thank Peter O'Reilly for copy-editing and formatting the manuscript.

Notes

1. Heron, "Asymmetric Bargaining and Development"; Heron and Murray-Evans, "Limits to Market Power"; Murray-Evans, "Regionalism and African Agency"; Nyaga Munyi, "Beyond Asymmetry". Namibia and Ghana both concluded interim EPAs at the end of 2007 but later refused to sign these agreements. Both countries concluded watered-down EPAs along with their respective regions in 2014.
2. Heron and Murray-Evans, "The EU and Africa".
3. The Singapore issues – government procurement, trade facilitation, investment and competition – were introduced onto the World Trade Organisation agenda at the Singapore Ministerial

in 1996 and subsequently became part of the Doha Round negotiations. All except trade facilitation were dropped from the Doha agenda following disagreements between developed and developing countries that culminated in the collapse of the Cancun Ministerial in 2003. These issues were mentioned only briefly in the 2000 Cotonou Agreement between the EU and the ACP countries but the EU subsequently insisted that they should be an important part of any 'comprehensive' EPA.

4. See, *inter alia*, Brown, "Restructuring North–South Relations"; Faber and Orbie, *Beyond Market Access*; Gibb, "Post-Lome"; Heron, *Pathways from Preferential Trade*; Heron and Murray-Evans, "Limits to Market Power"; Heron and Siles-Brügge, "Competitive Liberalisation and the 'Global Europe'"; Siles-Brügge, *Constructing European Union Trade Policy*; Ravenhill, "Back to the Nest."
5. Heron and Murray-Evans, "Limits to Market Power."
6. Siles-Brügge, *Constructing European Union Trade Policy*, 142.
7. Solignac Lecomte, *Options for Future ACP-EU*, 7.
8. European Commission, "Green Paper on Relations", xii.
9. European Commission, "European Community Support".
10. Heron, *Pathways from Preferential Trade*.
11. For a more detailed discussion of the central contradictions within the EU's approach to the EPAs and their consequences, see note 5 above; see note 10 above.
12. Hurrell, "Regionalism in Theoretical Perspective"; Breslin and Higgott, "Studying Regions: Learning from the Old".
13. Akokpari, "Dilemmas of Regional Integration"; Østergaard, "Classical Models of Regional Integration"; Qualmann, "Political, Legal and Economic Perspective"; Tekere, "Challenges for the SADC EPA Group"; Payne, *The Politics of the Caribbean Community*.
14. See note 2 above
15. See also, Heron, *Pathways from Preferential Trade*, 64–5.
16. European Commission, *Orientations on the Qualification*, 3.
17. Ibid., 9.
18. Ibid.
19. See also, Heron, *Pathways from Preferential Trade*, 68.
20. The other regional economic communities either contain a number of non-ACP countries (Community of Sahel-Saharan States [CEN-SAD] and Arab Maghreb Union [UMA]) or focus primarily on security and political dialogue (IGAD). While ECCAS was initially identified as the possible basis for an EPA, the eventual EPA group in Central Africa more closely reflected the smaller and more integrated Economic and Monetary Community of Central Africa (CEMAC).
21. A confidential interview with a former DG Trade official revealed that the Commission argued the case for the Democratic Republic of Congo – a member of three separate RECs – to be part of the Central Africa EPA configuration to give this region more market potential. In 2007, the Commission also insisted that Tanzania leave the SADC-minus group and join the EAC group instead (a customs union of which it was a member).
22. The SADC REC members were initially divided between the SADC-minus, Central Africa, and Eastern and Southern Africa EPA groups. Tanzania later joined the EAC EPA, dividing the SADC REC into a fourth EPA group.
23. See note 16 above.
24. Bilal and Ramdoo, "EPA Negotiations."
25. Signatures of the West Africa and EAC EPAs are still pending at the time of writing. This is in some doubt in both regions. In West Africa there has been opposition to the deal from Nigerian government and private sector actors since the terms were agreed in 2014. In the EAC, Tanzania indicated in advance of the scheduled signing of the region's EPA on July 18 2016 that it no longer wished to be part of the agreement, citing the uncertainty created by the United Kingdom's vote to leave the EU as a key reason for the decision.
26. Lesotho and Mozambique concluded subregional EPAs in 2007 before concluding a regional deal with the rest of the SADC EPA group in 2014. Zambia and Comoros initialled an EPA in 2007 but never signed or ratified this deal.
27. European Commission, *Orientations on the Qualification*.

28. These categorisations – low, moderate or high – are based on the authors' judgement, with brief justifications offered in Table 2. They are intended to provide an indication of the comparative degree of institutional congruence between the individual ACP groups and the model of economic integration on which the EU's approach to the EPAs was premised. The claim is not that the outcome of the negotiations could be read off solely on the basis of these categorisations, nor that each of the four variables carried the same weight in determining the negotiating outcome in each case. Rather, Table 2 offers a simplified picture of the institutional dynamics of each region, while the way in which these shaped the outcome of the negotiations is discussed in further detail and with greater nuance in the sections below.
29. Heron, "Asymmetric Bargaining and Development"; Nyaga Munyi, "Beyond Asymmetry".
30. South Centre, *EPA Negotiations in the Caribbean Region*, 5.
31. Ibid., 8.
32. Heron, "Asymmetric Bargaining and Development"; ECDPM, *Implementing the Economic Partnership Agreement*.
33. During the 30th Annual Conference of CARICOM Heads of Government, held in Guyana 2–4 July 2009, the decision was taken to rename the CRNM as the Office of Trade Negotiations (OTN) and to redefine its operational remit. Among other things, the OTN was re-incorporated into the CARICOM Secretariat. These changes are a direct result of the fallout from the EPA negotiations where the quasi-autonomous status of the CRNM was widely criticised in the region. The controversy surrounding the CRNM provides an interesting footnote to the issues explored in this article, not least the tension between the economic and political dimensions of the EPAs.
34. Bishop et al., "Caribbean Development Alternatives", 94–5.
35. Nyaga Munyi, "Beyond Asymmetry", 58–9.
36. Bishop et al., "Caribbean Development Alternatives", 95–6.
37. See note 2 above.
38. Hulse, "Actorness Beyond the European Union", 556–7.
39. Ibid., 558.
40. Lorenz, *Transformation on Whose Terms?*, 14.
41. Hulse, "Actorness Beyond the European Union," 556.
42. See Murray-Evans, "Regionalism and African Agency."
43. Ibid.
44. Ibid.
45. South Centre, *EPA Negotiations in Central African Region*, 2.
46. Babarinde and Faber, "EPAs and Integration in SSA."
47. Lorenz, *Transformation on Whose Terms.*
48. For and extended discussion, see note 10 above.
49. Julian et al., "EPA Update"; Roquefeul, "EPA Update."
50. South Centre, *EPA Negotiations in the Pacific Region*, 9.
51. Confidential interview, 9 September 2015.

Bibliography

Akokpari, John. "Dilemmas of Regional Integration and Development in Africa." In *The African Union and its Institutions*, edited by John Akokpari, Angela Ndinga-Muvumba, and Timothy Murithi, 85–112. Auckland Park: Fanele, 2008.

Babarinde, Olufemi and Faber Gerrit. "EPAs and Integration in SSA." In *Beyond Market Access for Development: EU African Relations in Transition*, edited by Gerrit Faber and Jan Orbie, 111–134. Abingdon: Routledge, 2009.

Bilal, San and Isabelle Ramdoo. "EPA Negotiations: The Honeymoon is Over …" *Trade Negotiations Insights* 10, no. 7 (2011): 22.

Bishop, Matthew Louis, Tony Heron, and Tony Payne. "Caribbean Development Alternatives and the CARIFORUM–European Union economic partnership agreement." *Journal of International Relations and Development* 16, no. 1 (2013): 82–110. doi:10.1057/jird.2012.5.

Breslin, Shaun, and Richard Higgott. "Studying Regions: Learning from the Old, Constructing the New." *New Political Economy* 5, no. 3 (2000): 333–352.

Brown, William. "Restructuring North–South Relations: ACP-EU Development Co-operation in a Liberal International Order." *Review of African Political Economy* 27, no. 85 (2000): 367–383.

ECDPM. *Implementing the Economic Partnership Agreements in the East African Community and the CARIFORUM Regions: What is in it for the Private Sector?* Discussion Paper No. 104, 2010.

European Commission. "European Community Support for Regional Economic Integration Efforts among Developing Countries." *Communication from the Commission*, COM (95) 219 final, 16 June, 1995.

European Commission. "Green Paper on Relations Between the European Union and the ACP Countries." *Communication from the Commission*, COM (96) 570 final, 20 November, 1996.

European Commission. *Orientations on the Qualification of ACP Regions for the Negotiation of Economic Partnership Agreements*, Brussels, 2001.

European Commission. "Trade and Development: Assisting Developing Countries to Benefit from Trade." *Communication from the Commission to the Council and the European Parliament*, COM (2002) 513 final, 18 September, 2002.

Faber, Gerrit, and Jan Orbie (eds.). *Beyond Market Access for Economic Development: EU–Africa Relations in Transition*. Abingdon: Routledge, 2009.

Gibb, Richard. "Post-Lomé: The European Union and the South." *Third World Quarterly* 21, no. 3 (2000): 457–481.

Heron, Tony. "Asymmetric Bargaining and Development Trade-offs in the CARIFORUM-European Union Economic Partnership Agreement." *Review of International Political Economy* 18, no. 3 (2011): 328–357.

Heron, Tony. *Pathways from Preferential Trade: The Politics of Trade Adjustment in Africa, Caribbean and Pacific*. London: Palgrave Macmillan, 2013.

Heron, Tony. *Pathways from Preferential Trade: The Politics of Trade Adjustment in Africa, Caribbean and Pacific*. London: Palgrave Macmillan, Forthcoming.

Heron, Tony and Peg Murray-Evans. "Limits to Market Power: Strategic Discourse and Institutional Path Dependence in the EU-ACP Economic Partnership Agreements." *European Journal of International Relations*, OnlineFirst (2016).

Heron, Tony and Peg Murray-Evans. "The EU and Africa: Trade, Development and the Politics of Interregionalism." In *Handbook on European Union Trade Policy*, edited by Maria Garcia, Sangeeta horana, and Jan Orbie. Cheltenham: Edward Elgar, Forthcoming.

HERON, Tony, and Gabriel SILES-BRÜGGE. "Competitive Liberalisation and the 'Global Europe' Services and Investment Agenda: Locating the Commercial Drivers of the EU-ACP Economic Partnership Agreements." *JCMS: Journal of Common Market Studies* 50, no. 2 (2012): 250–266.

Hulse, Merran. "Actorness Beyond the European Union: Comparing the International Trade Actorness of SADC and ECOWAS." *JCMS: Journal of Common Market Studies* 52, no. 3 (2014): 547–565.

Hurrell, Andrew. "Regionalism in Theoretical Perspective." In *Regionalism in World Politics: Regional Organization and International Order*, edited by Louise Fawcett and Andrew Hurrell, 37–73. Oxford: Oxford University Press, 1995.

International Trade Centre. *Trade Map: Statistics for International Business Development*. Accessed September 3, 2016. http://www.trademap.org

Julian, Melissa, Melissa Dalleau, and Quentin de Roquefeuil. "EPA Update." *Trade Negotiations Insights* 10, no. 2 (2011): 14–15.

Lorenz, Ulrike. *Transformation on Whose Terms? Understanding the New EU-ACP Trade Relations from the Outside In*. KFG Working Paper Series, no. 40, 2012.

Murray-Evans, Peg. "Regionalism and African Agency: Negotiating an Economic Partnership Agreement between the EU and Southern Africa." *Third World Quarterly* 36, no. 10 (2015): 1845–1865.

Nyaga Munyi, Elijah. "Beyond Asymmetry: Substantive Beliefs in Preference Formation and Efficiency of Asymmetrical Negotiations"." *New Political Economy* 21, no. 1 (2016): 49–68.

Østergaard, Tom. "Classical Models of Regional Integration – What Relevance for Southern Africa." In *Southern Africa After Apartheid: Regional Integration and External Resources*, edited by Bertil Odén, 27–47. Uppsala: Scandinavian Institute of African Studies, 1993.

Overseas Development Institute. *The Costs to the ACP of Exporting to the EU under the GSP*. London: Overseas Development Institute, 2007.

Payne, Anthony. *The Politics of the Caribbean Community 1961–79: Regional Integration Amongst New States*. Manchester, NH: Manchester University Press, 1980.

Qualmann, Regine. "Political, Legal and Economic Perspective." In *Regional Integration and Economic Partnership Agreements: Southern Africa at the Crossroads*, edited by Talitha Bertelsmann-Scott and Peter Draper, 47–58. Johannesburg: South African Institute of International Affairs, 2006.

Ravenhill, John. "Back to the Nest? Europe's Relations with the African Caribbean and Pacific Group of Countries." In *EU Trade Strategies: Between Regionalism and Globalism*, edited by Vinod K Aggarwal and Edward Fogarty, 118–147. London: Palgrave Macmillan, 2004.

Roquefeuil, Quentin de. "EPA Update." *GREAT Insights* 3, no. 2 (2014): 24.

Siles-Brügge, G. *Constructing European Union Trade Policy*. London: Palgrave Macmillan, 2014.

Solinac Lecomte, Henri-Bernard. "Options for Future ACP-EU Trade Relations." ECDPM paper sponsored by the Belgian Administration for Development Cooperation and the Swedish Ministry for Foreign Affairs, Working Paper 60, Maastricht.

South Centre. *EPA Negotiations in the Central African Region: Some Issues for Consideration*. Analytical Note SC/AN/TDP/EPA/9. Geneva: South Centre, 2007a.

South Centre. *EPA Negotiations in the Pacific Region: Some Issues of Concern*. Analytical Note SC/AN/TDP/EPA/11. Geneva: South Centre, 2007b.

South Centre. *EPA Negotiations in the Caribean Region: Some Issues of Concern*. Analytical Note C/AN/TDP/EPA/12. Geneva: South Centre, 2008.

Tekere, Moses. "Challenges for the SADC EPA Group." In *Regional Integration and Economic Partnership Agreements: Southern Africa at the Crossroads*, edited by Talitha Bertelsmann-Scott and Peter Draper, 65–71. Johannesburg: South African Institute of International Affairs, 2006.

Equal partnership between unequal regions? Assessing deliberative parliamentary debate in ACP-EU relations

Sarah Delputte and Yentyl Williams

ABSTRACT
This paper develops an analytical framework to assess the quality of deliberation in the ACP-EU Joint Parliamentary Assembly (JPA). Despite rhetoric on 'equal partnership' between ACP and EU countries, academic assessments of the Cotonou Agreement point to the lasting asymmetrical power relationship, most visible in the Economic Partnership Agreements (EPAs) negotiations. However, this paper assesses to what extent the JPA debate on EPAs can approach the ideal type of deliberation. The empirical investigation is based on participatory observation, semi-structured interviews and an analysis of primary documents, including the attendance lists of 29 JPA sessions, more than 40 resolutions and 120 parliamentary questions related to the trade-development nexus.

Introduction

One of the main debates that is currently taking place in EU development circles deals with the future of the partnership between the EU and the African, Caribbean and Pacific (ACP) Countries. After almost 60 years of cooperation, including several revisions, the central question relates to what will happen after 2020, when the current Cotonou Partnership Agreement expires. On this occasion, several evaluations of the past cooperation have been published.[1] At the end of 2015, the Commission also held a public consultation on the partnership and the ACP-EU relations after 2020.

The debate raises key questions on the nature of the relationship and the 'extent to which it remains valid for the future and offers a platform to advance joint interests'.[2] A key point of interrogation in this regard is whether the Cotonou Agreement has been an expression of an equal partnership, as it proclaims to be, or whether it is just a continuation of an asymmetrical partnership and a relic of the colonial past. Most academic literature on ACP-EU relations makes a rather different evaluation than the normative discourse of the EU itself, pointing to lasting power imbalances.[3] However, so far this literature has not paid attention to the expression of this relationship within the joint institutions that underpin the ACP-EU partnership, and certainly not to the specific institutional setting of the ACP-EU JPA. This is remarkable for several reasons. First, the JPA is the oldest and most institutionalised parliamentary assembly between the countries of the global North and South. Second, the parliamentary dimension has grown in importance both within and beyond the EU-ACP framework. Third, and most important in the context of this paper, arguably the ACP-EU JPA is the place in which real dialogue between the different parties is most likely to be approached, especially when compared to intergovernmental negotiations.

The results of the Commission's public consultation on the ACP-EU partnership after 2020 does not provide clear insights on the ACP-EU JPA as it appears that stakeholders are divided on the questions relating to the institutional set-up of the partnership. Although one part of the contributors see the joint institutions as relevant 'as they provide for genuine dialogue, strengthen the ACP-EU positions in the global arena and make ACP countries' political voice stronger',[4] others consider other regional and sub-regional organisations as far more relevant than ACP-EU cooperation. Apart from this division over the general institutional set-up, it is not clear how the specific role of the ACP-EU JPA is perceived. Hence, by focusing on the ACP-EU JPA, this paper aims to provide new insights and add to the existing policy-oriented and academic evaluations of ACP-EU relations.

When analysing the ACP-EU JPA the paper takes a deliberative approach to parliamentary debate. It draws on the definition of deliberation by Steenbergen et al.,[5] as a 'process in which political actors listen to each other, reasonably justify their positions, show mutual respect and are willing to re-evaluate and eventually revise their initial preferences through a process of discourse about competing validity claims'. The choice for this theoretical perspective to study the partnership follows from two main arguments. One argument is procedural, as the procedures of deliberation may allow for an equal debate in an asymmetrical relationship. The second argument is substantial as deliberation is considered to be a precondition for a critical and rational substantial debate between divergent views, interests and identities. This paper thus aims to assess the quality of deliberation in the ACP-EU JPA in order to evaluate the extent to which the JPA approaches the ideal type of an equal partnership.

Empirically, the paper focuses on the JPA debate on the trade-development nexus, and more specifically on the Economic Partnership Agreements (EPAs), one of the most exemplary issues for demonstrating the unequal partnership between the EU and the ACP countries. Hence the research question that this paper aims to answer can be narrowed down to the following: *to what extent does the JPA dialogue on EPAs approach the ideal type of deliberation?* In doing so, the paper also aims to offer new empirical insights into the substantive position of the JPA in recent years on the trade-development nexus, and more specifically on the EPAs.

The remainder of this paper is structured as follows. The next section provides the background on the role of the ACP-EU JPA and a brief review of the academic literature on ACP-EU relations. Subsequently, section three discusses the theoretical perspective of deliberation and develops an analytical framework to study deliberation in the ACP-EU JPA. Section four outlines the methodology used for the data generation and analysis. The analysis is based on participatory observation, 37 semi-structured interviews and an analysis of primary documents, including the attendance lists of 29 sessions, more than 40 resolutions, 120 publically available parliamentary questions to the Commission and the Council and responses by the Commission (hereafter referred to simply as parliamentary questions) related to the trade-development nexus over the past 15 years. Section five discusses the results of the analysis of deliberation in the ACP-EU JPA based on the five main criteria for ideal deliberation. Finally, the paper concludes with some general reflections on the main findings of this study, linking them to some broader questions relating to ACP-EU relations.

The JPA and ACP-EU relations

In the past decade one of the central debates on the EU's policies towards developing countries has focused on the character of the relationship between the EU and the ACP regions, and notably, the EU institutions' discourse centred on 'equal partnership'. This has been the case already since the 1970s with the entry into force of the Lomé Convention and it still dominates the EU discourse relating to the current Cotonou agreement. Indeed, Cotonou was designed to be a partnership between equals, to promote common interests and sustainable development, relying on an open dialogue amongst the parties.[6] However, this discourse on equal partnership has been strongly and widely criticised as mere rhetoric, which overshadows the asymmetrical power relationship that continues to characterise the ACP-EU framework. One of the central targets of this criticism is the EPAs. On the one hand, the EPA negotiations and specifically the inflexible approach of the Commission has been heavily criticised. Despite the EU's rhetoric on the promotion of norms such as development, ownership and equal partnership, its attitude is marked by a neo-imperialist,[7] or a hegemonic approach.[8] On the other hand, much criticism has been directed towards the substance of the EPAs as they are designed to promote the EU model of economic liberalism and lock in neoliberalism across the ACP regions, while restricting the policy space of the ACP governments.[9]

The existing literature mainly focuses on the intergovernmental dimension of the relationship and on main actors such as the European Commission, the EU Member States, the Council and to a lesser extent on the ACP countries themselves. Much less attention has been paid to other actors of the partnership, despite their growing importance and increased presence in the partnership and its revisions over time. Some attention has been paid to the role of Non State Actors (NSAs) and specifically to Civil Society Organisations (CSOs),[10] but hardly any attention has been paid to the parliamentarian dimension. Notable exceptions are an historical and institutional analysis of the ACP-EU JPA,[11] a policy orientated study of the European Centre for Development Policy Management[12] and an analysis of the ACP-EU JPA based on members' perceptions.[13] In the research on EPAs, which constitutes the empirical focus of this study, the JPA has not been considered either, except for an article on the perception of Eastern African policy-makers of the possible consequences of EPAs on regional integration,[14] and a book chapter on the promotion of core labour standards through the Cotonou and EPA process.[15] Finally, in the relatively new field of parliamentary diplomacy and interparliamentary cooperation, the ACP-EU JPA has largely been overseen also, apart from one chapter in an edited volume on inter-parliamentary institutions.[16]

This lack of attention to the parliamentary dimension of ACP-EU relations is remarkable for several reasons. First, the JPA is the oldest and most institutionalised parliamentary assembly between the countries of the global North and South. It was created to bring together an equal number of EU and the ACP parliamentarians for bi-annual meetings, rotating between the regions and to discuss issues of the three committees on political affairs; economic development, finance and trade and social affairs and environment, respectively. Indeed, it has served as a model for similar North-South parliamentary assemblies, such as the Euro-Mediterranean Parliamentary Assembly and the Euro-Latin American Parliamentary

Assembly. Second, the parliamentary dimension has grown in importance both within and beyond the EU-ACP framework. It has gained importance under the successive revisions of the Cotonou Agreement. For example, in the amendments of the political pillar after the 2005 review of Cotonou, the JPA was mentioned in Article 8 concerning the 'essential elements', implying the JPA should in the future be involved in the political dialogue. After the 2010 review, the role of ACP national parliaments as well as the oversight role of JPA was strengthened,[17] in line with the increasing focus on political dialogue over the successive conventions. Third, and most important in the context of this paper, arguably the ACP-EU JPA is the place in which real dialogue between the different parties is most likely to be approached. Shielded from power politics and lacking authority in terms of decision-making capacity, leaving more room for ideas and norms to be exchanged, deliberation is more likely to take place in this forum than in any intergovernmental negotiations.

Deliberation

The concept of deliberation has become increasingly central in political science debates since Habermas' discourse ethics.[18] Indeed, this has sparked much debate in the literature on discourse theory of deliberative democracy.[19] Today, it continues to be one of the most relevant concepts to assess the processes used to reach reasoned consensus by shedding light on blind spots in political analyses. Indeed, in contrast to rationalist approaches, a deliberative perspective recognises that parliamentary debates are more than 'cheap talk'.[20] Under specific conditions, deliberation can generate better-reasoned and informed positions that are, therefore, more legitimate and effective. Importantly, this paper employs the ideal type of deliberation as a heuristic tool and starts from the assumption that a real political debate will never fully reach the ideal type of deliberation. More specifically, this paper adopts a deliberative perspective on parliamentary debate for two reasons.

The first argument is *procedural* and emanates from the idea that deliberation is important to allow for an equal debate in an asymmetrical relationship. More specifically, according to Stie, 'procedures of deliberation can ensure that not only the strong and powerful but also weaker and less resourceful groups can influence outcomes'.[21] The second argument is *substantial* as deliberation is considered a prerequisite for a critical and rational debate between divergent views, interests or identities.[22] The differences in world views, interests and identities amongst ACP and EU countries are often large and in such a context deliberation is all the more necessary to be a able to agree on a common and valid normative framework as it enables actors to change their own world views, interests, identities.[23] Based on the existing literature on deliberation, an analytical framework has been developed (see Table 1) based on five main criteria identified for ideal deliberation i.e. the criteria that is necessary in order to arrive at valid norms,[24] or legitimate outcomes.[25] The analytical table allows us to study the quality of deliberation in the JPA and to assess *to what extent does the JPA dialogue on EPAs approach the ideal type of deliberation?*

The first criterion, *participation*, concerns the inclusion of all relevant affected parties. This criterion includes both a procedural and a substantial dimension. *Procedurally*, ideal deliberation requires the continuous participation of elected representatives. *Substantially*, opinions of the actors should be representative and include the needs, interests, preferences and positions of all concerned parties. According to Stie, these factors come closest to assessing participation – as democratic deliberation or elite deliberation – in modern democracies

Table 1. Quality of deliberation: analytical framework.

Criteria	Participation/Inclusion	Openness	Common good	Constructive politics	Power neutralising mechanisms
Guiding questions	Are all relevant affected parties included in the deliberation?	Are the deliberations transparent and communicated to wider public?	Does the deliberation refer to narrow constituencies' interests or the common good?	Does the deliberation lead to a consensus or do positional politics prevail?	Is the deliberation guided by power neutralising procedures?
Empirical indicators	Procedural: *Continuous* participation of *elected* representatives	Procedural: *Accessibility of policy documents* and background information	Substantial: *References to the common good* (in terms of the least advantaged)	Substantial: Positional politics (participants sit on their positions) vs. *consensus*	Procedural: *description of rules governing the deliberation* (that contribute to induce argumentative behaviour: predictable, continuous, understandable, consistent)
	Substantial: *Representativeness of opinions of actors* (inclusion of needs, interests, preferences, positions)	*Open sessions, minutes, voting results*			
		Substantial: Clear presentation of *perspectives (main dilemmas, visions, alternatives)*			
Data	Procedural: participants lists, interviews and participative observation	Procedural: ACP-EU JPA website, interviews and participative observation	Parliamentary questions, minutes, resolutions, interviews and participative observation	Parliamentary questions, minutes, resolutions, interviews and participative observation	Rules of procedures, interviews and participative observation
	Substantial: questions, minutes, resolutions, interviews and participative observation	Substantial: questions, minutes, resolutions, interviews and participative observation			

based on representative systems.[26] Second, ideal deliberation should be characterised by *openness* in order to allow for a free and transparent public debate and scrutiny. Existing literature already highlights that deliberative meeting places are identified by their openness and transparency.[27] Therefore, *procedurally*, the openness should be institutionalised through open sessions and the accessibility of the policy documents, background information, verbatim records and not merely minutes and voting results. *Substantially*, the public should be able to get a clear presentation of all the main dilemmas, visions and alternatives that circulate during deliberation. The third criterion is the '*common good*' and refers to whether there is a display of 'empathy, other-directedness, or solidarity that allows participants to consider the wellbeing of others and the community at large',[28] or purely narrow constituencies' interests in deliberation. In line with Rawls,[29] we understand the common good in terms of references to the least advantaged in society, as opposed to Mill's utilitarian definition based on the good of the greatest number of people.[30] Fourth, deliberation should involve *constructive politics*. Risse explains, 'the goal of discursive interaction is to achieve argumentative consensus with the other, not to push through one's own view of the world or moral values'.[31] As such, constructive politics is linked to the ability to reach reasoned or argumentative consensus through empathising and sharing a *common lifeworld*,[32] as opposed to sticking to uncompromising positional politics. The fifth and final criterion refers to the presence of *power neutralising mechanisms*, or put simply, the *rules of procedure*. Risse highlights that the more that rules prescribe non-hierarchical behaviour between actors, the more the rules should enable argumentation within the given framework.[33] This is an important criterion to assess whether not only the stronger more vociferous actors, but also the weaker and perhaps less powerful, can effectively contribute to argumentation to balance the tables in a partnership, which seeks to be equal.

In the table below these five main criteria are operationalised by means of sub-questions and corresponding empirical indicators. As explained in the introduction, the empirical focus is put on the JPA debate on the EPA negotiations. Additionally, it is indicated which data are used for each criterion. The next section outlines the methodology relating to the data generation and analysis in greater detail.

Methodology

The research presented in this paper is based on (1) document analysis, (2) semi-structured interviews and (3) participatory observation.

First, the document analysis is based on the attendance lists of 29 JPA sessions, more than 40 resolutions and 120 publically available parliamentary questions related to the trade-development nexus over the past 15 years. The choice for resolutions is motivated by the fact that these constitute the main outcome documents of the JPA and can thus be considered as the result of the deliberation. In contrast, parliamentary questions provide unique and exact insights into the concerns and preferences of the parliamentarians and offer a better understanding of the deliberation processes and the role and function of the JPA.[34] Especially for the criterion of the 'common good', the analysis of parliamentary questions was useful to reveal whether the deliberation refers to narrow constituencies' interests (or 'local interests') or to the common good (or 'broader policy concerns for the least advantaged in society'). For example, references to 'vulnerable groups', 'poor', 'women', 'ACP producers' were coded to decipher the level of commitment to the common good. The analysis happened through a systematic interpretation of these data, making use of codes. In doing so, we have employed an axial coding strategy[35] in order to relate the content of the resolutions and questions to the different criteria of the analytical framework.

For the 'participation' criterion we have also conducted an analysis of the attendance lists from the first JPA session in 2000 in Brussels until the 30th session in 2015 in Brussels. No data were available for the 7th session of 2004 and the 5th session in Brussels in 2002 was cancelled, so we have analysed the attendance lists of 29 sessions in between 2000 and 2015. A systematic comparison of these attendance lists enabled the calculation of the participation rates of ACP and EU members as well as their delegation continuity.

Second, the analysis is also based on semi-structured interviews conducted in 2010 and 2016 with 37 key ACP-EU JPA stakeholders, including JPA members and experts. The 2010 round of interviews included EP administration (3), civil society (2) and think tank (1) representatives as well as members of the European Parliament (MEPs) (8) and national ACP parliaments (10). The 2016 round of interviews included MEPs (2), EU officials (4) from the EEAS, DG DevCo, DG Trade and the EESC, EU NGOs (2), ACP Ambassadors (1) and ACP think tank representatives (1), as well as the JPA Secretariat on both the EU and ACP sides (3).[36]

Third and final, the insights also build on the authors' participatory observation during the 15th session of the JPA in Ljubljana in March 2008, the 19th session in Spain in March-April 2010 and the 30th session in Brussels in December 2015, as well as the standing Committees on Economic Development, Finance and Trade in Brussels, in October 2014, March 2015 and September 2015.

Analysis

This section will discuss the results of the analysis of deliberation in the ACP-EU JPA based on the five main criteria for ideal deliberation.

Participation

On participation, research on *procedural* indicators – *continuity* of participation and *representation* of political groups – reveals that participation is problematic due to striking differences on the EU and ACP sides. On the EU side, there is more or less stable participation during each legislature, although there are turnovers when elections are held every five years. While this was not deemed to be an issue per se, there was unanimous agreement amongst all interviewees on the disparity in participation when the JPA is held outside of Brussels. Some interviewees highlighted that MEPs are more active outside of the EU,[37] and that there is higher attendance in exotic places.[38] This acknowledgement has previously led to criticism of the JPA as a forum for 'political tourism'.[39] An analysis of the attendance lists[40] partly confirms this perceived imbalance. While the JPA sessions have gathered an average of 64% of the EU members of the JPA per session, some meetings have indeed attracted more MEPs than others. On the one hand, there is no significant difference in the average participation when the sessions take place in Brussels or Strasbourg (62%), in Europe (65%) or in an ACP country (63%). On the other hand however, we found evidence that attendance is indeed higher when JPA sessions take place at tourist destinations. The sessions with the highest MEP attendance rates[41] were the gatherings in Cape Town (2002, 89%), Barbados (2006, 84%), Rome (2003, 84%) and Tenerife (2010, 80%). In contrast, the lowest participation recorded was for the meetings in Strasbourg (March 2014, 27%, and December 2014, 42%), Brazzaville (2003, 38%) and Lomé (2011, 42%), where less than half of the EP members met their ACP counterparts.

On the ACP side, permanent participation is problematic as there are no permanent individual members, only permanent *country* members. Indeed, the list of the JPA members consists of the names of individual EP representatives and of the names of ACP *countries*. In formal terms, the ACP countries can delegate different MPs for each JPA session. Consequently their formal average attendance is rather high and higher than the MEPs attendance, namely 70% per session. Unlike the MEPs, attendance seems to be rather stable over the different sessions, and we found no peaks when the JPA took place at tourist destinations. However, when the sessions take place in Brussels or Strasbourg on the one hand, or another European city on the other, ACP attendance is slightly higher on average (73 and 72%, respectively) than JPA gatherings in ACP countries (67%). The largest part of ACP *countries* are also loyal participators: over the past 15 years, 77% of the ACP members have attended more than half of all the JPA sessions, while 61% have even attended more than 75% of the sessions. ACP countries are not obliged to appoint permanent MPs to the JPA and although the degree of individual permanence within their delegations is lower than on the European side, most of the loyal participating countries maintain a rather high degree of continuity within their delegations, sending the same MP to the JPA for several years, contributing to an enabling context for deliberation.

Where the EU side may lack on continuity, it makes up for it in *representation* due to the cluster of active and loyal MEPs who represent a nearly perfect reflection of the political groups in the EP. On the ACP side, most participants represent their respective governments by being delegates of the majority parties, but there are a few exceptions – whereby the opposition is also represented[42] – which are good signs for democracy, according to some interviewees. One interviewee expressed frustration with the ACP side because 'there is always an issue of government officials attending in parliamentarians' positions (...) [and] this loses focus on the objective'.[43] These issues impact deliberation precisely because of the nature of the Assembly to engage parliamentarians. However, Art.1 (2) JPA rules of procedure sets out the provisions whereby if a state may not be able to send parliamentarians due to 'forces majeures' – if parliament is suspended or doesn't exist – a representative may be nominated via letter by the speaker of the given parliament. This touches on the crux of the issue in representative systems of whether parliamentarians engage in democratic or elite deliberations. In this case, there is a fine line of demarcation, and perhaps often an interplay of both since parliamentary representatives, or government officials as nominated representatives, are part of an elite.[44]

Despite issues of procedural participation, on the *substantial* indicators, it seems rather straightforward to grasp the variety of different actors' opinions on both the possible positive and negative implications of the EPAs, as well as the more critical positions in the debate from the sum of the empirical research. However, there is variation on what can be grasped from resolutions to the parliamentary questions individually. More specifically, the parliamentary questions reflect the variety of opinions more explicitly than the resolutions. For example, while, the resolutions include many references to the different risks of EPAs, they have the tendency to refer to these in a more cautious manner. In general, the resolutions tend to address the potential risks of the EPAs, as opposed to taking a position on the topic. For example, one resolution states that 'many ACP countries fear that the current trend in the EPA negotiations and the adoption of agreements by subregions may undermine regional integration efforts'.[45] In the same vein, the resolution on 'EPA: problems and perspectives' also states the fact but does not take a position: 'negotiations conducted so far have revealed serious divergences between the ACP and the EU'.[46] Although the JPA refers to several marginalised groups – including NSA (10% of the resolutions), women's organisations (21%), civil society groups (19%) producer and consumer organisations (24 and 12%, respectively) – the JPA does not actively strive for their active participation in the majority of texts analysed.[47] Yet, EPA-specific resolutions had a much stronger correlation with being more participative by having significantly more references to these groups than the other resolutions on the trade-development nexus in general.

In contrast, parliamentary questions overtly indicate opinions on the EPAs, even questioning the fundamentals of the EU's neoliberal agenda. For example, one MEP asked, 'In view of the protests that have taken place (...) in Africa against the EPAs, is the Commission not willing to listen to the people (...) Free trade agreements have been a failure (...) so is the Commission going to shift its policy stance?'[48] Indeed, the more critical perspectives – on shortcomings, contradictions or counter-movements – are more easily grasped from parliamentary questions than resolutions, and they have often been additionally substantiated through participatory observation and interviews.

Openness

On openness, four issues were identified, which underscore that the JPA's relatively good openness (publically available documents, a dedicated website, etc.) is severely impacted by certain *procedural* impediments (navigating the JPA maze), which tangibly impact the accessibility of the Assembly. First, on minutes and voting results, there are no detailed minutes and the explanation of the voting results is on the European Parliament website for MEP's votes (when available), as opposed to the JPA website. Second, stakeholders have noted that committees may be easily accessible and on the agenda of the JPA, however information and policy documents on 'workshops' (Art. 27 JPA rules of procedure) are not.[49] Third, JPA plenary and committee sessions are open to the general public, although accreditation is needed and this in itself can be problematic in practice. One CSO stakeholder noted that 'access to documents is good but access to the forum is not easy. We've always had to fight for it and logistically it was always a challenge but friends within the JPA helped us'.[50] Fourth, while policy documents and background information are publicly available on the JPA website, there is limited accessibility due to the current layout of the website, the lack of clear categorisation of documents and their accessibility in advance of the sessions.[51] However, the JPA Secretariat has informed us that they do plan to revamp the website to make it more user-friendly. An additional element of accessibility is the possibility to web stream the plenary sessions live in the European Parliament, however this has proven to be too costly in ACP countries. The JPA Secretariat also mentioned plans to web stream committee meetings, although some stakeholders expressed preference that these remain off camera to allow for enhanced substantial openness.

Surprisingly, the aforementioned procedural issues did not significantly impact *substantial* openness as the documents reviewed displayed a full range of dilemmas, visions and alternatives, with the exception of the issue of ACP bloc voting. The ACP side of the JPA consistently vote as a bloc, which obscures the possibility to grasp the different substantial issues amongst the ACP parliamentarians themselves. However, in the resolutions and parliamentary questions, it is relatively straightforward to grasp the substantial issues on openness. For example, typical *dilemmas* referenced include the capacity constraints in ACP countries, regulatory barriers to trade and the impact of EU's Common Agricultural Policy reform.[52] Similarly, the resolutions include both global EU-ACP *visions* in the ACP context, which refer to achieving the objectives of the Cotonou Partnership Agreement (with reference to the relevant articles), and more JPA parliamentary-specific visions. For example, one innovative vision was the suggestion that national and regional parliaments set up functional stakeholder mechanisms.[53] Additionally, several JPA resolutions have made outright reference to *alternatives* with reference to Art. 37(6) Cotonou, which states that 'the Community (...) will examine all possible alternative possibilities' vis-à-vis the EPAs. Indeed, the overall perception from interviews is that openness is good.

Common good

On common good, the Assembly displayed continued concern on the social impacts of Cotonou. There are consistent and widespread references to vulnerable or marginalised groups across all data reviewed. For example in the parliamentary questions, some of the issues raised include: (i) the protection of the weakest economies in the SADC EPA and (ii) references to impact studies that predict a narrowing of social and economic policy spaces for ACP countries.[54] Interestingly, narrow interests appear more from interviews with JPA stakeholders than in official documents. For example, one interviewee explained, 'There is a near unanimous view on the EPA in the JPA and this is very surprising. The JPA has been consistent in emphasising the development dimension of EPA (...) [and] The JPA has tended to focus on social impact of Cotonou'.[55] The particular case referenced by this interviewee was the JPA deliberations on the EU Market Access Regulation (i.e. that countries would no longer benefit from preferential access to the EU market if they did not ratify the EPA by 1 October 2014), which was considered to be decisive in making the Commission extend the deadline for one year.[56] This is striking as it shows that the EP as an institution via the JPA, can agree on common good issues with its ACP parliamentarian counterparts, in stark contrast to the Commission and its ACP governmental counterparts. This can be explained by the nature of the JPA setting where, in contrast to intergovernmental negotiations, stakes are lower, allowing participants to behave less strategically and update their opinions based on arguments and new information. Moreover, in contrast to national parliaments, the JPA debates are less oriented towards voting or mobilising constituencies, but more towards aggregating new information and arguments and weighing positions.[57] Hence, majority votes to pass resolutions, including block voting on the ACP side, means that the Assembly is more prone to achieving consensus and divergence is less evident, and certainly not publicly available information.[58]

Participatory observation in JPA debates shows that there is a much more evident interplay of common good, expressed as empathy, solidarity and consideration of the other's well-being, than narrow interests. This was confirmed by interviewees, who conceded that this criterion ranges between good and satisfactory at the JPA. Also, the parliamentary questions paid a lot of attention to the least advantaged and the well-being of the ACP regions at large. For example, at several points in time, concerns have been raised about the conditions on which poor countries are eligible for debt relief.[59]

However, the analysis of the resolutions indicates more textual emphasis on 'products' and 'production', as opposed to vulnerable ACP producers. This undermines the claim that the JPA focuses on the social aspects of Cotonou. Indeed, remarkably, groups such as LDCs (in 48% of the resolutions), vulnerable states (36%), the poor (29%), indigenous persons (7%) and ACP farmers (17%) are not consistently referred to throughout the resolutions. Moreover, where references were made to the common good, there was evidence that this could be linked to local interests. For example, one interviewee pointed out to a perversion of the common good by linking narrow fisheries interests with the wider debate on sustainable development.[60] This raises the question, the common good from whose perspective? Can the solidarity at the JPA bridge EU and ACP interests or is it a euro-centric, or even euro-selfish construction of common issues?[61]

Constructive politics

On constructive politics, it is evident that the JPA is able to reach a consensus on EPAs. There is also clearly consensus both within the resolution texts and also across the texts over the years, especially on the 'development dimension' of EPAs and possible risks for sustainable development. Yet, despite an overwhelming consensus on the EPAs at the JPA, there were deeper more problematic concerns that consensus happened at the expense of content, and 'ACP self-censorship'.[62] This raises non-negligible issues relating to the qualitative elements of reaching argumentative consensus. Firstly, the quality of debates has been deemed to be weak based, in part, on the fact that only like-minded EU and ACP political parties meet each other and there is less of a constructive interaction with the entirety of political representatives. Indeed, side-meetings of informal groups of friends amongst EU and ACP parliamentarians – the 'Windhoek Dialogue' for the Conservatives, the 'International Socialists' and the 'ALDE-PAK' for the Liberals – mean that divergences are limited and based on ideology as opposed to EU vs. ACP lines. For example, EU and ACP parliamentarians may agree on hunting as a benefit (or not) for sustainable development within their informal groups of friends, but this cannot be gaged from the ACP block voting or the resolutions based on consensus. This is an example of deliberation within the remit of the JPA, but outside the formal context of debate, which is only evident from interviews and participatory observation. One MEP put it crudely that 'participants are generally optimistic and dreamers, therefore dreaming about a *common lifeworld*'.[63] Secondly, one interviewee recalled witnessing self-censorship on the side of ACP parliamentarians,[64] wherein they could not push their views too far because the EU side can call for a split vote i.e. the EU and the ACP sides can vote separately, as opposed to voting together as one house, and both must have a majority on both sides of the house in order for a resolution to pass. For this reason, it is no surprise that country oriented resolutions are harder to get consensus on, and that although LDCs are usually very nationalistic and less focused on the EU-ACP dimension, consensus is still reached. Linked to this latter critique, one interviewee described the JPA as 'a structure for giving pretense of democratic legitimacy and ACP endorsement of the EU position'.[65] From this perspective therefore, arriving at a rationally motivated consensus at the JPA is nevertheless based on EU preferences, world view and moral values. However, there is a finer line of demarcation due to the limited display of 'personal politics', wherein the majority of speakers make 'mediating proposals' that are appropriate for the JPA agenda.[66] This implies that in general,[67] members come to the Assembly with the *common lifeworld* spirit, less inclined to sit on their positions and less inclined to pursue openly argumentative deliberation since consensus is the given outcome.

Power neutralising mechanisms

On power neutralising mechanisms, it was interesting to note that institutional actors considered this criterion to be very good, in contrast to non-institutional EU and ACP experts who were more critical and expressly linked the rules of procedure to determining the outcomes and impact of the JPA deliberation. The JPA *rules of procedure* include 35 articles – stipulating the Public nature of proceedings, the Adoption of the Agenda, Seating arrangements, Official languages, Right to speak, Right to vote and methods of voting, Assembly resolutions and Amendments, Questions for written answer, Consultation with civil society, financial regulation amongst others – and 4 Annexes, which have been revised eight times since adoption on 3 April 2003. Overall, it can be considered to be clear and transparent. Indeed, interviewees largely considered the rules of procedure to be between satisfactory on the low end to very good on the high end. Even a more critical viewpoint explains, 'It is difficult with the EU and the ACP because there is mistrust and agenda setting. (...) Yet, there is nothing that obstructs expressing opinion'.[68] Even more critical JPA MEPs recognised, 'There is no hierarchy and no asymmetry',[69] and 'therefore no problem'.[70]

A closer look at the JPA rules of procedure *de jure* shows that the power neutralising mechanisms, nevertheless preserves asymmetries between the Parties. For example, Art. 10 JPA rules of procedure on seating arrangements was identified by one interviewee as perpetuating asymmetries between EU and ACP parliamentarians, whereby the former is referred to by their name and the latter by their country.[71] Similarly, Art. 19 on amendments also states that 'An ACP representative with the right to vote, a political group or ten members may table amendments' also underlines this difference between ACP on the one hand and MEPs who represent their political groups. In addition, Art. 20 and 21 on 'Questions for written answer' and 'Question time', respectively, there is a burden on the European Commission (and the ACP-EU Council of Ministers) to respond, but no equivalent burden on the ACP side to respond to issues raised at the JPA. However, in practice, the ACP Secretariat is not an equal vis-à-vis the Commission, and indeed there is no equivalent follow-up on the ACP side. This additional obligation to follow-up on the EU side, and lack of it on the ACP side in practice, gives concessions to the ACP and underscores the inequality of partnership as opposed to equality.

A closer look at rules of procedure de facto, that is mastery of these rules, shows that in practice it is a double-edged sword. For example, in committees, all members are equal vis-à-vis speaking time, but in the plenary session the *d'Hondt* method is applied therefore larger groups on the EP side have more speaking time. However, the ACP side is larger overall and has the decisive vote. As such, the power at the JPA is equivalent to the ACP voting as a bloc – which is consistently the case – regardless of the difference in speaking time. Indeed, stakeholders on both the EU and ACP side have recognised the JPA *rules of procedure* as a benefit to the ACP, and as an extension, some believe this guarantees a 'debate between equals'.[72] From this perspective, the rules of procedure means that the ACP side does not merely rubber-stamp the resolution on the table because working methods mean that both sides must work towards compromise. The only way around this, whereby a resolution does not pass, is when a majority vote occurs through a vote by separate EU and ACP houses, the so-called split vote. One interviewee perfectly summed up, 'rules of procedure are important in political process and they can advantage or disadvantage parties but it is the mastery of these rules that matter'.[73]

Conclusions

By studying the EU-ACP JPA, this paper aimed to provide new insights and add to the existing policy-oriented and academic evaluations of ACP-EU relations. Fleshing out the deliberative framework allowed us to respond to the key question: *to what extent does the JPA dialogue on EPAs approach the ideal type of deliberation?* By focusing on five key criteria for deliberation – participation, openness, common good, constructive politics and power neutralising mechanism – this analysis shed light on the fact that real dialogue between different parties is not always guaranteed. Or, the JPA dialogue on EPAs struggles to approach the ideal type of deliberation, even if there is overwhelming consensus on EPAs at the JPA.

This is largely due to a number of recurrent critical issues across the different criteria. On the criteria of *participation*, there is *procedural* continuity which creates an enabling environment for deliberation, however there remains a fundamental distinction between representing their political parties and ACP parliamentarians representating their country. *Substantially*, the parliamentary questions are more inclusive of the variety of all actors' opinions, compared to the resolutions. On *openness*, given the high-level nature of the Assembly, the *procedural* openness of the JPA means that it is relatively accessible, despite the fact that the results of the votes are not publicly available digitally. Additionally, ACP bloc voting limits the *substantial* openness to the individual parliamentary positions during the debate. In relation to the *common good,* there is a tension between the interviewees' perceived solidarity in the JPA and the parliamentary questions about broader policy concerns for the least advantaged on the one hand, and the actual prevalence of narrow interests linked to the trade-development nexus evidence from the resolutions on the other hand. Regarding *constructive politics*, despite an overwhelming consensus on the EPAs at the JPA, there were deeper more problematic concerns that consensus happened at the expense of content, and 'ACP self-censorship. Finally, despite several amendments to the *rules of procedure* over the years, the asymmetry between the EU and ACP parliamentarians has never been overcome.

This was the first attempt at a more holistic and systematic analysis of deliberation at the JPA, which led us to develop the 'Quality of deliberation analytical framework'. Applying the criteria in the framework to the extensive empirical data of the JPA enabled us to come to a deep and thorough understanding of the nature of the debate. However, we have also identified a number of areas that merit further research, which are largely linked to further investigating divergence at the JPA. For example, *procedurally*, the use of ACP bloc voting or 'self-censorship', the presence of representatives of ACP opposition parties and the JPA split vote can fundamentally impact the outcome on deliberation.

Additionally, *substantially*, deliberations on non-resolutions, failed resolutions and debates without resolutions are another layer of untapped empirical data, which could provide an even deeper understanding of the complex nature of deliberation at the JPA. Currently, our analysis demonstrates the ccomplementarity of the variety of parliamentary instruments/ arenas for deliberation, including questions, resolutions, plenary debates and workshops to name a few. However, a key pitfall remains follow-up debates at the national parliamentary level.

Finally, these new findings have raised some deeper and unanswered issues on the power, impact and relevance of the JPA, which ought to be develop in further research, especially leading up to the expiry of Cotonou in 2020. Deliberation in the JPA has shown that ideas do not always travel in reciprocal directions, which brings into question the fundamentals of equal partnership between unequal regions. In other words, this questions the foundations of the Cotonou Agreement, namely the ability to 'discuss issues' and 'facilitate greater understanding between the peoples of the European Union and those of the ACP' (Art. 17 Cotonou).

Disclosure statement

No potential conflict of interest was reported by the authors.

Notes

1. See Gomes, "Reshaping an Asymmetrical Partnership"; Carbone, "Rethinking ACP-EU Relations"; Keijzer and Negre, "Outsourcing a Partnership?" and Pape, "An Old Partnership."
2. European Commission, "Towards a New Partnership."
3. Goodison, "The European Union"; "EU Trade Policy"; Flint, "The End of a Special Relationship?"; Storey, "Normative Power Europe?"; Hurt, "Co-operation and Coercion?"; Farrell, "A Triumph of Realism"; and Langan, "A Moral Economy Approach."
4. European Commission, "Towards a New Partnership," 13.
5. Steenbergen et al., "Measuring Political Deliberation," 21.
6. Carbone, "Rethinking ACP-EU Relations."
7. Steven, "The EU, Africa and Economic Partnership Agreements," 441–58; and Goodison, "The European Union."
8. Williams, "Shifting Between Hegemony and Dominance?"; "The EU as a Foreign Policy Actor."
9. Flint, "The End of a Special Relationship?" 79–92; and Hurt, "Co-operation and Coercion?"
10. Carbone, "Theory and Practice of Participation," 241–55; and Hurt, "Civil Society and European Union Development Policy."
11. Delputte, "Talking Shop or Relevant Actor."
12. Corre, *Parliaments and Development*.

13. Delputte, "The ACP-EU Joint Parliamentary Assembly."
14. Delputte, "EPA's: Welkome stimulans."
15. Kerremans and Martins-Gistelinck, "Labour Rights in EPAs."
16. Delputte, "Talking Shop or Relevant Actor."
17. Delputte, "The ACP-EU Joint Parliamentary Assembly"; "Talking Shop or Relevant Actor."
18. Steenbergen et al., "Measuring Political Deliberation," 21.
19. Stie, "Assessing Democratic Legitimacy," 1.
20. Bächtiger, "Debate and Deliberation in Legislatures."
21. Ibid., 3–4.
22. Habermas, "Between the Facts and Norms"; and Risse, "Let's Argue!" 1–39.
23. Risse, "Let's Argue!" 2.
24. Habermas, "Between the Facts and Norms".
25. Stie, "Assessing Democratic Legitimacy."
26. Ibid., 4–6.
27. Ibid., 13.
28. Steenbergen et al., "Measuring Political Deliberation," 26.
29. Rawls, *A Theory of Justice*.
30. Mill, *Utilitarianism*. See also Steenbergen et al., "Measuring Political Deliberation," 26.
31. Risse, "Let's Argue!" 10.
32. Ibid.
33. Ibid., 19.
34. See Martin, "Parliamentary Questions, the Behaviour of Legislators, and the Function of Legislatures" on the merits of analysing parliamentary questions.
35. 'The process of relating categories to their subcategories is termed 'axial' because coding occurs around the axis of the category, linking categories at the level of properties and dimensions', see Strauss and Corbin, "Basics of Qualitative Research."
36. In the 2016 round of interviews, it was not possible to conduct semi-structured interviews with ACP parliamentarians due to time constrictions. However, the authors' participatory observation at the 2016 sessions, complimented by the interviews with ACP officials and experts, provided ample information.
37. Expert interview with EU institution and EU NGO, 13 July 2016.
38. Expert interview with EU institution (DG Trade), 14 July 2016.
39. See Delputte, "The ACP-EU Joint Parliamentary Assembly," 241–60.
40. For this analysis, we have considered data from the first JPA session in 2000 in Brussels until the 30th session in 2015 in Brussels. No data were available for the 7th session of 2004 and the 5th session in Brussels in 2002 was cancelled, so we have analysed the attendance lists of 29 sessions in between 2000 and 2015.
41. The inauguration session in Brussels in 2000 also recorded a high attendance rate (84%).
42. Namibia and Zambia were both noted as countries that send representatives of the ruling and oppositions party. However, as there is only one Head of Delegation, this does not guarantee that the opposition can take the floor.
43. Expert interview with EU NGO, 19 July 2016.
44. In interviews with an expert and MEP, both recognised JPA members as being part of the elite, although the MEP did not want to be recognised as such and called for more pluralism through broader participation of different interest groups, including young people, farmers and civil society amongst others. Expert interview with EU institution, 13 July 2016 and expert interview with MEP, 13 July 2016.
45. Resolution on 'experiences from the European regional integration process relevant to ACP countries' (2008), point 21.
46. Resolution on 'EPA: problems and perspectives' (2004), point B.
47. Just over half the texts reviewed had 0–3 references to these groups, 10% of the texts had between 6 and 9 references, while the bulk of ten or more references were in a quarter of the texts.
48. MEP Joao Ferreira, 31st session of the JPA, Windhoek, Namibia, 13–15 June 2016.

49. Expert interview with EU institution, 12 July 2016.
50. Expert interview with EU NGO, 13 July 2016.
51. Note that this can also impact participation.
52. See in particular, the resolution on 'EPA: problems and perspectives' (2004), point 18 and Resolution on 'EPAs and their impacts on ACP states' (2009), point N.
53. Resolution on 'EPAs' (2002) point 6 and Resolution on the 'review of negotiations on EPAs' (2006) point 21.
54. See the parliamentary session from the JPA plenary session in Windhoek, Namibia, 13–15 June 2016, http://www.europarl.europa.eu/intcoop/acp/2016_namibia/pdf/1096273en.pdf and the Committee session questions, Brussels, Belgium, 7–9 December, http://www.europarl.europa.eu/intcoop/acp/2015_acp2/pdf/1080041en.pdf.
55. Expert interview with JPA Secretariat, 22 July 2016.
56. Ibid.
57. See also Bächtiger, "Debate and Deliberation in Legislatures" for a thorough discussion on the question why parliamentary contexts can enable genuine deliberation.
58. For example, in the 32nd session of the JPA in Nairobi, Kenya there were divergences over a resolution on Gabon, which was not passed. However, without participatory evidence or 'openness' via local media, the issues that led to this divergence may not necessarily come to the fore. Moreover, they certainly won't be available from merely analysing resolutions.
59. Question by MEP Mikel Amezaga and response by the Commission, 17th session, Prague, Czech Republic, 6–9 April 2009.
60. Expert interview with EU NGO, 13 July 2016.
61. Ibid.
62. Ibid.
63. Expert interview with MEP, 12 July 2016.
64. Expert interview with EU NGO, 13 July 2016.
65. Expert interview with ACP think-tank, 8 July 2016.
66. Steenbergen et al., "Measuring Political Deliberation," 30.
67. Indeed, the aforementioned example on the failure to have a resolution on Gabon is an exception, 32nd JPA in Nairobi, Kenya 19–21 December 2016.
68. Expert interview with EU NGO, 19 July 2016.
69. Expert interview with MEP, 12 July 2016.
70. Expert interview with MEP, 13 July 2016.
71. Expert interview with EU institution, 19 July 2016.
72. Ibid.
73. Expert interview with ACP Ambassador, 13 July 2016.

Bibliography

Bächtiger, André. "Debate and Deliberation in Legislatures". In *The Oxford Handbook of Legislative Studies*, edited by Kaare Strøm, Thomas Saalfeld, and Martin Shane, 145-166. Oxford: Oxford University Press, 2014.

Carbone, Maurizio. "Rethinking ACP-EU Relations After Cotonou: Tensions, Contradictions, Prospects." *Journal of International Development* 25, no. 5 (2013): 742–756.

Carbone, Maurizio. "Theory and Practice of Participation: Civil Society and EU Development Policy." *Perspectives on European Politics and Society* 9, no. 2 (2008): 241–255.

Corre, Gwénaëlle. "Parliaments and Development: The Icing on the Cake? What Parliamentary Capacity can mean for Cooperation." *Brief*, no. 9 (2004): 1–12.

Delputte, Sarah. "EPAs: A Welcomed Boost for Cooperation or a Possible Source of Disintegration? Perceptions from the East African Political Elite." *Res Publica* 51, no. 4 (2009): 489–518.

Delputte, Sarah. "The ACP-EU Joint Parliamentary Assembly Seen by its Members: Empowering the Voice of People's Representatives?" *European Foreign Affairs Review* 17, no. 2 (2012): 241–260.

Delputte, Sarah. "Talking Shop or Relevant Actor: The ACP-EU Joint Parliamentary Assembly." In *Parliamentary Dimensions of Regionalisation and Globalisation: The Role of Inter-Parliamentary*

Institutions, edited by Oliver Costa, Clarissa Dri, and Stelios Stavridis, 189–210. Basingstoke: Palgrave Macmillan, 2013.

European Commission. "Public Consultation. Towards a New Partnership between the EU and the ACP Countries after 2020." Accessed October 6, 2015. http://ec.europa.eu/europeaid/public-consultation-eu-acp-new-partnership_en

European Commission. "Towards a New Partnership between the European Union and the African, Caribbean and Pacific Countries after 2020. Summary Report of the Public Consultation". Brussels. Accessed March 18, 2016. https://ec.europa.eu/europeaid/sites/devco/files/summary-report-public-consultation-eu-acp-20160318_en_0.pdf

Farrell, Mary. "A Triumph of Realism Over Idealism? Cooperation between the European Union and Africa." *Journal of European Integration* 27, no. 3 (2005): 263–283.

Flint, Adrian. "The End of a Special Relationship? The New EU–ACP Economic Partnership Agreements." *Review of African Political Economy* 36, no. 119 (2009): 79–92.

Goodison, Paul. "The European Union: New Start or Old Spin?" *Review of African Political Economy* 32, no. 103 (2005): 167–176.

Goodison, Paul. "EU Trade Policy and the Future of Africa's Trade Relationship with the EU." *Review of African Political Economy* 34, no. 112 (2007): 247–266.

Gomes, Patrick I. "Reshaping an Asymmetrical Partnership: ACP-EU Relations from an ACP Perspective." *Journal of International Development* 25, no. 5 (2013): 714–726.

Habermas, Jürgen. *Between the Facts and Norms: Contribution to a Discourse Theory of Law and Democracy*. Cambridge, MA: MIT Press, 1998.

Hurt, Stephen. "Civil Society and European Union Development Policy." In *New Pathways in Development: Gender and Civil Society in EU Policy*, edited by M. Lister and Maurizio Carbone, 109–122. Aldershot: Ashgate, 2006.

Hurt, Stephen. "Co-operation and Coercion? The Cotonou Agreement between the European Union and ACP States and the End of the Lomé Convention." *Third World Quarterly* 24, no. 1 (2003): 161–176.

Hurt, Stephen. "The EU–SADC Economic Partnership Agreement Negotiations: 'Locking In' the Neoliberal Development Model in Southern Africa?" *Third World Quarterly* 33, no. 3 (2012): 495–510.

Keijzer, Niels, and Mario Negre. "Outsourcing a Partnership? Assessing ACP–EU Cooperation under the Cotonou Partnership Agreement." *South African Journal of International Affairs* 21, no. 2 (2014): 279–296.

Kerremans Bart, and Myriam Martins-Gistelinck. "Labour Rights in EPAs: Can the EU-CARIFORUM EPA Be a Guide?" In *Beyond Market Access for Economic Development. EU-Africa Relations in Transition*, edited by Geritt Faber and Jan Orbie, 304–321. London: Routledge, 2009.

Langan, Mark. "A Moral Economy Approach to Africa-EU Ties: The Case of the European Investment Bank." *Review of International Studies* 40 (2014): 465–485.

Maes, Marc. "EPAs, the EU and ACP – An Uneven Partnership." Accessed October 1, 2014. http://www.equaltimes.org/epas-the-eu-and-acp-an-uneven?lang=en#.Vw5T3uYXZ2E

Martin, Shane. "Parliamentary Questions, the Behaviour of Legislators, and the Function of Legislatures: An Introduction." *The Journal of Legislative Studies* 17, no. 3 (2011): 259–270.

Mill, John Stuart. *Utilitarianism*. Oxford: Oxford University Press, 1998.

Pape, Elisabeth. "An Old Partnership in a New Setting: ACP–EU Relations from a European Perspective." *Journal of International Development* 25 no. 5 (2013): 727–741.

Rawls, John. *A Theory of Justice*. Cambridge, MA: Belknap Press of Harvard University Press, 1971.

Risse, Thomas. "Let's Argue!." *International Organisation* 54, no. 1 (2000): 1–39.

Steenbergen, Marco R., André Bächtiger, Markus Spörndli, and Jürg Steiner. "Measuring Political Deliberation: A Discourse Quality Index." *Comparative European Politics* 1 (2003): 21–48.

Stevens, Christopher. "The EU, Africa and Economic Partnership Agreements: Unintended Consequences of Policy Leverage." *The Journal of Modern African Studies* 44, no. 3 (2006): 441–458.

Stie, Anne Elizabeth. "Assessing Democratic Legitimacy from a Deliberative Perspective." ARENA Working Paper 6. Oslo: Centre for European Studies, 2008.

Storey, Andy. "Normative Power Europe? Economic Partnership Agreements and Africa." *Journal of Contemporary African Studies* 24, no. 3 (2006): 331–346.

Strauss, Anselm, and Juliet Corbin. *Basics of Qualitative Research: Grounded Theory Procedures and Techniques*. Newbury Park, CA: Sage, 1990.

Williams, Yentyl. "Shifting between Hegemony and Dominance? A Neo-Gramscian Analysis of the EU as a Structural Foreign Policy Actor: The Singular Case of the Cariforum-EU Economic Partnership Agreement." *Bruges Regional Integration & Global Governance Papers*, no. 1, 2–35. Bruges: United Nations University and College of Europe.

Williams, Yentyl. "The EU as a Foreign Policy Actor: Shifting between Hegemony and Dominance." *Caribbean Journal of International Relations and Diplomacy* 3, no. 1 (2015): 7–33.

Feigned ambition. Analysing the emergence, evolution and performance of the ACP Group of States

Niels Keijzer

ABSTRACT
In 1975 the Africa, the Caribbean and Pacific (ACP) Group of States was created after the then 46 states concluded a cooperation partnership with the European Economic Community. This article draws on the literature on international organisation (IO) independence and performance to analyse the ACP Group's evolution and functioning over time. Its findings show that whereas the ACP Group has generally failed to deliver on its supra-national objectives, its members have used Group membership as a means to accessing European Union benefits. This confirms recent research that dependent and non-performing IOs may serve important funding and patronage purposes to their members.

Introduction

In June 2015 the Africa, the Caribbean and Pacific (ACP) Group of States celebrated its 40th anniversary, four decades during which the Group grew from 46 to 79 states and became 'the largest inter-governmental association of developing countries with a permanent Secretariat'.[1] The ACP Group was founded in June 1975, a few months after negotiations between the 46 states and Europe concluded with the adoption of the Lomé Convention. As per its history and main constituting motivation, the ACP Group derives a large part of its identity from its relationship with Europe, which since 2000 is governed by the Cotonou Agreement. In 2017 negotiations will start to determine the future of ACP-European Union (EU) cooperation after the expiration of the Cotonou Agreement in 2020. In deliberating on its future relations with and beyond Europe, the ACP Group has been reflecting on its own institutional development and organisational structures. At their 2012 Summit in Malabo, Equatorial Guinea, the ACP Group conveyed its commitment to '(…) deepening and enhancing the ACP-EU relationship as a unique North-South Development Cooperation model, while developing diversified South-South and other partnerships'.[2]

ACP-EU cooperation is no stranger to the scholarly literature on EU external action and until today remains a key feature of European development cooperation and Africa-EU relations. Key foci in the literature include the effectiveness of the EU's long-standing asymmetrical trade preference scheme and subsequent Economic Partnership Agreement (EPA) negotiations, as well as the evolution of development cooperation practice from non-interference and recipient discretion towards conditionality and political dialogue.[3] As per both the aims and nature of this body of literature, it predominantly analyses the ACP Group from a European perspective, while neglecting the question as to how the ACP Group itself developed over time. This article draws on the literature on the performance of international organisations (IOs) to analyse the ACP Group's evolution since the founding of the Group, with particular attention to its four central organs (alternatively referred to as 'institutions') and permanent secretariat.

Available information on the inner-workings of the ACP Group is scarce, which required a flexible research design combining information gathering with exploring perceptions of ACP Group functioning and performance. The analysis presented in this article draws on a review of both public and grey sources, after which ten semi-structured interviews with ACP officials were conducted in Brussels in the period July–September 2015.[4] ACP Secretariat officials and Ambassadors were contacted with the aim to cover all three regions and include both Least-Developed Countries as well as richer members. As per its research design, the article does not present conclusive evidence on the functioning of ACP institutions. Through its historical overview and analysis of perceived functioning of ACP Group's structures and processes, it contributes to the literature on IO performance as well as facilitates further research inquiry and increased understanding of ACP-EU relations.

The remainder of this article is structured in four sections. The first section analyses the literature on the (non-)performance of IOs as a means to analysing the expected interests of ACP states in Group membership. Section two describes the emergence of the ACP Group. Section three presents the research findings on the functioning of the ACP institutions. Section four further analyses the evolving mandate of the Group's permanent secretariat and the effects of related EU support. Section five concludes.

International organisation independence and (non-)performance

The social science literature on IOs performance can be divided into two strands: an economistic group guided by concepts of instrumental rationality and efficiency, and a sociological group focused on legitimacy and power. The first strand defines IOs as mechanisms through which states act, while the second analyses IOs as agents with power independent of the states that created them.[5] Recent research evidence confirms the latter strand of literature that IOs should be considered as independent agents.[6] A study comparing institutional design characteristics of thirty regional integration arrangements identified economic interdependence and the passage of time as important explanatory variables for predicting IO independence, indicating that IOs evolve over time in a way that matches functional needs. Yet the authors and other recent scholarly contributions recognise the need for qualitative studies to assess under what conditions formal design aspects promoting *de jure* independence are translated into *de facto* independence, and how this independence facilitates IO performance. [7]

Studies have sought to analyse the performance of IOs, which can be defined as the extent to which they achieve stated objectives in a cost-effective and responsive manner. [8] A recent analysis comparing available IO assessments shows considerable variation in performance across IOs with similar mandates, resources and membership.[9] The Yearbook of IOs identified 1454 intercontinental membership organisations and 6612 regionally oriented membership organisations.[10] The sheer number of IOs challenges efforts to attribute specific outcomes to the performance of individual IOs, which is why much of the literature measures performance in terms of processes and the production of outputs that may or may not promote the IO's formal objectives.[11] In view of these methodological challenges and the availability of information, the literature on IO performance concentrates on a number of 'usual suspects', particularly those IOs with economic mandates that make performance measurement more straightforward.[12]

The literature identifies various factors internal or external to the IO concerned that may explain for good or bad performance. Examples of internal factors include the IO leadership and resourcing, while external factors include the degree of member consensus, as well as external support.[13] While earlier studies suggested that IO independence may lead to dysfunctional behaviour[14], recent research argues that this finding has only been examined through studies of individual IOs and is not adequately supported by comparative analysis. While noting that only some IOs have gained sufficient independence to engage in deviant behaviour, recent cross-IO analysis identifies opportunistic behaviour by member states as the primary obstacle to IO performance. Well-performing IOs were seen to mitigate this challenge by means of adequate independence, promoted through institutionalised non-state alliances and the technical complexity of their activities.[15] This is complemented by recent case studies describing how selected members collude with the IO secretariat to achieve outcomes at the expense of other members, moving beyond the conceptualisation of a binary IO-membership relation.[16]

Like other developing countries, the 79 ACP States are party to a multitude of regional and IOs. Since membership and participation costs can be substantial, recent research has sought to analyse what drives states to continue their membership of ineffective IOs. Examples of such IOs include various Regional Economic Communities, which feature considerable bureaucracies and formalised meeting structures yet generally have made only limited progress in delivering on their mandates. These IOs are typically strongly dependent on their members, while not featuring strong multi-stakeholder linkages or delivering technical substance so as to enable progress.[17] This research suggests that non-performing or even dysfunctional IOs may still benefit members by producing two interlinked benefits: facilitating access to external funding, and opportunities for private gain including employment and travel.[18] This implies that IOs may also serve to promote aims for which they were not formally created. IOs may be favoured even when they may not be the most efficient or effective ones, but may instead serve normative ends and be 'created not for what they do but for what they are'.[19] Permanent secretariats, meeting structures and other visible structures are key to conveying such an image.

Throughout the past decades, group membership has enabled ACP states to access and consolidate EU development cooperation and trade on better terms than non-ACP countries. Its negotiation dynamics with Europe and resulting first Lomé Conventions have been characterised by John Ravenhill as 'collective clientelism', 'a relationship in which a group of weak states combine in an effort to exploit the special ties that link them to a more powerful state or group of states'.[20] The ACP Group's image and supra-national goals, regardless of whether the ACP Group performed in pursuing these, also served the EU's interests by helping to justify this 'special relationship' with the ACP vis-à-vis non-ACP developing countries. This in turn supported the EU's own financial and political support to ACP institutions which represented a key factor in its development during the past and present decade. Gray's second assumed IO benefit of patronage would particularly relate to the special interests of the diplomatic officials of those of the 79 countries based in Brussels, the staff of the permanent secretariat, visiting officials from ACP countries as well as other direct beneficiaries.

Guided by the literature on IO independence and (non)performance, this article will analyse perceptions of the performance of the ACP Group against its stated objectives, but also further analyse to what extent it delivers on the two types of benefits associated to non-performing IOs.

The emergence of the ACP group

The ACP Group's nature and identity is highly intertwined with the European project, and rooted in the association policy of the European Economic Community (EEC) towards its overseas countries and territories as set out in the 1957 Treaty of Rome.[21] Amidst its preparations for joining the EEC during the early 1970s, the United Kingdom had encouraged Commonwealth countries to join the existing former French and Belgian African colonies' association to the European project.[22] Instead of choosing from what they perceived as a set of European offers, the group of countries resolved to jointly negotiate a new cooperation agreement with Europe.[23] Although it was their decision to negotiate together, Europe largely prescribed the composition of the ACP Group through the 1973 United Kingdom's EEC accession treaty that defined which Commonwealth states were 'associable' to the existing EEC-Africa cooperation framework.[24] Frey-Wouters observed that at the time of the Group's creation, 'the ACP countries share[d] very little economic and commercial organization' and were vulnerable in their isolated economic and political cooperation with the EEC.[25]

The sequence of first concluding the convention and subsequently creating the Group meant that the first Lomé Convention was agreed between the EEC and the states of the ACP Group.[26] Article 1 of the Group's constitutive Georgetown Agreement in fact required aspiring members of the Group to first accede to the Lomé Convention.[27] Another example of the links between the ACP Group and its partnership with Europe was that the term in office of the Group's Secretary General coincided with the duration of the Lomé I Convention.[28] Article 2 of the Georgetown Agreement sets out a total of seven objectives for the Group, of which the first three are related to the implementation of the Lomé Convention and the remaining four present broad objectives on solidarity, as well as promoting individual and group cooperation interests. The latter include the supra-national aims

> to contribute to the development of greater and closer trade, economic and cultural relations amongst the ACP States and amongst developing countries in general, and to this end to develop the exchange of information amongst the ACP States in the fields of trade, technology, industry and human resources.[29]

Conferences were held in the late 1970s to operationalise and advance these ambitions, yet failed to go beyond generic statements of intent.[30] Revisions to the Georgetown Agreement were made in 1992 and 2003 and mainly sought to 'catch up' with the substance of EU-ACP cooperation agreements.

The Georgetown Agreement provides the ACP Group with legal personality, while its Headquarters Agreement with the Belgian Kingdom guarantees diplomatic immunity to senior personnel of its permanent secretariat, as well as documentary and communications immunity. The ACP Group has since 1981 held Observer Status at the UN, which recognises the Group as an IO.[31] Although in a legal sense it exhibits the characteristics of an IO, i.e. 'being associations of more than one state, undertaking common tasks and fulfilling concrete ends and objectives for which they were created', already at an early stage it was argued that the ACP was primarily created to receive special favours from Europe.[32]

The Oxford Companion to Politics of the World typifies the Lomé Conventions and the Cotonou Agreement as a 'legally binding contractual agreement based on partnership, reciprocity, and equal benefits between the EU and the ACP states'.[33] This characterisation underlines that it is not just the broad cooperation agenda and broad membership that sets the partnership apart from others, but also the approach to governing the partnership. Given its historical rooting in the EEC's association policy, the introduction of joint ACP-EEC structures and new discourse around 'partnership' in Lomé I sought to bring balance to an otherwise asymmetrical relationship.[34] Although much of the literature presents Lomé as a conceptual and rhetorical break with the idea of association, archival analysis of the Lomé I negotiations concludes that the three largest EEC members were instrumental in shaping the Lomé accord and that the essence of the post-colonial Yaoundé relationship remained unchanged. The resulting Lomé I Convention would reflect the concept of collective clientelism, yet the archival analysis nuances the ACP states' negotiation strength implied in that concept by showing that ACP preferences were only influential when they reflected those of the influential EEC members.[35]

Following the four Lomé Conventions covering the period 1975–2000, EU-ACP relations are presently governed under the Cotonou Agreement. The legally binding agreement confirmed the special status of the relationship, yet also sought to fundamentally reform it in response to the disappointing results of the Lomé Conventions, and the need to phase out trade preferences that were non-compliant with WTO rules. As a means to reforming relations, the Cotonou Agreement introduced the principle of differentiation to reform all three cooperation pillars. Direct European Development Fund (EDF) contributions were progressively reduced for those ACP states that classify as Upper Middle and High-Income Countries. Trade relations also became increasingly differentiated as per the outcomes of trade negotiations with six regional groups, with the Caribbean agreeing to a more comprehensive trade agenda and other sub-regions pursuing trade in goods agreements. Finally, political dialogue at the national level was strengthened and governance reform incentivised through additional aid, while the EU further invested in its political partnership at the regional level, particularly with Africa.[36] As is described below, although the ACP Group's structures and processes have poorly performed throughout their lifetime, the Cotonou Agreement's differentiation policy has aggravated this underperformance by reducing direct EU benefits to several of its members.

The organisation of the ACP

The Georgetown Agreement created two organisational structures that it refers to as the Group's 'organs': the ACP Council of Ministers and the ACP Committee of Ambassadors (COA). In terms of composition and procedures these largely mirrored joint EEC-ACP structures that were set up in 1975 under Lomé I, which in turn were based on structures created by the first Yaoundé Convention in 1962.[37] Article 3 of the agreement states that the ACP organs were to be assisted by a General Secretariat. Shridath Ramphal of Guyana played an instrumental role in the realisation of the Group's Brussels-based secretariat by persuading the European partners to use EDF reserves to co-finance the building.[38] In 2003 the Revised Georgetown Agreement created the Summit of ACP Heads of State as the third organ of the

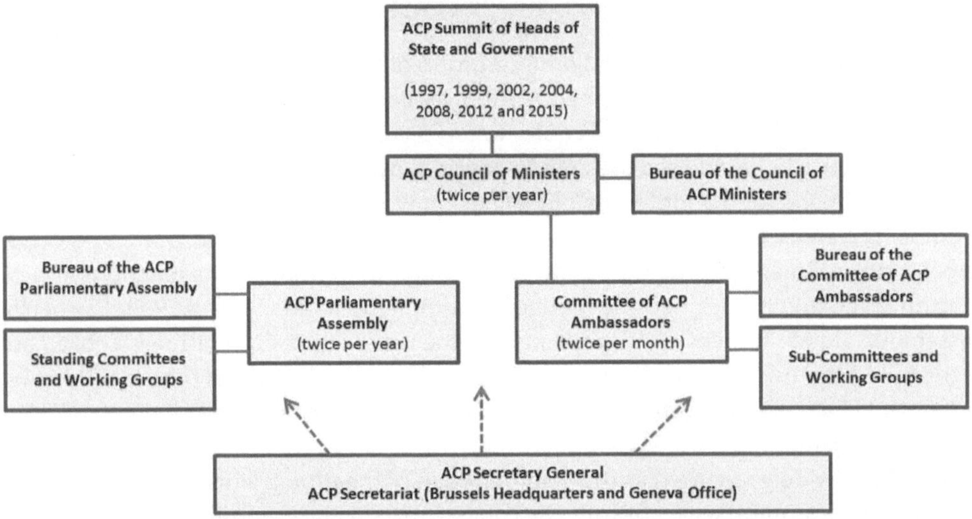

Figure 1. Organisational structure of the ACP Group. Source: own elaboration based on ACP 2012: 15

group and announced plans to establish an ACP Parliamentary Assembly. Figure 1 presents the current setup.

The following paragraphs present findings from the analysis of the literature and interviews with regard to the performance of the Group's four organs, followed by an analysis of the Group's permanent secretariat.

The Council of Ministers

The Council of ACP Ministers is the main decision-making body of the ACP Group. Working under the Summit of the Heads of State, the Council defines the broad outlines of the work to be undertaken to achieve the Group's objectives. It consists of a member of the Government of each of the ACP States or its designated representative, and meets twice a year in regular session. Its agenda is prepared by the Brussels-based Committee of ACP Ambassadors (COA).[39] Although Article 10 of the Georgetown agreement allows for the Council to adopt decisions by a two-thirds majority, in practice decisions are made by consensus.[40] Absence of consensus typically leads to additional consultations in search of a compromise, as in practice ACP states would choose to vote only in exceptional cases.[41]

Council meetings typically produce a set of agreements and decisions, yet no precise instructions are made to ensure follow-up. ACP ministerial attendance in Council meetings has been poor for a long time, with ACP states frequently choosing to delegate lower ranking officials or the head of their Brussels mission.[42] This is indeed no recent phenomenon, since already in 1981 only 18 of the then 46 sent their minister to the 13th ACP Council of Ministers.[43] A recent COA chair acknowledged that there is broad awareness among Ambassadors that their committee is failing to organise and prepare Council meetings in a way that would allow ministers to engage and make decisions.[44] This awareness has however to date not translated into reform.

The COA

In the course of the negotiations for Lomé I, a group of Brussels-based Ambassadors of ACP states regularly met to prepare its negotiation sessions with the EEC.[45] The Georgetown Agreement transformed this ad hoc coordination process into a formal meeting structure, and through Article 17 required the COA to adopt its own rules of procedure. The COA subsequently prepared and adopted its 'guidelines on working methods' on 27 January 1981 to guide its plenary meetings as well as its various sub-committees and working groups.[46] As per its formal mandate, the COA assists the Council of Ministers in its functions and carrying out any mandate assigned and monitors the implementation of the ACP-EU Partnership Agreement. Similar to the Council of Ministers, the work of the Committee is coordinated by the Bureau of the COA that consists of nine members: one for each of the six ACP regions, the current chairperson as well the incoming and previous chairs.[47] The chairperson's term is limited to six months.

The COA is widely regarded as the leading organ of the group. Since it is the only organ that meets on a regular basis, as it convenes twice a month, the Committee's role has moved beyond its 'decision preparing' mandate to effectively making such decisions. The low frequency of Council meetings has led to the COA de facto furthering the Group's objectives between Council sessions, so that 'in practice, the Committee of Ambassadors plays the role of decision-maker, and even during a Council of Ministers meeting, the majority of delegates are actually ambassadors'.[48] Ambassadors also adopt ACP Group statements on recent developments within the ACP, such as natural disasters, contested general elections or internal conflicts, which are posted on its website. Such statements by the Group do not result in any follow-up beyond Brussels, and one interviewee indicated that they mainly serve a 'signalling' function.[49]

The Committee's strong position does not mean that it asserts itself in an effective and goal-oriented manner. The current rules were adopted at a time when the Group had 46 members, and the requirement of decision by consensus is in practice interpreted as requiring unanimity.[50] This need for unanimity has frequently delayed decisions, such as in cases where previously absent states asked for discussions to be reopened, or by small minorities of ACP states blocking decisions.[51] The frequent absence of ambassadors at regular meetings is related to the fact that many have demanding mandates, which may include the full Benelux group of countries as well as UN and IOs based in Geneva and Rome.[52] Others nonetheless observed that embassies were starting to send staff of lower level of seniority to sub-committees and working groups, suggesting a more recent downward trend.[53] Several examples of cumbersome decision-making were presented by the interviewees. These included a proposed trip to Vanuatu by some ACP Ambassadors after the cyclone Pam in April 2015, as well as the adoption of a joint ACP-EU position for the 2015 Addis Ababa UN Financing for Development conference, both of which were blocked by a small minority of ACP states. Whereas the latter case lead to an all-ACP position being adopted instead, the former case was an example of how ACP Ambassadors failed to agree on how to use the Secretariat's budget.[54]

Beyond these specific examples, interviewees described Committee meetings as formalistic, inefficient and ego-centred as opposed to results-oriented. Meetings can last as long as two days, in part due to the fact that ambassadors may address their colleagues during meetings for excessive amounts of time, not shying away from restating points already made.

This happens in spite of the COA guidelines allowing the Chairman to propose a time limit on interventions, which one interviewee argued was symptomatic of the ACP Group's 'culture of rule-breaking'.[55] Mailafia argues that the low effectiveness of the COA is due to the ambassadors' mandates of promoting and protecting national interests, so that progress can only be made on a lowest common denominator basis.[56] Interviewees added that because of the nature of their mandates, ambassadors are unlikely to openly criticise or plead for COA reform as this may have a negative bearing on their bilateral relations with other states.[57]

The ACP summit

Article 9 of the revised Georgetown Agreement states that the Summit of ACP Heads of State and Government 'shall lay down the general policy of the ACP Group and issue the Council of Ministers with the directives relative to its implementation'.[58] ACP Summits have so far been held in 1997, 1999, 2002, 2004, 2008, 2012 and 2016. The first two summits played a key role in preparing the Group's positions during the negotiation of Cotonou. The most recent four summits focused on the Group's future development and its future beyond 2020. Each Summit leads to the adoption of a negotiated document addressing various international developments, own initiatives as well as reactions to European actions and plans. Although the revised Georgetown agreement states otherwise, interviewees and studies confirm that the Summit-hosting country does not play a role in connecting the Summits or representing the Group in international fora, thus weakening its strategising function (Babb and Babb 2006, 70).[59]

While there is no direct role for the EU, the ACP has strongly relied on EDF funding for organising summits. The EU Court of Auditors launched investigations into the management of EDF support to the 2008 Accra summit, and pending these investigations the EU was unable to provide funding for the 2012 summit.[60] The hosting country of Equatorial Guinea stepped in by providing additional financing equivalent to euro 249,879.[61] Although no official records are available, media reporting indicates that recent ACP Summits performed poorly in terms of attracting Heads of State presence. A total of 15 heads of state attended the 2012 summit, with lower-level participation from other ACP States and 13 states sending no delegation whatsoever.[62] The hosting government of Suriname was unable to host the ACP Summit foreseen for 2014, with the Ebola outbreak in West Africa stated as the reason for the cancellation. Following a long search for an ACP state willing to take over, the summit was finally held in Papua New Guinea June 2016, yet attendance levels were again poor.[63]

The ACP parliamentary assembly

The ACP Parliamentary Assembly first convened back to back with the ACP-EU Joint-Parliamentary Assembly (JPA) in Mali of 2005 when its founding charter was adopted (ACP 2005). This charter clarifies that the Assembly is not new but formalises and reaffirms the existing inter-parliamentary cooperation mechanism within the ACP Group. The ACP Parliamentary Assembly was created after the JPA's image with similar aims, objectives and procedures. The Assembly is currently not financed by the ACP states but is instead financed by the EDF and 'piggybacks' on JPA sessions.[64] There is no publicly available reporting on its proceedings and effectiveness, but the ACP Council of Ministers is informed on the Assembly's activities through the Secretary General's annual report. In view of the low profile of the

Assembly in current discussions on the future of the Group, its existence seems to mainly depend on continued EU funding of the JPA.

The ACP secretariat

The 1975 Georgetown Agreement defined the Secretariat's role as assisting the COA and the Council of Ministers. The Council was tasked to determine its organisational structure and staffing based on a proposal from the COA. The 2003 Georgetown agreement defines four roles for the Secretariat: (1) carrying out tasks assigned by the four principal organs, (2) contribute to the implementation of their decisions, (3) monitor the implementation of the ACP-EU Partnership Agreement; and (4) service the organs of the ACP Group and, as appropriate, the joint institutions established under the ACP-EU Partnership Agreement.[65] The Secretariat's senior personnel is appointed by the COA, while the secondary staff, secretaries and local agents, as well as the chief of cabinet are appointed by the Secretary General (SG). Changes to the organisational structure can be agreed by the Council of Ministers meeting during one of its regular sessions and are prepared by the COA.[66] Figure 2 depicts the institutional setup of the ACP Secretariat during the 1990s.

In earlier decades the organisation was structured differently than the Georgetown Agreement required since no Deputy Secretary General (DSG) was appointed. The main reason was lack of resources as well disagreement over other appointments among ACP states, notably that of the SG.[67] Following the adoption of the Cotonou Agreement, the Group agreed to abolish the DSG post and formalise the creation of the four Assistant Secretary General (ASG) posts as reflected in the 2003 revised Georgetown Agreement. This was facilitated by an increase in the EU's financial contribution to the Secretariat and its change to a fixed-rate funding system.[68] The Secretariat's structure was subsequently split

Figure 2. The organisational structure of the ACP Secretariat: pre-Cotonou. Source: adapted from Mailafia (1997: 78)

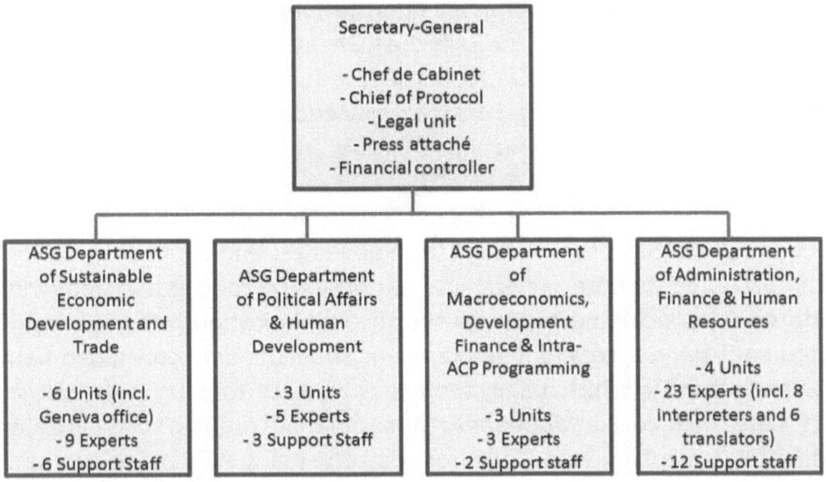

Figure 3. The organisational structure of the ACP Secretariat: since Cotonou. Source: adapted from EPG (2014).

into four pillars, one for each ASG (see Figure 3). Another important change was the opening of an ACP Secretariat office in Geneva, which was established in December 2001 as an EU-funded project to assist the ACP Group in WTO negotiations. As of May 2015, a total of 92 posts were available at the secretariat, of which 75 were filled.[69]

Although it is the most visible feature of the ACP, the Group's permanent Secretariat was deliberately designed with a low profile and has a subordinate position to the Brussels-based ACP diplomatic representatives.[70] This contrasts with some of the earlier literature suggesting that the Secretariat could play a crucial role in supporting the countries in managing the demanding EEC-ACP relationship.[71] The Secretariat and its Secretary General (SG) has no right of initiative but are confined to responding to specific requests from the states. Interviewees confirmed that it is not straightforward for the ACP SG to put anything on the agenda of the Council meeting because the agenda is controlled by the COA.[72] Malaifia argued that 'the status of the Secretary-General is, in truth, more that of Secretary than General'.[73] Despite this limited formal mandate the SG remains the central figure in the ACP Group and enjoys privileged access to EU officials. This explains why the process of electing a new SG has been a recurring source of tension between ACP regions.[74] These tensions were referred to be interviewees as reflecting a low level of trust between different ACP sub-regions, which one interviewee illustrated by the absence of information exchange between the regional groups during the EPA negotiations.[75] Interviewees further noted that the introduction of the ASGs had further politicised the Secretariat as they had no specific job profiles and suggested they mainly served patronage functions towards the ACP sub-regions who they represent.[76]

As for its technical tasks, the Secretariat is frequently unable to compile good quality reports in a timely manner due to the refusal of ACP states to share information on areas they consider sensitive, or because they view the Secretariat as lacking the authority to effectively advance their interests.[77] There were also issues of available human resource capacity, with interviewees describing the Secretariat as greying, with many staff members having been in the same position for decades and largely consisting of administrators rather than technicians.[78] These internal factors affecting performance interacted with the external influence of the Group's members through the COA. Interviewees noted that micro-management of the Secretariat by the COA, for instance requiring the SG to seek COA agreement before using the Secretariat's travel budget, was needed because the Secretariat would otherwise not use it in an effective manner.[79] The Secretariat's problems are not of a recent nature, given that a first ad hoc COA to investigate Secretariat's problems completed its work as early as 1981.[80] Despite its long-standing challenges and subordinate position, interviewees did stress that the Secretariat was far from powerless and could act autonomously. It was specifically noted that the Secretariat avails of several sources and networks that the ambassadors do not, including its direct lines of communication with the EU. One ambassador noted not having access to memoranda of understanding concluded between the Secretariat and other IOs, which mainly serve to enable EDF funding to these IOs.[81]

The ACP states' financial contributions to the secretariat's running costs have always been erratic. More fundamentally, essentially from day one many ACP states were unwilling to commit to the institutionalisation of the Group as few perceived it as viable in the long term.[82] Since 1977, the running costs of the ACP Secretariat are co-financed by the EU. Today's EDF rules allow for a maximum of 50% of the budgeted running costs of the Secretariat to be financed by the EU, while it provides additional funding for operational activities such as studies, institutional meetings, conference or seminars organised by the Secretariat.[83] It has been observed that despite its own co-financing, the EU has never cut EDF funding to ACP states that failed to timely make their financial contributions to the Secretariat.[84] In 2015 the Secretariat operated with a total budget of 15.3 million euro, and a total of 43 ACP states had developed arrears in payment. In May that same year a total of eleven ACP countries had accumulated such long-standing arrears that they were placed under formal sanctions. This group ranged all the way from Least-Developed Country, the Central African Republic, to High-Income Country, Antigua and Barbuda. Interviewees noted that sanctions are in practice not enforced since Ambassadors of ACP states with arrears generally continue to come to the Secretariat, pick up documents, take the floor during meetings, etc.[85]

As a result of the differentiation of development finance under the Cotonou Agreement, many ACP states in the Upper Middle and High-Income Country categories witnessed their direct development finance benefits eroding, thus also reducing the returns of their Group membership contribution. One example concerns Botswana which received 83.5 million euros during the period 2007–2013, which was reduced to 33 million euros for the period 2014–2020, while Mauritius saw its national envelop shrink by 90% for the same period. Similar cuts were made in richer Caribbean states, with the balance moved to the regional programmes.[86] One interviewee had been asked by the President's office for an assessment of the benefits of membership, while another wondered whether the small grant was a good deal in exchange for an intrusive political dialogue with the EU.[87] Evidence supporting ACP states' declining Group support included pressure by some to close down the Secretariat's Geneva office, as well as the launch of a study to reform the contribution key for determining ACP states' financial contribution to the Secretariat.[88]

The ACP secretariat's development cooperation mandate

The 2012 & 2016 Summit and various ACP strategising processes of recent years consistently included statements on the ACP Group's desire of taking an ambitious 'next step' and diversify relations beyond Europe, plans which imply a greater role for the Secretariat. In contrast, during the past four decades the Secretariat remained a largely subordinate and dependent body whose available resources and capacity failed to grow at a pace that was commensurate to the Group's increasing membership and its widening cooperation agenda. In the absence of ACP reforms of their own Secretariat, EDF- financed programmes have particularly since the adoption of Cotonou supported the Secretariat's changing role and capacity. Through its support, the EU helps implement the Secretariat's strategy under the following overall objective: *'transforming the Secretariat into a modern organisation which is adapted to the current priorities of the ACP Group of States and which is an effective and efficient organisation in terms of internal business processes'.*[89] The formulation lacks precision as to what these ACP priorities may be, while applying private sector terminology to describe an envisaged organisation that is capable in a managerial sense.

Although the Secretariat was created to support the ACP organs, the Group has also allowed its Secretariat to enter into direct responsibilities for the implementation of the EDF. Through the Cotonou Agreement, the Secretariat was designated as 'Regional Authorising Officer' for the component of the EDF that finances intra-ACP cooperation (EU 2014). The intra-ACP budget amounted to 20% of the total budget of the 9th EDF, as well as 12% of the budgets for EDF10 and EDF11. Parts of these funds are channelled through other IOs, such as UN agencies and the African Union, while others fund specific intra-ACP cooperation programmes that are managed by separate Project Implementation Units (PIUs), while administered by the Secretariat. Many of these PIUs organise meetings or commission studies, thus creating additional patronage opportunities for ACP states.[90] As per its increased responsibilities, the Secretariat considers to fulfil a 'double mandate':

> (1) its institutional mandate, i.e. to serve the Organs of the ACP Group of States, the ACP-EU Joint Institutions and the ACP Member States, and (2) its role of implementing institution of some important "all ACP" projects funded under the intra-ACP resources.[91]

Assessment of the Secretariat's functioning in recent years shows that the two sides of its mandate do not easily co-exist: its human resources are largely absorbed by the need to organise meetings that are estimated at 300 per year, and expenditures under the intra-ACP budget are insufficiently linked to ACP Group's own objectives.[92] The intra-ACP budget also acts as a legal 'loophole' for EU financing of the African Peace Facility that EU law prevents from being financed through the EU's budget. An independent evaluation observed a mismatch between the Group's ambition and the objectives of the intra-ACP budget: 'There is currently no example of an ACP state being mandated to represent the interest of the ACP Group of States in the governance structure of an IO or fund receiving Intra-ACP funding'.[93] The Secretariat further observed in its 2012 strategy that its increased EDF management tasks may have contributed to 'the fact that the ACP may sometimes be misperceived as a creation of the EU, and that its organizational and institutional provisions do not advance these activities/actions'.[94] Since the signing of the Cotonou Agreement the EU has funded several studies, trainings and technical assistance measures to strengthen the Secretariat's roles in the area of EDF management and to ensure its compliance with international standards. The assistance thus predominantly focused on the second aspect of the Secretariat's mandate as presented above. Although it observes certain challenges such as posts remaining vacant and declining ACP state contributions, the EU argues that critical aspects of the Secretariat's procedures have been strengthened through its support, such as the introduction of programme budgeting and an accrual accounting system.[95] Interviewees confirmed this and observed that Secretariat staff no longer use individual approaches to managing intra-ACP projects, but that procedures are becoming more streamlined and standardised.[96] Although this strengthened capacity internal factors would support implementation of future EU financed projects, they are less relevant to supporting the supra-national ambitions of the ACP Group.

Conclusions

Drawing on the literature on IO independence and (non-)performance, this article has analysed the emergence of the ACP Group's institutions and their evolution and performance over the past decades. Its starting observation is that since the Group's creation its institutional design and rhythm have been closely tuned to its cooperation partnership with Europe. When viewed from the objectives set out in the Georgetown Agreement, the ACP Group has performed at a suboptimal level and is characterised by a dominant yet ineffective COA and a subordinated as well as under-resourced Secretariat. The findings nonetheless indicate that ACP states differ in the extent to which they engage in the Group, while the Secretariat's role has evolved through its EDF-implementation responsibilities. Although the EU has formally chosen not to directly involve itself in the ACP Group's internal affairs, the EU implicitly does so by providing support to the Secretariat's expanding aid management mandate. The article's findings detect further potential for future research on how IO mandate and strategies are interlinked with external support, and in the process may affect the IO's independence and its relations with its members.

How then to explain the persistence of the Group and continued (though erratic) member state financial support and transaction costs in terms of attending and contributing to meetings? This article's findings confirm recent research that dependent and non-performing IOs may serve important funding and patronage purposes to their members. The existence of the ACP Group and its supra-national ambitions has allowed the EU to legitimise its different treatment of ACP versus non-ACP developing countries. The absence of clear intra-ACP benefits and the indications of non-performance suggest that the continuing relevance of the ACP Group as an IO to its members is more related to its effective provision of patronage and EU funding benefits, than to its performance in relation to the Group's formal mandate. The findings show parallels with the concept of collective clientelism used to analyse ACP-EEC negotiations and outcomes, yet specify that the ACP states' engagement in the Group is largely confined to their Brussels-based Secretariat and diplomatic representatives and moreover strongly differs from one ACP state to the next. The findings also suggest a linkage between the ACP states' individual returns from their cooperation partnership with the EU and their investment in and engagement with the ACP Group as an IO. This is confirmed by eroding support to the Group by those richer ACP states that in recent years have seen their direct benefits decline as a result of Cotonou's differentiation policy, while the 'regionalisation' of trade preferences has further reduced the direct benefits of ACP Group membership. In conclusion, the Group's future is more likely to be shaped by the outcome of the upcoming post-Cotonou negotiations with Europe than by its own independent actions.

Disclosure statement

No potential conflict of interest was reported by the author.

Acknowledgement

The interviews conducted for writing this article were conducted in the context of research project led by the European Centre for Development Policy Management (ECDPM). Initial findings were published in the final report of this project: Bossuyt, Jean, Niels Keijzer, Alfonso Medinilla and Marc de Tollenaere. *The future of ACP-EU relations: A political economy analysis*, Maastricht, 2016.

Notes

1. ACP, *The ACP Group*, 1.
2. ACP, Sipopo Declaration, 13.
3. E.g. Kühnhardt, 'The EU and ACP Countries'; Elgström, 'Partnership in Peril'; Arts and Dickson, *EU Development Cooperation*.
4. The interviewees concerned six ACP ambassadors (Interviews 1–6), three staff members of the ACP Secretariat (7–9), and one independent ACP consultant (10).
5. Barnett and Finnemore, 'The Politics, Power and Pathologies'; Gutner and Thompson, 'The Politics of IO Performance'.
6. Dijkstra, 'Collusion in International Organisations'.
7. Haftel and Thompson, 'The Independence of International Organizations'; see also Lall, 'Beyond Institutional Design'; Dijkstra, 'Collusion in International Organisations'.
8. Lall, 'Beyond Institutional Design'.
9. Ibid.
10. UIA, 'Number of International Organisations'.
11. Gutner and Thompson, 'The Politics of IO Performance'.
12. Gray, 'Patronage Explanations,' 3; Haftel and Thompson, 'The Independence of International Organizations'.
13. Barnett and Finnemore, 'The Politics, Power and Pathologies'; Gutner and Thompson, 'The Politics of IO Performance'.
14. Barnett and Finnemore, 'The Politics, Power and Pathologies'.
15. See note 8 above.
16. See note 6 above.
17. Barnett and Finnemore, 'The Politics, Power and Pathologies'; Gray, 'Patronage Explanations'.
18. Gray, 'Patronage Explanations'.
19. Barnett and Finnemore, 'The Politics, Power and Pathologies,' 703.
20. Ravenhill, *Collective Clientelism*, 22.
21. Slocum-Bradley, 'Constructing and De-Constructing the ACP'; Langan, 'The Moral Economy of EU Association'.
22. Mut-Bosque, *Setting the Framework*, 287.
23. Green, 'The Child of Lomé,' 6.
24. Hewitt, 'The Lomé Conventions,' 24, 25.
25. Frey-Wouters, *The European Community*, 260.
26. The same approach was used for all subsequent EU-ACP agreements.

27. In 2003 the agreement was revised to also allow ACP Group membership based on geographic proximity. This allowed for Cuba's accession, since it did not sign the Cotonou Agreement, as well as for South Africa, Sudan and Equatorial Guinea which did not ratify subsequent revisions.
28. Matheson, 'Institutional Capacity and Multiple Conditionality,' 142.
29. ACP, *Georgetown Agreement*, 1.
30. Ravenhill, *Collective Clientelism*, 315.
31. Babb and Babb, *Study on the Future*, 71.
32. Mut-Bosque, *Setting the Framework*, 304; Hewitt, 'The Lomé Conventions,' 25.
33. Krieger, *The Oxford Companion*, 507.
34. Drieghe, 'Lomé I herbekeken,' 223; Kühnhardt, 'The EU and ACP Countries,' 240.
35. Drieghe, 'Lomé I herbekeken,' 77–88, 234.
36. For a detailed discussion of the reforms introduced under Cotonou, see Arts and Dickson, *EU Development Cooperation*.
37. Drieghe, 'Lomé I herbekeken,' 33.
38. Miller, 'Paradigms in Caribbean Trade,' 3.
39. ACP, 'Strategy for Renewal,' 17.
40. Interview 1.
41. Mgbere, 'Cooperation Between the European Community,' 278.
42. Matheson, 'Institutional Capacity and Multiple Conditionality'; Mgbere, 'Cooperation between the European Community'.
43. Ravenhill, *Collective Clientelism*, 319.
44. Mahase-Moiloa, 'Acceptance Statement,' 8.
45. Ramphal, 'ACP Beginnings'.
46. ACP, 'Guidelines on Working Methods'.
47. Ibid.
48. Babb and Babb, *Study on the Future*, 74; Mgbere, 'Cooperation between the European Community'.
49. Interview 1.
50. Interview 1, 3.
51. Mgbere, 'Cooperation between the European Community,' 177.
52. Interview 3, 9.
53. Interview 5.
54. Interview 2, 5.
55. Interview 1, 3, 5, 6.
56. Mailafia, 'Europe seen from Africa,' 236.
57. Interview 2, 3, 5, 8.
58. ACP, *Georgetown Agreement (2003)*, 6.
59. Interview 5.
60. Interview 7.
61. EU, 'Action Document – 2014'.
62. Interview 7.
63. Interview 7.
64. ACP, 'Strategy for Renewal,' 39.
65. ACP, *Georgetown Agreement (2003)*, 10.
66. Mgbere, 'Cooperation between the European Community,' 186.
67. Matheson, 'Institutional Capacity and Multiple Conditionality'; Mgbere, 'Cooperation between the European Community'.
68. European Court of Auditors, *Annual Report*.
69. Personal Communication.
70. Matheson, 'Institutional Capacity and Multiple Conditionality,' 142–3.
71. See note 25 above.
72. Interview 8.
73. Mailafia, 'Europe seen from Africa,' 236.

74. Matheson, 'Institutional Capacity and Multiple Conditionality,' 132; Mgbere, 'Cooperation between the European Community,' 185.
75. Interview 10.
76. Interview 3, 5.
77. Matheson, 'Institutional Capacity and Multiple Conditionality,' 181; Mgbere, 'Cooperation between the European Community,' 316.
78. Interview 7, 8, 10.
79. Interview 5, 8.
80. Mailafia, *Europe and Economic Reform in Africa*, 77.
81. Interview 5.
82. See note 30 above.
83. EU, 'Action Document – 2015,' 10.
84. Matheson, 'Institutional Capacity and Multiple Conditionality'.
85. Interview 8.
86. Interview 6.
87. Interview 1, 5.
88. Interview 2, 6.
89. EU, 'Action Document – 2015,' 6.
90. Interview 10.
91. ACP, 'Strategy for Renewal,' 9.
92. SACO, *Evaluation of the EDF*, 5.
93. SACO, *Evaluation of the EDF*, 46.
94. ACP, 'Strategy for Renewal,' 40.
95. EU, 'Action Document – 2015,' 5, 6.
96. Interview 7, 8.

Bibliography

ACP. *The Georgetown Agreement on the Organization of the African, Caribbean and Pacific Group of States*. Georgetown, 1975. http://www.archive.caricom.org/jsp/secretariat/legal_instruments/georgetownagreementonacp.jsp?null&prnf=1.

ACP. "Guidelines on Working Methods of the ACP Committee of Ambassadors," January 27, 1982. http://www.acp.int/content/guidelines-working-methods-acp-committee-ambassadors.

ACP. *The Georgetown Agreement. Amended in Accordance with the Council of Ministers' Decision Adopted at Its 55th Session Held in Brussels from 24 to 26 November 1992*, 1992. http://www.epg.acp.int/fileadmin/user_upload/Georgetown_1992.pdf.

ACP. *The Georgetown Agreement. As Amended by Decision No.1/LXXVIII/03 of the 78th Session of the Council of Ministers, Brussels, 27 and 28 November 2003*. Brussels: ACP, 2003. http://www.epg.acp.int/fileadmin/user_upload/Georgetown2003.pdf.

ACP. "Signing of the Charter to Create the ACP Consultative Assembly," April 15, 2005. http://www.acp.int/content/parliamentary-assembly.

ACP. *Sipopo Declaration. 7th Summit of ACP Heads of State and Government*. Sipopo: ACP, 2012. http://www.acp.int/sites/acpsec.waw.be/files/Final%20ACP2806512%20Rev%208%20Draft_Sipopo_Declaration.pdf.

ACP. *Strategy for Renewal and Transformation 2011–2014*. Brussels: ACP Secretariat, 2012. http://www.acp.int/sites/acpsec.waw.be/files/Strategy%20for%20Renewal%20and%20Transformation%202011-2014.pdf.

ACP. *The ACP Group of States in the Post-2015 Development Era, Promoting Partnership for Sustainable Development in ACP Regions and Countries*. Brussels: ACP Secretariat, 2015.

Arts Karin, and Anna K. Dickson (eds.). *EU Development Cooperation: From Model to Symbol*. Manchester, NH: Manchester University Press, 2004.

Babb, Glenn, and Tracey Babb. *Study on the Future of the ACP Group*. Brussels: ACP Secretariat, 2006.

Barnett, Michael, and Martha Finnemore. "The Politics, Power, and Pathologies of International Organizations." *International Organization* 53, no. 4 (1999): 699–732.

Drieghe, Lotte. "Lomé I herbekeken: naar een geopolitiek intergouvernementalistische analyse van de eerste Conventie tussen de Europese Economische Gemeenschap en de Afrikaanse, Caribische en Stille-Zuidzeelanden op basis van een archiefonderzoek." PhD diss., Ghent University, 2011.

Dijkstra, Hylke. "Collusion in International Organisations: How States Benefit from the Authority of Secretariats." *Global Governance*, forthcoming.

Elgström, Ole. "Partnership in Peril? Images and Strategies in EU-ACP Economic Partnership Agreement Negotiations." In *External Perceptions of the European Union as a Global Actor*, edited by Sonia Lucarelli and Lorenzo Fioramonti, 137–149. London: Routledge, 2010.

EU. "Action Document for the 'Institutional Support to the ACP Secretariat and Its Geneva Antenna'," 2014. https://ec.europa.eu/europeaid/sites/devco/files/action-document-institutional-support-acp-secretariat-20141124_en.pdf.

EU. "Action Document for the "Institutional Support to the ACP Secretariat and Its Geneva Antenna (2016–2018)," 2015. https://ec.europa.eu/europeaid/sites/devco/files/ad2-part2-intra-acp-2015_en.pdf.

EU. "Memorandum to the Members of the EDF Committee – Annual Action Programme Covered by the Programming Documents Intra-ACP Cooperation – 10th EDF Strategy Paper and Multi-Annual Indicative Programme for the European Development Fund in Favour of Intra-ACP Cooperation for 2011," 2011. http://www.gtai.de/GTAI/Content/DE/Trade/Fachdaten/PRO/2012/01/P20016.pdf.

European Commission. "Green Paper on Relations between the European Union and the ACP Countries on the Eve of the 21st Century – Challenges and Options for a New Partnership. COM (96) 570 Final, 20 November 1996," Brussels: EU, 1996.

European Court of Auditors. *Annual Report Concerning the Financial Year 2000*. Luxembourg: ECA, 2001.

European Economic Community. *Partnership in Africa: The Yaoundé Association. Community Topics 26*. Brussels: European Communities Information Service, 1962.

Frey-Wouters, Ellen. *The European Community and the Third World: The Lomé Convention and Its Impact*. New York: Praeger, 1980.

Gray, Julia C. "Patronage Explanations for the Survival of International Organizations," 2016. https://mershoncenter.osu.edu/media/media/publications/misc-pdfs/grayj.pdf.

Green, Reginald Herbold. "The Child of Lomé: Messiah, Monster or Mouse?" In *The Political Economy of EEC Relations With African, Caribbean And, Pacific States*, edited by Frank Long, 3-31. Oxford: Pergamon Pr., 1980.

Gutner, Tamar, and Alexander Thompson. "The Politics of IO Performance." *The Review of International Organizations* 5, no. 3 (2010): 227–248.

Haftel, Yoram Z., and Alexander Thompson. "The Independence of International Organizations." *Journal of Conflict Resolution* 50, No. 2 (2006): 253–275.

Hewitt, Adrian. "The Lomé Conventions: Myths and Substance of the Partnership of Equals." In *Europe & Africa: Issues in Post-colonial Relations*, edited by Noel Buxton and Margaret Cornell. *Noel Buxton Lectures 1980*. London: Overseas Development Institute, 1981.

Lall, Ranjit. "Beyond Institutional Design: Explaining the Performance of International Organizations", *International Organization*, forthcoming 2017.

Langan, Mark. *The Moral Economy of EU Association with Africa*. London: Routledge, 2016.

Krieger, Joel (ed.). *The Oxford Companion to the Politics of the World*. 2nd ed. Oxford: Oxford Univ. Press, 2001.

Kühnhardt, Ludger. "The EU and the ACP Countries." In *Routledge Handbook of the Economics of European Integration,* edited by Harald Badinger and Volker Nitsch, 238–252. Routledge, 2015.

Mahase-Moiloa, Mpeao. "Acceptance Statement by the Ambassador of the Kingdom of Lesotho, Mrs. Mpeo Mahase-Moiloa as the Incoming President of the ACP Committee of Ambassadors," 2015. http://www.acp.int/sites/acpsec.waw.be/files/Statement_Amb%20Moiloa_Committee%20of%20Ambassadors.pdf.

Mailafia, Obadiah. "Europe Seen from Africa." In *Rethinking the Future of Europe: A Challenge of Governance*, edited by Stefan Schepers and Andrew Kakabadse. Basingstoke: Palgrave Macmillan, 2014.

Mailafia, Obadiah. *Europe and Economic Reform in Africa: Structural Adjustment and Economic Diplomacy*. 1st ed. London: Routledge, 1997.

Matheson, James Henry Edward. "Institutional Capacity and Multiple Conditionality in ACP-EU Development Cooperation." PhD diss., London School of Economics and Political Science (United Kingdom), 1997.

Mgbere, John Chinwi. *Cooperation Between the European Community and African, Caribbean and Pacific Countries (1957–1990): A Study in Group Diplomacy*. Phd diss.: London School of Economics and Political Science (University of London), 1994.

Miller, Keste Oswald. "Paradigms in Caribbean Trade Diplomacy: Negotating the CARIFORUM–EC Free Trade Agreement." Phd diss., University of Westminster, 2010.

Mut Bosque, María. "Setting the Framework for the Relations between the Commonwealth and the European Union." Phd diss., Universitat Internacional de Catalunya, 2014.

Ramphal, Shridath. "ACP Beginnings, Speech. ACP Eminent Persons Group – Caribbean Regional Consultations," November 1, 2013. http://www.epg.acp.int/fileadmin/user_upload/EPG_Caribbean_SpeechRamphal.pdf.

Ravenhill, John. *Collective Clientelism: The Lomé Conventions and North-South Relations*. The Political Economy of International Change. New York: Columbia Univ. Pr., 1985.

SACO. *Evaluation of the EDF Support through the Intra-ACP Cooperation*, Unpublished report, 2013.

Slocum-Bradley, Nikki. "Constructing and De-constructing the ACP Group: Actors, Strategies and Consequences for Development." *Geopolitics* 12, no. 4 (2007), 635–655.

Union of International Assocations (UIA). "Number of International Organizations by Type, Edition 51, 2014/2015 (Data Collected in 2013)", 2014. https://www.uia.org/sites/uia.org/files/misc_pdfs/stats/Number_of_international_organizations_by_type_2013.pdf.

OPEN ACCESS

Promoting sustainable development or legitimising free trade? Civil society mechanisms in EU trade agreements

Jan Orbie, Deborah Martens, Myriam Oehri and Lore Van den Putte

ABSTRACT

This study critically reflects on the involvement of civil society actors in the sustainable development chapters of recent EU trade agreements. It discusses how civil society mechanisms may legitimise the underlying neoliberal orientation of the agreements through co-optation of critical actors. Starting from a critical perspective and drawing on evidence from innovative survey data, qualitative interviews and participatory observations, it concludes that, despite overall criticism, there is no clear evidence of co-optation. While being aware of the risks their participation entail, EU participants take a constructive position. Nevertheless, diverging perspectives between non-profit and business actors risk reinforcing existing power asymmetries.

Introduction

In response to growing concerns and contestation about the sustainable development implications of free trade agreements, the European Union (EU) has included a sustainable development (SD) chapter in its recent trade agreements. This chapter typically creates institutionalised mechanisms for civil society participation. These civil society mechanisms aim to discuss and monitor the sustainable development dimension of the trade agreement. It has been argued that they constitute an original and distinctively European approach to promoting labour rights, environmental principles and economic development through trade. Each of the trading partners organises its own domestic mechanisms, which then meet annually in the transnational mechanism. The number of mechanisms is likely to increase dramatically in the coming years and decades, given the growing volume of trade agreements being concluded.

While very little is known about the functioning and relevance of these mechanisms, some criticism has already been voiced by civil society actors, academics, Members of the European Parliament and the European Economic and Social Committee (EESC).[1] Most call for institutional improvements, such as more efficient management, more representative composition of the participants, better feedback mechanisms with the governments and budgetary support for travel and practical organisation. Some of these shortcomings have been (partly) acknowledged by EU officials.[2]

The above-mentioned shortcomings all have in common that they are compatible with the dominant neoliberal paradigm that free trade contributes to sustainable development and that civil society mechanisms ought to play a role in this process. Instead of these institutional shortcomings, and in line with the general objective of this collection, we aim in this article to explore a much-needed fundamental critique of how the civil society mechanisms may contribute to legitimising the underlying free trade orientation of the agreement. In particular, with the deadlock of the World Trade Organization (WTO) Doha Round and the increasing importance of bilateral and regional trade agreements, it is important to critically reflect on the opportunities and limits of civil society mechanisms in (European) trade agreements as well as on their potential incorporation into a neoliberal paradigm.[3] This tension between resisting free trade agreements for their (alleged) adverse impact on sustainable development, on the one hand, and using the agreements' mechanisms for the purpose of improving sustainable development or at least preventing harmful consequences, on the other, will be situated theoretically and illustrated empirically in this study.

Thus, our critical evaluation involves both a theoretical and an empirical dimension. Theoretically, we discuss how and why the involvement of civil society in international trade agreements may be problematical. Specifically, we point to the danger of co-optation, whereby critical voices are being silenced and induced to be more constructive. This entails the 'insider-outsider dilemma' for civil society organisations: should they reform the system 'from within' by participating in the mechanisms established by the agreement, knowing that this may equally serve to legitimise the entire free trade agreement?

Empirically, we examine the experiences of the European members of the civil society mechanisms. Evidence comes from an innovative survey (conducted in August and September 2016) with EU business, labour, environmental and other representatives participating in the civil society mechanisms established in the EU trade agreements.[4] In addition to the survey, we draw on 15 qualitative interviews conducted in Brussels, Colombia, Costa Rica, Honduras and Peru with civil society actors participating in civil society mechanisms, as well as participatory observation in the EU-Colombia-Peru and EU-Central America domestic and transnational civil society meetings held in 2015 and 2016.

Whereas both the theoretical and the empirical parts focus on the civil society mechanisms and how these may serve to legitimise the free trade agreements, they are embedded within a broader critical analysis of the trade-sustainable development nexus. As such, three critical questions recur in the theoretical and empirical parts: the impact of (EU) free trade agreements on sustainable development, the relevance of the sustainable development chapters in EU agreements and most importantly the role of the civil society mechanisms in this regard.

Our data reveal the insider-outsider dilemma that European civil society members, especially those from labour and other non-profit organisations, are facing through their involvement in the mechanisms. While these organisations hold (very) critical views on the impact of (EU) free trade agreements on sustainable development, they also actively participate in the mechanisms *and* acknowledge the pitfalls of co-optation. The position of business representatives is more straightforward: they hold more positive evaluations across the board, both on the benefits of free trade and the role of the civil society mechanisms (business representatives even recognise their potential to legitimise free trade).

The article is structured as follows. First, we provide an overview of the mechanisms and their rationale. Second, we draw from several strands of the critical studies literature to situate the possibly problematic role of civil society mechanisms in EU trade agreements. Third, we address the same issue based on empirical findings from the survey and interviews. Finally, we formulate provisional conclusions and questions for further research.

Institutional criticisms

The establishment of civil society mechanisms in the context of EU trade agreements is a recent phenomenon. The first EU trade agreement to create a separate mechanism involving civil society was the EU-CARIFORUM Economic Partnership Agreement (EPA), which was concluded in 2008. This agreement includes commitments on labour and environmental standards and sets up a transnational civil society mechanism, known as the Consultative Committee. The new generation of EU trade agreements, launched by the 'Global Europe' strategy,[5] of which the EU-Korea agreement was the first in 2011.[6] Three changes were carried through in these new generation agreements: first, labour and environment provisions were grouped in a separate SD chapter; second, in addition to a transnational mechanism, each agreement establishes domestic civil society mechanisms; third, the legal provisions concerning the set-up of these mechanisms are elaborated in more detail.

Even though there is some variation in the legal texts, the civil society mechanisms created in the new generation of EU trade agreements are characterised by three recurrent features. First, a domestic civil society mechanism is set up in which representatives of three constituencies (labour, environment and business) of each Party (the EU and its trading partner(s)) participate. This is often called the Domestic Advisory Group (DAG). Second, a transnational civil society mechanism is created where the members of the domestic mechanisms and/ or other actors from both the EU and its trading partner(s) meet annually. Third, there is some interaction between these two mechanisms and the intergovernmental body (comprising officials of the EU and its trading partner(s)). This body meets annually to discuss the implementation of the SD chapter.

Currently, civil society mechanisms have been activated in the framework of the agreements with Korea, Peru-Colombia, Central America, Moldova, Georgia and the CARIFORUM states.[7] Although the mechanisms are a relatively new phenomenon, several aspects have already been criticised by a variety of actors. A first cluster of criticism concerns the organisation of the mechanisms, which are viewed as too improvised.[8] It has also been suggested that the domestic mechanisms should convene more frequently, for instance through videoconferencing, to ensure substantial progress and continuity.[9] Another avenue recommended to ensure continuity and better organisation is creating a coordinating mechanism such as a secretariat.[10] Whereas the EESC fulfils this role for the EU DAGs, there is no equivalent body for the EU's trade partners.[11] This limited secretarial support reflects a general lack of budgetary resources for the organisation of the mechanisms.[12]

A second area of criticism concerns the composition of the mechanisms, and more specifically the selection procedures. Although there are no indications that the European Commission deliberately excludes critical voices, the selection procedures are not transparent. This is all the more so in the EU's partner countries, where representatives are not always independent from the government, for example in Peru, Colombia and Honduras.[13] Furthermore, there is a lack of awareness of the existence and role of these mechanisms, affecting the level of civil society participation.[14] The lack of financial resources also has a significant impact on some civil society actors' opportunities to attend meetings.[15]

A third criticism relates to the accountability of governments. It is often unclear whether and how governments follow up on the outcomes of these mechanisms. If participants feel that their views are not taken into account, this may lower their satisfaction and lead to 'consultation fatigue', which risks undermining the efforts invested in the civil society mechanisms.[16] Moreover, it is not always clear whether domestic mechanisms in third countries are operational and effective.[17]

All of these criticisms refer to flaws in the functioning of the mechanisms and concentrate on institutional improvements. As such, they do not fundamentally question the underlying assumptions that free trade contributes to sustainable development and that civil society mechanisms can be instrumental for this purpose. In the remainder of this article, we aim to go beyond institutional criticisms and critically analyse how the mechanisms may legitimate free trade by reducing civil society opposition through co-optation. The next parts will attempt to address this question from a theoretical and an empirical perspective.

Critical reflections

In order to provide a more profound critique, this part will draw from several theoretical strands in academic literature and situate the potentially problematic role of civil society mechanisms within broader critiques of the free trade – sustainable development nexus.

Free trade and sustainable development

Even though there is no consensus on the impact of economic globalisation on sustainable development,[18] there are concerns that free trade can have detrimental consequences for labour and environmental conditions. Liberalisation can lead to a race-to-the-bottom as countries and firms are tempted to engage in social dumping in order to increase their competitiveness.[19] Likewise, it can create incentives for industry to produce in an ecologically unsustainable manner in order to reduce production costs.[20]

Moreover, a conventional preoccupation with liberalisation largely assesses immediate economic benefits of enhanced market access while neglecting longer-term costs such as reduced regulatory policy autonomy.[21] In fact, several authors evaluate the prevailing global trade governance as ultra-restrictive on policy space and as having a negative impact, especially on developing countries.[22] Bilateral free trade agreements, even more than the multilateral WTO rules, may limit governments' scope to adopt measures aimed at enhancing social policy or increasing environmental protection.[23]

Although EU leaders assume that free trade brings economic growth, which can reduce social injustice and environmental degradation and mitigate other crises,[24] it is still unclear whether the EU is actually able to 'square current neo-liberal trade policy with the preservation of ecological and social diversity'.[25] Such doubts are based on the observation that EU trade policy-making features unequal power relations in which corporate interests dominate at the expense of social and environmental voices.[26] Accordingly, EU free trade is at risk of fulfilling neoliberal demands while leaving sustainable development aspects behind. The EU's free trade agenda has been particularly criticised in relation to the EPAs with the African, Caribbean and Pacific group of countries. Reviewing a number of studies on the 'dangers of premature liberalisation' and the limits to policy space as a result of these agreements in West Africa, Langan and Price point out that the neoliberal trade agenda is also subscribed to by African elites.[27] The EU's neoliberal trade agenda has been further radicalised since the 2006 Global Europe trade strategy, which launched a range of bilateral free trade agreements with Asian and Latin American countries,[28] and more recently the negotiations with Canada, Japan and the US. While earlier critiques concerned the impact of the EU's free trade agreements within developing countries,[29] the protests against the EU-US Transatlantic Trade and Investment Partnership (TTIP) have sparked growing concerns about policy space for sustainable development objectives within the EU.[30]

In order to mitigate the potentially negative effects of trade agreements on sustainable development, the European Commission added a chapter on environment and social aspects in the EU-CARIFORUM EPA and has included a SD chapter in its bilateral trade agreements since the agreement with Korea (see *supra*). The growing discursive attention to sustainable development is also illustrated by the 2015 'Trade for all' strategy. Here, it is emphasised that '[t]he EU has been leading in integrating sustainable development objectives into trade policy and making trade an effective tool to promote sustainable development worldwide'.[31]

Nevertheless, it seems the SD chapters in EU trade agreements do not go far enough in ensuring that free trade does not hamper sustainable development, let alone contribute to it. To start, they have been criticised on the grounds that their purposes are too vague[32] and for being designed in such a 'soft' way that they are, for example, not able to deal adequately with labour violations.[33] The European Commission claims that this reflects its cooperative approach in dealing with labour and environmental issues. A DG Trade official formerly in charge of sustainable development argued that the EU's goal is to deal with the root causes of violations of labour rights rather than with the symptoms, as the US does by having a binding dispute settlement system for labour violations.[34] Furthermore, these provisions are designed in a conservative and flexible way: conservative because there are no specific requirements for modifications to domestic law, as long as core labour rights are not systematically violated and softening of domestic labour laws does not have an impact on trade and investment; and flexible because they leave ample discretion for the governments as regards implementation of the labour protection commitments at the domestic level and the functioning of the civil society mechanisms.[35] This is in sharp contrast to economic concessions, which are generally formulated in a much more binding and precise way.

From a more negative stance, one could even argue that the chapter is only included to ensure support for the free trade agreement, a practice that can be observed in other parts of the world. By way of illustration, during negotiations on the North American Agreement on Labor Cooperation, a side agreement to the North American Free Trade Agreement (NAFTA) between the US, Canada and Mexico, in 1993, voices from labour expressing reservations towards the NAFTA became more silent.[36] Similarly, the North American Agreement on Environmental Cooperation, NAFTA's other side agreement concluded in 1993, helped to mobilise support for the NAFTA from environmental groups.[37] In the same vein, van Roozendaal[38] argues that in the case of the EU-Korea agreement, the inclusion of labour standards could be regarded 'as a symbolic act to increase the support for free trade agreements without expectations that they would be effective'. This critical perspective might also hold true for other agreements concluded by the EU. Given the increasing contestation of EU trade policy and the growing power of the European Parliament in this area, the inclusion of SD chapters has become all the more important in order to guarantee public and political support for trade agreements.

Civil society participation

Adding a sustainable development dimension to EU trade agreements is not always enough to legitimise these intergovernmental accords. In fact, a political institution can be questioned per se by the broader public as political support for an institution is not predetermined but has to be granted. Allowing participatory practices can be a way of obtaining support for a system.[39] At the same time, however, they entail risks for those participating.[40] More precisely, participation can be either transitive or intransitive, moral, amoral, or immoral, free or forced and spontaneous or manipulative. In essence, whereas transitive forms of participation are oriented towards a specific goal, intransitive forms are reduced to a partaking process without any predefined purpose. Moreover, participation can pursue ethically or unethically defined goals. Free participation, furthermore, can be distinguished from a form of participating in which people are asked or pushed into partaking in operations which are not of interest to them, purely for the sake of participation.[41]

This manifestation of participation can also be understood as 'co-optation', which, in the context of policy-making, describes a process where states aim to divert the goals or demands of civil society (groups) to serve different, less transformative agendas. It can, furthermore, characterise a process by which civil society (groups) are co-opted into working 'from within' and thus cooperate with state actors to pursue certain goals.[42] Finally, in contrast to spontaneous participation, in manipulated forms of participation participants do not feel they are forced into doing something, but are led to actions which are inspired or directed by manifestations of power outside their control.[43] This last dimension is in line with the Foucauldian notion of governmentality, which assumes a form of power which, while outside the sphere of formalised and centralised power structures, nevertheless enables control to be exerted over society.[44] Accordingly, and even somewhat counter-intuitive to its rhetoric of empowerment, participation leaves room for fundamental criticism. In this regard, Cooke and Kothari[45] speak of participation's 'tyrannical potential', which is manifested in the illegitimate or unjust use of power through inclusive practices.

In light of these potentially negative effects of participation, three kinds of reactions to invitations for participation can be distinguished: inside, outside and inside-outside responses. Whereas the first type describes a strategy to defend vested interests from within by critically participating in certain initiatives, the outside response is characterised by actors' decision to 'opt out'; this means engagement outside the forum in order to build alternatives. The inside-outside response can be described as an oscillation between the two positions, comprising simultaneous or sequential engagement from within and protest from the outside.[46]

Given these alternatives with their respective advantages and disadvantages, actors find themselves in a dilemma. This insider-outsider dilemma surrounding participatory practices is of particular relevance for civil society actors. From a Gramscian point of view, civil society can be seen as a sphere which either stabilises and reinforces or transforms governmental hegemony.[47] As extant literature illustrates, the involvement of civil society can help to improve the democratic legitimacy of global governance in general[48] and EU trade policy in particular.[49] Accordingly, participation by civil society actors entails the same risks as outlined above. In the context of trade liberalisation, the peril of being co-opted might be particularly imminent for non-profit actors such as environmental, human and labour rights groups as they are, in contrast to business, traditionally more critical towards the neoliberal agenda.[50] Apart from that, it is more difficult for non-governmental organisations (NGOs) than for firms to defend their interests due to limited resources in terms of personnel and funding.[51]

The case of the WTO demonstrates a form of civil society participation which can be described as co-optation. In fact, the transformative potential of global civil society such as NGOs has been 'taken in' by the multilateral trade institution and its dynamics. In essence, civil society engagement against the WTO's neoliberal agenda from within the WTO has not resulted in alternative discourses and perspectives in debates and deliberation. Instead, civil society actors have themselves adopted technocratic and neoliberal forms of advocacy over the years.[52]

Inhibiting the potential of civil society for purposes of a neoliberal nature might also be a strategy applied by the EU. With the inclusion of critical civil society actors in a trade instrument, the democratic legitimacy of this instrument is likely to increase. Put differently, reservations that civil society actors have towards EU trade agreements can be undermined by the possibility to participate in policy-making in the context of these agreements. Such an assertion is substantiated with regard to the new generation of EU trade agreements. The limited literature on this topic has indeed suggested that the civil society mechanisms are 'at risk of legitimising free trade deals'.[53] Creating support for the trade agreement and assuring its ratification has been referred to as the mechanisms' 'instrumental purpose'.[54]

Co-optation is further manifested in the limited power given to civil society groups in the context of EU trade policy. At the EU level, despite the access that was granted to NGOs via the Civil Society Dialogue within DG Trade, these actors have not been able to influence trade policy outcomes in any real sense.[55] A similar picture is revealed in the context of civil society mechanisms in EU trade agreements: while EU domestic and transnational mechanisms convene in practice, participating civil society cannot articulate enforceable rules for the governments. As a recent study illustrates, '[i]nitial assessments from stakeholders indicate that participation is time-intensive but recommendations and provisions are non-enforceable'.[56] This limitation underlines the restricted role of civil society actors in relation to sustainable development in the context of EU trade agreements. In summary, a critical perspective suggests that providing civil society with a role in trade agreements, but at the same time restricting their influence in policy-making, may be a way of silencing potential criticism of neoliberal orientations.

This theoretical exploration will inform the empirical insights in the following part, which analyses the positions of the European members of the civil society mechanisms. Again, the critical evaluation of the civil society mechanisms will be related to broader questions on (EU) free trade agreements and the sustainable development chapters.

Empirical perspectives

Free trade and sustainable development

When asked about their opinions of the 'impact of free trade on sustainable development', labour representatives as well as other non-profit organisations such as environment, development, human and animal rights organisations' replies vary slightly from positive to extremely negative, but the main tendency is towards the negative (see Figure 1, Non-profit).[57]

What is perhaps surprising is that non-profit organisations are only *moderately* negative on the consequences of free trade (see Figure 1) and EU trade agreements (see Figure 2) for sustainable development. The option 'extremely negative' was indicated only a few times, whereas more than one third of these representatives were neutral or even positive on the relevant questions. Non-profit organisations are neither unanimously nor radically negative about these issues. Despite tendencies towards the critical end of the spectrum, a significant minority assesses the impact of (EU) trade agreements positively and only a very small minority makes an extremely negative evaluation (see Figures 1 and 2).

This might lead to the conclusion that these civil society organisations have become less critical through their co-optation within EU mechanisms. If we consider the anti-TTIP and anti-CETA protests, which took place at the time when the survey was held (August-September 2016) and are remarkably strong both in terms of intensity (heavily anti-trade) and scope (proliferation of civil society organisations mobilising against these agreements), we might have expected a more outspokenly negative evaluation by labour, environmental, development, human rights and animal welfare organisations. In other words, non-profit organisations participating in the mechanisms seem generally less critical of free trade and EU trade agreements than most civil society organisations that are campaigning on trade issues. Nevertheless, it would be premature to conclude that this more positive inclination

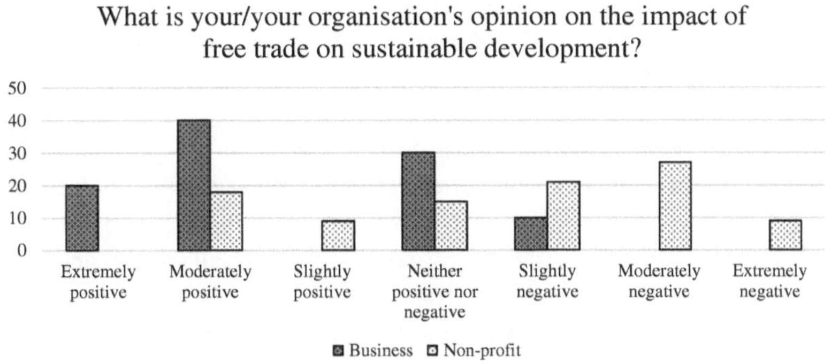

Figure 1. Opinion on impact of free trade on sustainable development (in percentages; business n = 10, non-profit: n = 32).

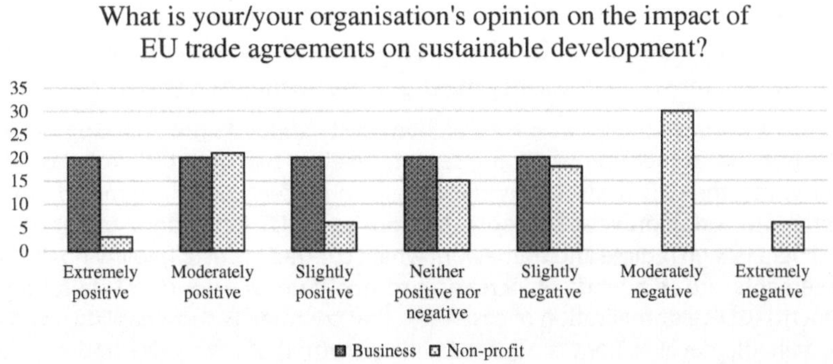

Figure 2. Opinion on impact EU trade agreements on sustainable development (in percentages; business n = 10, non-profit: n = 32).

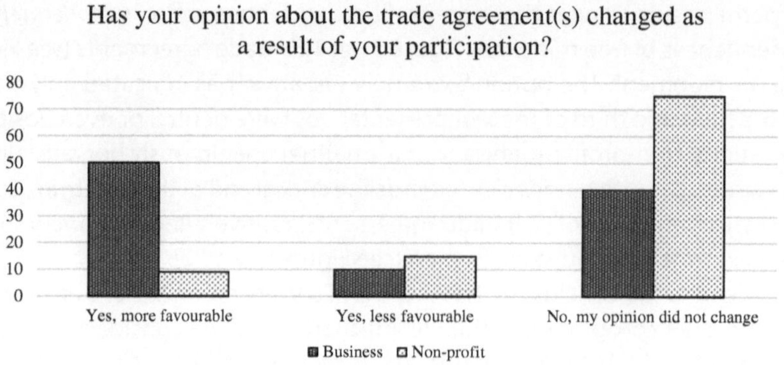

Figure 3. Changed opinions about the free trade agreement (in percentages; business n = 10, non-profit: n = 32).

of the participants in the civil society mechanisms is caused by co-optation. Our methodology does not make it possible to make a pre–post measurement (before/after participation) or to use a control group (non-participants). We did, however, ask the civil society participants whether participation in the mechanisms had changed their evaluation of the EU trade agreement. On this question, most non-profit organisations indicated that they had not changed their views (see Figure 3). There may also be a self-selection effect in that organisations that are radically against free trade agreements do not participate in the mechanisms because they are not willing to do so or because they have not been selected by the European Commission.

Importantly, further qualitative data suggest that civil society representatives are aware of the dangers of co-optation. Even respondents who are very critical of free trade and EU free trade agreements in general attempt to be actively involved in the mechanisms in order to make the best of the situation. Several interviewees from civil society acknowledge that their participation in the mechanisms may have the (in their eyes) perverse effect of legitimising the free trade agreement as a whole. As one respondent who is a member of an environmental organisation wrote:

> 'It's primarily a tool by the Commission to show that the EU is integrating environmental and social issues in trade agreements.'

Non-profit organisations seem to be clearly aware of the pitfalls as well as the opportunities that the civil society mechanisms offer and seem to be struggling with the 'inside-outside dilemma' that these pose for them. One NGO representative who has experience with several transnational and domestic civil society mechanisms formulated this as follows:

> A cabaret artist portrays the EU as a kind of 'humanist capitalist': not shooting on people at the border but letting them drown in the sea; and feeling bad about it. So full of contradictions. Hence, yes, the CSD [civil society dialogue] can be seen as an attempt by the institutions to promote and improve sustainable development, BUT this is done under the premise of a trade liberalisation regime and framework which contradict sustainability goals. FTAs (free trade agreements) are an agenda of increasing competition, of resource exploitation, of false measurements (GDP, externalisation of costs), etc. that contradicts sustainability goals. In other words, sustainable development is equated with growth; that is why DG Trade can organise those kinds of CSDs and include sustainable development chapters. So they have appropriated and incorporated sustainability…

Furthermore, the same person argued that 'the core of the trade agreement has not changed just because there are consultative bodies [involving civil society] or DAGs set up; if there is any impact, it is limited [...].' Another development NGO representative stated that he finds it important to negotiate on the conclusions of the meetings until the very last minute, even if he is very critical of the impact of free trade and EU trade agreements on policy space for sustainable development. From our observations of the EU-Peru-Colombia and EU-Central America mechanisms, some representatives of non-profit organisations attempt to use the mechanism to highlight shortcomings in third countries' compliance with labour, environmental and human rights standards. In so doing, they criticise the impact of the EU trade agreement in this regard, trying to get the most out of it. Others attend the civil society mechanisms, yet are more passively involved or work behind the scenes.

When discussing their role in the EU-Peru-Colombia DAG, one member from another development NGO illustrated the insider-outsider dilemma in very literal terms as follows:

> Look where we are standing now... Before, we were shouting against the agreement on the streets; today, we are helping to implement it inside this building.[58]

Two years earlier, another participant in these mechanisms had expressed it as follows:

> You see, this is a governmental process and then we're asked to come in to basically defend these free trade agreements. Now many of us [...] have substantial conflicts and issues with the kind of free trade agreements and the economic agenda behind it. And for the Commission, for the government, this is a way to say we're smoothing the edges and we get civil society in there and they can help us to address the worst issues. But the fundamental drivers and the way we design trade relations remain contentious. At least for us, [...] it's a way to invite the protest on the street into the agreement.[59]

One opponent of the EU-Central America trade agreement decided, after opposing the agreement as a whole, to join the civil society mechanisms because then at least they would still have a platform available to fight possible negative consequences of the agreement.[60] He too decided to participate in the civil society mechanisms, not in spite of but because of his opposition to it.

Civil society mechanisms

When considering the survey questions on participants' evaluation of the civil society mechanisms, a mixed picture emerges. When asked to rate their experience with the civil society mechanisms according to a number of statements ranging from 'strongly disagree' to 'strongly agree', non-profit organisations not only endorsed the critical statements but also (moderately) subscribed to the opportunities that the mechanisms offer. Three statements in the survey relate to the critical perspective: whether the civil society mechanisms are there 'to guarantee ratification of the agreement', 'to reduce opposition to the agreement' and 'to legitimise the agreement with the larger public'. Each of these statements relates to the possible function of the mechanisms as legitimising free trade instead of promoting sustainable development. Notwithstanding some exceptions, the large majority of respondents from non-profit organisations agree with these statements. Again, however, a constructive position emerges: only a slight minority 'strongly agrees', and overall evaluations are rather moderate (see Table 1).

More surprisingly, these rather negative evaluations go together with positive assessments of the mechanisms. Our data illustrate that these representatives recognise potential

Table 1. Business and non-profit evaluating the civil society mechanisms (in percentages; business n = 10, non-profit: n = 32).

	The meetings that I attended are a mechanism to…															
	Reduce opposition to the agreement		Legitimise the agreement with the larger public		Guarantee ratification of the agreement		Build alliances with other civl society organisations		Have impact on decision-making		Discuss with officials		To present new ideas		Promote sustainable development	
	Business	Non-profit	Business	Non-profit	Business	Non-profit	Business	Non-profit	Business	Non-profit	Business	Non-profit	Business	Non-profit	Business	Non-profit
Strongly agree	0	6	0	6	10	6	10	16	0	6	0	3	10	3	0	0
Agree	50	25	40	25	20	16	30	25	60	25	60	41	30	28	30	31
Somewhat agree	10	31	30	28	20	22	30	38	20	41	10	31	20	34	30	38
Neither agree nor disagree	40	19	30	19	40	25	20	13	10	9	20	16	30	19	30	13
Somewhat disagree	0	3	0	9	10	6	0	6	10	6	10	9	0	9	10	6
Disagree	0	9	0	13	0	19	10	3	0	9	0	0	10	6	0	9
Strongly disagree	0	6	0	0	0	6	0	0	0	3	0	0	0	0	0	3

benefits of the civil society mechanisms. Not only are non-profit organisations 'only' moderately critical about the mechanisms in terms of legitimising free trade, but they also accept that these can promote sustainable development, foster discussions on the topic and most of all contribute to building alliances with other organisations. Although these respondents are not overly enthusiastic about these functions, they do recognise their potential.

Also in the blank spaces that respondents could fill in, this 'critical but constructive' position of non-profit organisations becomes clear. While a few comments relate to the insider-outsider dilemma and the risk of legitimising free trade (see *supra*), most of them express frustrations with the practical functioning and impact of the mechanisms. Some refer to the mechanisms' limited dynamic and the absence of a real impact: As a representative of a non-profit development organisation participating in the EU-CARIFORUM Consultative Committee claims,

> [t]here is not much life in between the meetings… They seem to be one-off events.

A similarly disillusioned opinion on the impact of civil society mechanisms is expressed by a labour representative member of several mechanisms:

> The meetings are not working and do not amount to anything. But if we would leave, there would be a void and we can't do that.[61]

Along the same line, a member of a non-profit organisation participating in the EU-Central America transnational meeting and its EU DAG claims:

> The meetings I attended are mostly to 'tick the box' on the mechanism of the agreement. They have been mostly processes where we focus more on the mechanism itself than on the content of discussions.

This is confirmed by a statement of a non-profit organisation member who participates in the EU-CARIFORUM Consultative Committee and the EU DAG of the EU-Colombia-Peru agreement:

> Sometimes, the discussion is more about the governance of the groups and less about the implementation of the agreements. After the meeting, there is not really an agenda for joint activities for the members of the groups in order to strengthen the exchange and the cooperation among them to monitor the implementation of the agreements. Lack of funding makes it sometimes difficult for the members of the groups to attend the relevant meeting and also to have the human resources to follow in detail the implementation of the agreements.

A member of another non-profit organisation who has participated in the EU-CARIFORUM Consultative Committee several times describes its limitations as follows:

> The mechanism in the CARIFORUM EPA has not really been very active; it is rather formal. As there is minimal interest on both the Caribbean and the European side in genuinely implementing this agreement, and there was very little private sector interest as well, there are few incentives to engage and therefore this civil society mechanism is not very active/effective as there is little to fight for or against.

Limited interest on both sides of the EPA is also observed by a business representative attending the EU-CARIFORUM Consultative Committee:

> The follow-up to the meetings is slow and there are no concrete outcomes. There is a lack of interest from the EU side and too high expectations from the Cariforum side.

As already touched upon in the previous two quotes, there are also concerns about the limited accountability of the governments. Limited interaction between civil society members and the Parties to the agreement is further substantiated in the following quotes:

> I have always found that the Sustainable Development Committee members (i.e. the intergovernmental body members) are reluctant to engage in a real discussion with DAG members and civil society during joint meetings. Sometimes they do not even accept having a dialogue with DAG members.

Like his labour counterpart, an environmental organisation representative to the EU DAG of the EU-Korea agreement emphasises the European Commission's passive role:

> The EU Korea DAG allows business, labour and civil society to express their views on certain environmental and labour issues related to trade. That is really all it is. The Commission attends, listens and does nothing.

In addition, there are comments on the representativeness of the mechanisms, especially on the limited presence of trade unions. To illustrate, a member of a non-profit organisation who has experience with five types of EU trade agreements' civil society forums notes the following:

> The key problem is lack of full involvement of all sectors of civil society (NGOs, trade unions), particularly in the EU trading partners' DAGs. Employers' federations are always represented.

A labour representative who attends several EU DAGs puts it as follows:

> The EU-Korea DAG is the most advanced one (even though problems of representation in the composition of the Korea DAG persist). The composition of the Central America DAG is still not defined and there is a lack of representation of trade unions in Central American countries.

Thus, the bulk of these comments concern criticism within the system, in line with the 'inside response' (see *supra*). This confirms once more that civil society participants have not given up on the possibilities that the civil society mechanisms are offering, and that they are intent on improving these mechanisms. However, as also stated above, this does not mean that these participants are not aware of the potentially legitimising effect of their participation in the mechanisms. Therefore, here too it is difficult to conclude that co-optation has taken place.

The perspectives of the business sector representatives deserve special mention as they diverge from those of the representatives of non-profit organisations. In essence, business groups are generally (very) positive about free trade, the EU trade agreement and the civil society mechanisms. Compared to the non-profit organisations, they are more positive about the impact of free trade on sustainable development (see Figure 1). Although they evaluate the impact of EU agreements slightly less favourably than the impact of free trade in general, a divergence with the other representatives continues to exist. This may not be surprising since it reveals a traditional socio-economic cleavage in European politics between labour and capital on the benefits of free trade.[62]

More surprisingly, business representatives also tend to evaluate the civil society mechanisms in terms of legitimising the free trade agreement. They largely agree with those statements that we considered to endorse the critical perspective, i.e. that the mechanisms serve 'to guarantee ratification of the agreement', 'to reduce opposition to the agreement' and 'to legitimise the agreement with the larger public'. As such, the polarisation between business and the other participants on the merits of free trade for sustainable development disappears when it comes to recognising the broader liberal agenda behind the mechanisms.

However, one may assume that the motivations behind these assessments are different, in line with the above-mentioned divergent assessments of the impact of free trade and EU trade agreements on sustainable development. While business representatives are more

Table 2. Business and labour evaluating the civil society mechanisms (in percentages; business n = 10, non-profit: n = 32).

	The meetings that I attended are a mechanism to...							
	Have an impact on decision-making		Discuss with officials		Criticise the sustainable development dimension of the agreement		Promote sustainable development	
	Business	Labour	Business	Labour	Business	Labour	Business	Labour
Strongly agree	0	13	0	13	0	25	0	0
Agree	60	13	60	38	0	25	30	13
Somewhat agree	20	38	10	50	20	25	30	50
Neither agree nor disagree	10	0	20	0	60	13	30	0
Somewhat disagree	10	13	10	0	10	0	10	13
Disagree	0	25	0	0	10	13	0	25
Strongly disagree	0	0	0	0	0	0	0	0

likely to support the mechanisms' legitimising role as necessary to guarantee the more important objectives of the trade agreement, non-profit organisations tend to view the legitimising function from a more critical perspective and are warier about co-optation, as illustrated above.

At the same time, business groups recognise the more 'mainstream' or 'free trade oriented' purposes of the mechanisms. The respondents (moderately) agree on all the statements that point to purposes and criticisms 'within the system'. However, a closer look at the data reveals subtle differences between business and labour representatives (see Table 2). For instance, the former agree more than the latter on the mechanisms' function 'to have an impact on decision-making' and 'to discuss with officials'. Business groups are also much less convinced than their labour counterparts that the mechanisms serve 'to criticise the sustainable development dimension of the agreement'. Business is also much more optimistic than labour about the mechanisms' aim 'to promote sustainable development'.

In sum, the survey data suggest that business groups recognise that the mechanisms play a role in legitimising the EU trade agreements while at the same time providing opportunities to discuss with officials and impacting on decision-making. This more positive evaluation of the civil society mechanisms is in line with their more optimistic assessment of the benefits of free trade for sustainable development in general. It also resonates with the different responses of business and non-profit organisations to the question 'Has your opinion about the trade agreement(s) changed as a result of your participation in the meeting(s)?' As can be seen from Figure 3, while most respondents indicate that their opinion has not changed, a majority of business representatives indicate that their opinion of the trade agreement has become more favourable.

Conclusion

This study aimed to critically reflect on a recent phenomenon in EU trade policy, namely the involvement of civil society actors in the EU's trade-sustainable development nexus. More precisely, it discussed how transnational and domestic civil society mechanisms provided for in the new generation of EU trade agreements may be a way to legitimise the underlying neoliberal orientation of the agreements. Starting from critical perspectives and drawing on evidence from a survey, qualitative interviews and participatory observations, we arrive at the balanced conclusion that non-profit civil society actors recognise the pitfalls of participatory practices in EU agreements, but also see the opportunities that they may offer for the promotion of sustainable development.

Therefore, we conclude that the approach adopted by non-profit actors has been constructive. Rather critical views on the impact of free trade and EU trade agreements on sustainable development have not prevented them from participating in the mechanisms; at the same time, rather critical evaluations of the purposes of the mechanisms have not withheld them from acknowledging the opportunities to discuss and monitor sustainable development. In short, both the vices and virtues are recognised. However, it is too early to evaluate whether this constructive position also entails co-optation. The non-profit actors involved seem clearly aware that they are walking a tightrope between legitimising free trade and obtaining results for the cause they represent.

Moreover, non-profit organisations, and particularly labour representatives, are rather critical about the civil society mechanisms. The large majority indicate that they have not become more favourable towards the trade agreement. In addition to criticisms concerning the institutional dimension of the meetings (e.g. financial support and representativeness), they also point to frustrations with limited impact and lack of substantive dialogue. In the absence of tangible progress, these actors' critical but constructive position may modify into a more radical rejection of the trade agreement. Instead of co-optation, one might equally expect a radicalisation of the positions on free trade and the EU agreements, especially if existing frustrations are not seriously addressed.

While not providing clear evidence of co-optation, the findings did reveal another critical issue, namely the discrepancy between business groups and non-profit organisations. Business representatives evaluate the civil society mechanisms more positively. For instance, they recognise the value of the mechanisms in terms of networking with officials and having an impact. Several business representatives also indicate that they have become more favourable towards the trade agreement since their participation. Therefore, there is a risk that the civil society mechanisms further reinforce the existing asymmetric power relationship between business and non-profit organisations when it comes to trade policy influence[63], rather than balancing them in favour of sustainable development.

This study contributes to extant literature which critiques EU trade governance[64] and assesses the transformative power of civil society actors in the context of international trade[65] by collating the perspectives of the civil society actors participating in the civil society mechanisms established in recent EU trade agreements. While it partly reveals fundamental criticism of these mechanisms, it would probably go too far to describe them as a form of 'tyranny', as suggested by Cooke and Kothari[66] on participatory approaches in development policy. Nevertheless, they may certainly be regarded as a double-edged sword in the sense that they may well entail co-optation in the longer run. The decision of critical groups to participate in EU civil society mechanisms undermines the power of their peers who have deliberately decided to stay outside the system in order to challenge it. What is more, 'empty' engagement from within runs the risk of fragmenting a constituency as the 'outsiders' might feel betrayed by the 'insiders'. Therefore, civil society actors are well advised to jointly reflect on potential negative effects that participation in civil society mechanisms might have on their constituency as a whole.

In order to better understand reservations about civil society mechanisms in EU trade agreements, future research would need to assess the rationales of those civil society groups and actors who decide to stay outside. It would also be of interest to investigate the perceptions of civil society on the other side of the agreements. Given the countries' different cultural and political heritages and, to some extent, the lack of experience with social and civil society dialogues, such an assessment is necessary to obtain a complete picture of the potential and limits of the civil society mechanisms in EU agreements.

Disclosure statement

No potential conflict of interest was reported by the authors.

Funding

This article was published with the financial support of the Belgian University Foundation.

Acknowledgements

The authors would like to thank the participants of the workshop on 'EU Contributions to Equitable Growth and Sustainable Development in the Post-2015 Consensus' in April 2016, Leicester University, as well as the editors of this issue, Mark Langan and Sophia Price, and the anonymous reviewers for their valuable comments.

Notes

1. EESC, *Briefing Note to the Attention of Mr. Dumitru Fornea*; Montoute, "Civil Society Participation in EPA Implementation"; Van den Putte et al., "What Social Face of the New EU Trade Agreements?"; Altintzis, "Civil Society Engagement and Linkages"; and Harrison et al., "Labour Standards in EU Free Trade Agreements."
2. Personal interview EU officials, 15 April 2015 and 4 August 2016.
3. Hopewell, "Multilateral Trade Governance," 37.
4. It comprised close-ended questions about the opportunities and limits of civil society mechanisms and blank spaces for comments. Out of the 126 listed participants, not all of whom participate effectively, 42 completed the survey, generating a response rate of almost 50% of effective participants in the mechanisms.
5. European Commission, *Global Europe*.
6. The EPAs with the West African States (ECOWAS) and the East African Community (EAC), which are awaiting approval at the time of writing, include very similar provisions to those pertaining to CARIFORUM. Interestingly, the EPA concluded between the EU and the Southern African Development Community (SADC), approved by the European Parliament in 2016, does not refer to any civil society involvement whatsoever.
7. In the near future, such mechanisms will also be created for the agreement with Ukraine. The number of civil society mechanisms is likely to increase exponentially, as some trade agreements have yet to enter into force, e.g. with Ecuador, Singapore, Vietnam, Canada, ECOWAS and EAC; some are still being negotiated (e.g. with the US, Japan, India and the Philippines); and some will be updated (Mexico, Tunisia) or (re)launched (e.g. Mercosur, Indonesia) in the near future.
8. Orbie et al., *Civil Society Meetings*.
9. Van den Putte et al., "What Social Face of the New EU Trade Agreements?"
10. Montoute, "Civil Society Participation in EPA Implementation."
11. EESC, *Briefing Note to the Attention of Mr. Dumitru Fornea*; and see note 8 above.

12. Harrison et al., "Labour Standards in EU Free Trade Agreements."
13. Altintzis, "Civil Society Engagement and Linkages"; and EESC, *Briefing of the EESC Secretariat.*
14. See note 11 above.
15. See note 10 and 11 above.
16. Muguruza, "Civil Society and Trade Diplomacy."
17. Orbie and Van den Putte, "Labour Rights in Peru."
18. Mosley, "Globalisation and the State."
19. Brown et al., "International Labour Standards and Trade."
20. Paul, "Cost of Free Trade"; and Porter, "Trade Competition and Pollution Standards."
21. Heron, Asymmetric Bargaining and Development Trade-offs," 336.
22. Chang, *Kicking Away the Ladder*; Chang, "Policy Space in Historical Perspective"; Dicaprio and Gallagher, "Shrinking of Development Space"; and Rodrik, "Save Globalisation from Cheerleaders."
23. De Ville et al., *TTIP and Labour Standards*; Rodrik, *The Globalization Paradox*; Shalden, "Development for Market Access"; and UNCTAD, *Trade and Development Report 2014*.
24. European Commission, *Commission Staff Working Document; Europe 2020;* and *Trade for all.*
25. Ford, "EU Trade Governance and Policy," 580.
26. See also Dür and De Bièvre, "Inclusion Without Influence?"
27. Langan and Price, "Extraversion and the West African EPA."
28. Holden, "Neo-liberalism by Default?"
29. Del Felice, "Power in Discursive Practices."
30. De Ville and Siles-Brügge, *The Truth About TTIP*.
31. European Commission, *Trade for all*, 22.
32. See note 12 above.
33. Adriaensen and González-Garibay, "The Illusion of Choice"; and Vogt, "Arrangements and Labor Rights."
34. Hencsey in Van den Putte, "Transcripts Social Face Trade," 10.
35. See note 17 above, 18.
36. Finbow, *Limits of Regionalism*, 54.
37. Allen, "The North American Agreement on Environmental Cooperation," 127–8.
38. van Roozendaal, "Labour Standards as an 'Afterthought," 12.
39. Kröger, *Europeanised or European?*
40. Luhmann, *Legitimation Durch Verfahren*, 151–3.
41. Rahnema, "Participation," 116.
42. See also Jaffee, "Weak Coffee: Certification," 270.
43. See note 41 above.
44. See also Kurki, "Governmentality and EU Democracy Promotion."
45. Cooke and Kothari, *Participation: The New Tyranny*.
46. See note 42 above, 279–81.
47. Cox, "Civil Society Turn of the Millennium," 4–5.
48. Scholte, "Civil Society and Global Governance."
49. Meunier, "Trade Policy and Political Legitimacy."
50. see also note 44 above.
51. See note 26 above, 86.
52. See note 3 above, 37.
53. Ulmer, "Trade Embedded Development Models," 319.
54. See note 8 above, 26.
55. Coffey, *Evaluation DG Trade CSD*; Slob and Smakman, *A Voice, Not a Vote* and see note 26 above.
56. See note 53 above, 318.
57. When participants are asked about the impact of EU trade agreements in general and of the specific agreement in which they have been involved, the same moderately critical tendency emerges.
58. Personal interview participant EU DAG of the EU Peru-Colombia agreement, 7 April 2016.
59. Personal interview European NGO, 19 June 2014.

60. Personal interview European NGO, 1 March 2016.
61. Personal interview European labour representative, 6 December 2016.
62. Burgoon, "European Union's 'Fair Trade'," 647.
63. See note 26 above.
64. See note 25 above.
65. See note 3 above.
66. See note 45 above.

Bibliography

Allen, Linda. "The North American Agreement on Environmental Cooperation: Has It Fulfilled Its Promises and Potential? An Empirical Study of Policy." *Colorado Journal of International Environmental Law and Policy* 23, no. 1 (2012): 121–199.

Adriaensen, Johan, and Monserrat González-Garibay. "The Illusion of Choice: The European Union and the Trade-labor Linkage." *Journal of Contemporary European Research* 9, no. 4 (2013): 542–559.

Altintzis, Yorgos. "Civil Society Engagement and Linkages in Eu Trade Policy." In *Linking Trade and Non Commercial Interests: The Eu as a Global Role Model?*, edited by Tamara Takacs and Angelos Dimopoulos. The Hague: Centre for the Law of EU External Relations, 2013.

Burgoon, Brian. "The Distinct Politics of the European Union's 'Fair Trade' Linkage to Labour Standards." *European Foreign Affairs Review* 14, no. 5 (2009): 643–661.

Brown, Drusilla, Deardorff Alan, and Robert Stern. "International Labour Standards and Trade: A Theoretical Analysis." Post-printed from *Fair Trade and Harmonization: Prerequisited for Free Trade*, edited by Jagdish N. Bhagwati and Robert E. Hudec, 1–48. Cambridge: MIT Press, 1996.

Chang, Ha Joon. *Kicking Away the Ladder: Development Strategy in Historical Perspective*. London: Anthem Press, 2002.

Chang, Ha Joon. "Policy Space in Historical Perspective with Special Reference to Trade and Industrial Policies." *Economic and Political Weekly* 41, no. 1 (2006): 627–633.

Coffey. *Evaluation of Dg Trade's Civil Society Dialogue in Order to Assess Its Effectiveness, Efficiency and Relevance*. Luxembourg: Publications Office of the European Union, 2014.

Cooke, Bill, and Uma Kothari. *Participation: The New Tyranny?* London: Zed Books, 2001.

Robert, Cox. "Civil Society at the Turn Ofthe Millenium: Prospects for an Alternative World Order." *Review of International Studies* 25 (1999): 3–28.

Del Felice, Celina. "Power in Discursive Practices, the Case of the Stop Epas Campaign." *European Journal of International Relations* 20, no. 1 (2012): 145–167. Online First Version. doi: 10.1177/1354066112437769.

De Ville, Ferdi, and Gabriel Siles-Brugge. *TTIP: The Truth about the Transatlantic Trade and Investment Partnership*. Hoboken: Wiley, 2015.

De Ville, Ferdi, Jan Orbie, and Lore Van den Putte. *In-depth Analysis: TTIP and Labour Standards*. Brussels: European Parliament, 2016.

Dicaprio, Alisa, and Kevin P. Gallagher. "The Wto and the Shrinking of Development Space." *The Journal of World Investment & Trade* 7, no. 5 (2006): 781–803.

Dür, Andreas, and Dirk De Bièvre. "Inclusion without Influence? Ngos in European Trade Policy." *Journal of Public Policy* 27, no. 1 (2007): 79–101.

EESC. *Briefing Note to the Attention of Mr. Dumitru Fornea for Trade Policy Committee Dinner Organized by the Dutch Eu Presidency, Discussion about the Trade and Sustainable Development Chapters in Eu Trade Agreements, including Civil Society Monitoring Mechanisms (18 April 2016)*. 2016.

EESC. *Briefing of the EESC Secretariat on the Functioning of Domestic Advisory Mechanisms in Eu Trade Agreements', on File with the Author (Brussel 19 April 2016)*. 2016.

European Commission. *Global Europe: Competing in the World*. Brussels: European Commission, 2006.

European Commission. *Commission Staff Working Document: Trade as a Driver of Prosperity*. COM (2010) 1269. Brussels: European Commission, 2010.

European Commission. *Europe 2020: A Strategy for Smart, Sustainable and Inclusive Growth*. COM (2010) 2020. Brussels: European Commission, 2010.

European Commission. *Trade for All: Towards a More Responsible Trade and Investment Policy*. Luxemburg: Publications Office of the European Union, 2015.

Finbow, Robert. *The Limits of Regionalism. Nafta's Labor Accord*. Surrey: Ashgate, 2006.

Ford, Lucy. "Eu Trade Governance and Policy: A Critical Perspective." *Journal of Contemporary European Research* 9, no. 3 (2013): 578–596.

Harrison, James, Mirela Barbu, Liam Campling, Ben Richardson, and Adrian Smith. "Labour Standards in Eu Free Trade Agreements: Working towards What End?" *GREAT Insights* 5, no. 6 (2016): 32–34.

Heron, Tony. "Asymmetric Bargaining and Development Tradeoffs in the Cariforum-European Union Economic Partnership Agreement." *Review of International Political Economy* 18, no. 3 (2011): 328–357.

Holden, Patrick. "Neo-liberalism by Default? The European Union's Trade and Development Policy in an Era of Crisis." *Journal of International Relations and Development*, Online First Version (2015). doi: 10.1057/jird.2015.10.

Hopewell, Kristen. "Multilateral Trade Governance as Social Field: Global Civil Society and the WTO." *Review of International Political Economy* 22, no. 6 (2015): 1128–1158.

Jaffee, Daniel. "Weak Coffee: Certification and Co-optation in the Fair Trade Movement." *Social Problems* 59, no. 1 (2012): 267–285.

Kurki, Milja. "Governmentality and EU Democracy Promotion: The European Instrument for Democracy and Human Rights and the Construction of Democratic Civil Societies." *International Political Sociology* 5, no. 4 (2011): 349–366. doi:10.1111/j.1749-5687.2011.00139.x.

Kröger, Sandra. *Europeanised or European? Representation by Civil Society Organisations in EU Policy Making*. Colchester: ECPR Press, 2016.

Langan, Mark, and Sophia Price. "Extraversion and the West African EPA Development Programme: Realising the Development Dimension of ACP–EU Trade?" *The Journal of Modern African Studies* 53, no. 3 (2015): 263–287.

Luhmann, Niklas. *Legitimation Durch Verfahren*. Frankfurt am Main: Suhrkamp Verlag, 1983.

Meunier, Sophie. "Trade Policy and Political Legitimacy in the European Union." *Comparative European Politics* 1, no. 1 (2003): 67–90.

Montoute, Annita. "Civil Society Participation in EPA Implementation: How to Make the EPA Joint CARIFORUM-EC Consultative Committee Work Effectively?" In *ECDPM Discussion Paper 119*. Maastricht: ECDPM, 2011.

Mosley, Layna. "Globalisation and the State: Still Room to Move?" *New Political Economy* 10, no. 3 (2005): 355–362.

Muguruza, Mikel. *Civil Society and Trade Diplomacy in the "Global Age": The European Case: Trade Policy Dialogue between Civil Society and the European Commission*. Washintgon DC: Inter-American Development Bank, 2002.

Orbie, Jan, Deborah Martens, and Lore Van den Putte. *Civil Society Meetings in European Union Trade Agreements: Features, Purposes, and Evaluation*. CLEER Papers. Edited by Tamara Takács. The Hague: Centre for the Law of EU External Relations, 2016.

Orbie, Jan, and Lore Van den Putte. "Labour Rights in Peru and the Eu Trade Agreement: Compliance with the Commitments under the Sustainable Development Chapter." In *ÖFSE Working Paper Series*. Vienna: Austrian Foundation for Development Research, 2016.

Rodrik, Dani. *The Globalization Paradox: Why Global Markets, States, and Democracy Can't Coexist*. Oxford: Oxford University Press, 2011.

Rodrik, Dani. "How to Save Globalisation from Its Cheerleaders." *The Journal of International Trade and Diplomacy* 1, no. 2 (2007): 1–33.

Joel, Paul. "The Cost of Free Trade." *Brown Journal of World Affairs* XXII (2015): 1–19.

Porter, Gareth. "Trade Competition and Pollution Standards: "Race to the Bottom" or "Stuck at the Bottom"." *The Journal of Environment & Development* 8, no. 2 (1999): 133–151.

Rahnema, Majid. "Participation." In *The Development Dictionary: A Guide to Knowledge as Power*, edited by Wolfgang Sachs. London: Zed Books, 1992.

Scholte, Jan Aart. "Civil Society and Democratically Accountable Global Governance." *Government and Opposition* 39, no. 2 (2004): 211–233.

Shalden, Kenneth. "Exchanging Development for Market Access? Deep Integration and Industrial Policy under Multilateral and Regional-bilateral Trade Agreements." *Review of International Political Economy* 12, no. 5 (2005): 750–775.

Slob, Anneke, and Floor Smakman. *A Voice, Not a Vote. Evaluation of the Civil Society Dialogue at Dg Trade*. Rotterdam: ECORYS, 2007.

Ulmer, Karen. "Trade Embedded Development Models." *The International Journal of Comparative Labour Law and Industrial Relations* 31, no. 3 (2015): 303–326.

UNCTAD. *Trade and Development Report 2014: Global Governance and Policy Space for Development*. Geneva: UNCTAD, 2014.

Van den Putte, Lore. 2015. "What Social Face of the New European Union Trade Agreements?" *Transcripts*, June 23. Brussels.

Van den Putte, Lore. "The European Union's Trade-labour Linkage. beyond the 'Soft' Approach?" PhD diss., Ghent University, 2016.

Van den Putte, Lore, Jan Orbie, Fabienne Bossuyt, Deborah Martens, and Ferdi De Ville. "What Social Face of the New Eu Trade Agreements? Beyond the 'Soft' Approach." *ETUI Policy Brief*, no. 13/2015 (2015).

van Roozendaal, Gerda. "Labour Standards as an 'Afterthought' in Trade Agreements: The South Korea Case." Paper presented at the 2016 EUIA conference, Brussels, May 11–13, 2016.

Vogt, Jeffrey. "Trade and Investment Arrangements and Labor Rights." In *Corporate Responsibility for Human Rights Impacts: New Expectations and Paradigms*, edited by Lara Blecher, Nancy Kaymar Stafford, and Gretchen C. Bellamy. ABA Book Publishing, 2014.

The EU's Economic Partnership Agreements with Africa: 'Decent Work' and the challenge of trade union solidarity

Stephen R. Hurt

ABSTRACT
The European Union (EU) has in recent years adopted the International Labour Organisation's Decent Work Agenda in its external trade and development policy. It is portrayed as a way to mitigate any negative impacts on labour. However, African trade unions have campaigned against the EU's Economic Partnership Agreements (EPAs). It is argued that their stance highlights the limitations of incorporating the Decent Work Agenda into trade agreements, which, instead, are seen as central to the process of entrenching economic liberalisation. As a result, the article considers the prospects for transnational labour solidarity to resist EPAs.

Introduction

During the 1990s, the European Union (EU) and the US led an unsuccessful attempt to try and include labour standards into the multilateral rules on trade regulated by the World Trade Organisation (WTO).[1] This was a campaign which was supported by the International Confederation of Free Trade Unions (ICFTU). It was argued that nation states were increasingly powerless to protect labour rights and therefore 'the leadership of the ICFTU felt that … the only strategy left for labour was to try and make the existing international institutions as least harmful to labour as possible'.[2] However, a number of trade union movements in the Global South were critical of ICFTU's support of this approach. Such divisions have continued to be apparent in the negotiation of preferential trade agreements (PTAs) and their potential to ensure core labour standards.

This article considers how these tensions have played out in the case of the EU's negotiation of PTAs with regions in the Global South. As the direction of EU trade policy has shifted towards bilateralism, so the inclusion of labour standards, and in particular the Decent Work Agenda as articulated by the International Labour Organisation (ILO), have featured increasingly prominently in its trade and development policy with African, Caribbean and Pacific (ACP) states. Van den Putte and Orbie describe how provisions on labour have featured particularly strongly in all the EU's trade agreements since its first full Economic Partnership Agreement (EPA) with the Caribbean (CARIFORUM) was agreed in 2008.[3] The specific focus of this article is the recently signed EPA between the EU and the Southern African

Development Community (SADC), which is the first comprehensive EPA signed with a group of African states.

The rest of the article is organised as follows. In the next section, I introduce the key aspects of the Decent Work Agenda. Here, I demonstrate how it has become an increasingly central feature of the current global development orthodoxy, encapsulated most obviously in the recently agreed Sustainable Development Goals (SDGs). I then trace how this has been reflected in the EU's trade and development policy. Here, I argue that the inclusion of 'decent work' in recent trade agreements provides a rhetorical justification for an approach that actually reflects the interests of European capital. The focus then turns to the EPA negotiations between the EU and SADC. Here, I outline how the labour movement, although it remains weak in many states across the region, has to varying degrees of intensity, pursued a strategy of resistance in response to the negotiation of an EPA. I also show how this critical stance taken by African trade unions in relation to EPAs has also been articulated at both the continental and regional levels. I then consider the prospects for transnational labour solidarity in response to the EU's trade agenda and the SADC EPA in particular. I argue here that these prospects have been compromised in the past because the European labour movement has been more convinced by the significance of the inclusion of labour standards in trade agreements. Only in the last few years, it has demonstrated both a more critical stance on EPAs and more explicit solidarity with the labour movement in Africa. The article then concludes by considering the options available to trade unions in how they respond to the inclusion of the Decent Work Agenda in PTAs.

'Decent Work' and the global development orthodoxy

Decent work has featured increasingly prominently in the emerging orthodoxy on global development. The idea of 'decent work' was set out as the ILO's primary goal in 1999 by the then Director-General, Juan Somavía.[4] It was central to a reorientation of the ILO's main focus, whereby they would seek to work more actively in tandem with other institutions of global governance. The theme of 'decent work' became the central concept for this new approach and was organised around four key objectives. These were the promotion of core labour standards at work, a focus on decent employment and income, enhancing social protection and a commitment to social dialogue.[5] The aim was to make 'decent work' a universal principle, which at the same time would be sufficiently flexible for it to be interpreted in relation to local context.[6] As a result, the ILO's definition of 'decent work' has remained rather imprecise and vague. It was reaffirmed as being at the core of the ILO's focus in a key declaration in 2008.[7] Within the ILO's tripartite structure, employers have continued to be effective in preventing a more concrete definition or set of indicators from being adopted.[8] Despite these limitations, 'decent work' as an idea has become embedded within the new 'common sense' on global development.

In contrast to the Millennium Development Goals (MDGs) agreed in 2000, 'decent work' does feature in the SDGs.[9] The SDGs could be argued to be relatively more transformative than the MDGs, given that they are a global agenda, rather than essentially a justification for North–South aid programmes.[10] Goal 8 of the SDGs is to 'promote inclusive and sustainable economic growth, employment and decent work for all'.[11] It is acknowledged in the SDGs that employment on its own is not a guarantee for poverty reduction. As Teichman argues, however, the SDGs themselves do not 'suggest what policy measures would mitigate precarious, low-paid employment for women, youth, or other members of society'.[12] Moreover, in Africa the creation of meaningful jobs remains a real challenge despite the higher growth rates achieved in many parts of the continent since the early 2000s.[13]

Since the introduction of the Decent Work Agenda the EU has enhanced its co-operation with the ILO. In fact, it has been convincingly argued that 'by aligning itself with the ILO's broader decent work discourse and programmes, the European Commission acquired a distinctive role in global social governance'.[14] In general, EU development policy has closely followed the emerging Post-Washington Consensus (PWC) since the early 2000s. The PWC seeks to overcome some of the limitations of the neoliberal development model that dominated policy-making during the 1980s. In particular, it acknowledges that neoliberalism had failed to create a sufficient number of productive employment opportunities in many countries in the Global South. The response within the PWC has been to focus on improving education so that there is an increased supply of more skilled labour in developing countries.[15]

At the same time, as this article demonstrates, the PWC still retains a belief that trade liberalisation remains a key driver of development. What remains in question, therefore, is where the demand for this more highly skilled labour will come from. The ILO's Decent Work Agenda is portrayed as the missing link. It becomes the key to ensuring that these qualitative improvements in the supply of labour will result in better quality employment opportunities. This is certainly the view of Guy Ryder, the current Director-General of the ILO, who in a recent statement argued that 'decent work' is the key to making progress on reducing both inequality and poverty.[16] Similarly, the United Nations Development Programme has argued recently that the ILO's Decent Work Agenda 'and the human development framework are mutually reinforcing'.[17] In the next section, I outline in more detail how the EU has sought to combine the ILO's Decent Work Agenda with its negotiation of EPAs with ACP states.

Understanding 'decent work' in the EU's trade and development policy

The idea of promoting 'decent work' in the EU's trade and development policy is part of the broader claim made since the beginning of the twenty-first century, that a social dimension to globalisation should guide Europe's external relations. This was set out in a European Commission communication, which argued that the EU's external policies should be concerned with 'maximising the benefits of globalisation for all social groups in all its partner countries and regions'.[18] Pascal Lamy, EU Trade Commissioner at the time, was one of the leading proponents of such a view. For example, in a speech in 2004 he suggested that:

> On globalisation, I think we face a twofold task: first, of harnessing globalisation, of using this force to produce growth and jobs, and better regulation in the name of justice. And secondly, to ensure that we also ensure that development and more specifically the interests of developing countries are fully considered.[19]

Thus, it was suggested that the values of the European social model should be promoted, if not directly exported, to other parts of the world. In terms of its trade strategy specifically, this has resulted in the EU focusing on the four pillars of the ILO's Decent Work Agenda and in particular core labour standards.[20] A 2006 communication from the Commission confidently asserted that this commitment would ensure that 'trade liberalisation should help to achieve goals such as high growth, full employment, poverty reduction and the promotion of decent work'.[21]

In terms of the EU's relationship with ACP states, the Decent Work Agenda does feature in the Cotonou Agreement between the two parties, which was agreed in 2000. Most notably, Article 50 includes the commitment of all signatories to recognise the ILO's core labour standards and not to use them as a disguised form of trade protectionism.[22] However, in reality this did not lead to significant outcomes in practice. In particular, the implementation of core labour standards by ACP states has not featured in political dialogue prompted by the Cotonou Agreement.[23] What we have seen in more recent years, however, is an apparent increase in the commitment to the Decent Work Agenda in trade agreements concluded by the EU. The EPA signed with CARIFORUM includes a chapter on 'social aspects' and the more recent agreement concluded with the SADC grouping includes a 'trade and sustainable development' chapter. In both of these cases clear references are made to a commitment to the ILO's Decent Work Agenda.[24] The EU also highlight the role that Aid for Trade (AfT) can play in ensuring that trade agreements support the goals of the Decent Work Agenda.

Alongside these policy developments in the EU's external relations, a new way of conceptualising the EU as a global actor, 'normative power Europe' (NPE), entered the academic debate.[25] It was suggested that we can identify five central norms inherent to the European project: peace, liberty, democracy, the rule of law and respect for human rights.[26] The NPE approach led to an increased focus on the importance of ideas in conceptualising the EU's external relations; but at the same time, in doing so, it failed to provide an adequate appreciation of Europe's material interests, which feature quite explicitly in the case of trade negotiations. Moreover, it puts too much faith in the rhetorical construction of the claims made by the EU itself as to its normative agenda. As Sjursen suggests, there is a danger that NPE analysis 'leaves researchers vulnerable to the charge of being unable to distinguish between their own sympathy for the European project and their academic role as critical analysts'.[27] Rather, the negotiation of reciprocal trade agreements with ACP states, demonstrates the EU's overarching ideational commitment to neoliberalism, albeit in the form of the PWC. This ideational position means that in reality 'the negotiation of EPAs brings the EU's material self-interest and the framing of its normative goals closer together'.[28]

Hence, what we have witnessed in recent decades is the emergence of what should be more accurately understood as 'corporate Europe', rather than 'social', or 'normative power' Europe. In terms of this being reflected in the EU's external relations, a clear turning point came with the publication by the European Commission of its 'Global Europe' strategy in 2006.[29] As Bieler makes clear, this new trade policy was primarily driven by a desire to boost the competitiveness of the EU economy, but at the same time it was also justified by the Commission in terms of the developmental benefits it would confer on its trade partners.[30] Given the neoliberal ideology at the heart of EU policy-making, trade is seen as a positive-sum game where all participants benefit. As a result, European policy-makers genuinely believe that they can 'enhance Europe's profits but also achieve ethical objectives associated with livelihood creation, employment, and trickle-down poverty elimination for poorer citizens in former colonies'.[31] Hence, in the case of the negotiation of EPAs with ACP states, the EU's ambitious strategy to include behind-the-border issues, rather than simply the liberalisation of trade in goods, represented 'a concerted attempt to secure much "deeper" roots for the neoliberal development model'.[32] Although it has faced significant resistance to these more comprehensive EPAs, the Commission's current trade strategy makes it clear that by including rendezvous clauses in the most recently concluded EPAs, they remain firmly committed to the eventual inclusion of services and investment.[33]

However, at the same time as the material interests of EU policy have become increasingly explicit, clauses on sustainable development, including a focus on the ILO's Decent Work Agenda, have become common in recent EU trade agreements. By incorporating elements from the ILO's Decent Work Agenda into its external trade agreements, the EU is seeking to provide a rhetorical justification for an approach that is based on reciprocal trade liberalisation. The inclusion of AfT also forms part of this discursive process. As Langan and Scott argue, AfT has helped legitimate the reciprocal trade liberalisation that is central to EPAs despite the fact that 'the development credentials of AfT measures implemented by the EU are doubtful'.[34] In so doing, the EU hopes to assuage any critics who may highlight potential downsides to this approach. As a way of justifying its development policy this is not a new political strategy. As Langan reminds us, the EU has a long history of including specific measures within its relationship with ACP states to legitimate the developmental claims of its policies.[35]

In essence then, there are significant problems with the concurrent rise of an agenda that is increasingly driven by the needs of European capital, and the commitment to ensuring the ILO's Decent Work Agenda is also advanced. The main aim of this article, however, is not to focus on demonstrating the gap between rhetorical EU policy claims and the reality of the impact of EPAs in relation to the Decent Work Agenda. Prior research has already done an excellent job in this regard. For example, Orbie notes how the peculiar institutional set-up of the EU, whereby the Commission has competency for trade policy-making, means that it becomes more likely that any commitment to social norms will be secondary to material interests.[36] Meanwhile, Langan in a more forceful and compelling critique, focuses on two specific economic sectors (poultry production and cut-flowers) to highlight the gap between the EU's discourse on 'decent work' and the actual outcomes of its trade and development policies to Africa.[37] Instead, I want to explore these tensions in relation to the response of trade unions to the EPA negotiations between the EU and SADC. In doing so, I will assess the resultant challenges posed to transnational solidarity between the labour movement in Europe and Southern Africa. The next section begins by considering the views of trade unions within the SADC region to the negotiation of an EPA with the EU.

Trade unions within SADC and EPA negotiations

Member states of SADC have been negotiating a new trade agreement with the EU since EPA negotiations began with regional sub-groups of the larger ACP group in 2004.[38] After missing the original deadline of 31 December 2007, negotiations finally came to a conclusion recently when an EPA was officially signed on 10 June 2016.[39] Only seven SADC member states were involved in the EPA negotiations and hence the negotiating group is often referred to as SADC-Minus.[40] As noted in the previous section, 'decent work' features in a number of the articles within the text of this EPA. In particular, Article 8 refers to 'decent work for all as a key element of sustainable development for all countries and as a priority objective of international cooperation'.[41] Meanwhile, Article 11 suggests that the signatories to the agreement may cooperate on 'the trade aspects of labour or environmental policies in international fora, such as the ILO Decent Work Agenda and MEAs'.[42]

Hence, we see the inclusion in the final agreement of the discourse aligned to the normative developmental agenda identified in the previous section. At the signing ceremony in Kasane, Botswana, the EU Trade Commissioner, Cecilia Malmström, reinforced this message in a speech where she argued that:

> It's a pragmatic deal based on a realistic collective assessment of everyone's relative strengths. As a result it will allow all six countries to shelter products and sectors from competition where needed in some cases forever, in other cases over long timelines. That makes it strongly pro-development. As do the provisions on workers' rights and protecting the environment. The EPA favours sustainable development – not growth at all costs![43]

Similarly, during the ratification process of the SADC EPA in the European Parliament in September 2016, the MEP acting as chief rapporteur, Alexander Graf Lambsdorff, suggested that 'the language on human rights and sustainable development is one of the strongest that you will find in any EU agreement'.[44]

African trade unions have felt rather marginalised within the process of the negotiations. The Southern African Trade Union Coordination Council (SATUCC) and a range of other civil society organisations have expressed frustration at their lack of involvement in the SADC EPA negotiations.[45] To a large extent this is a product of the limited strength of many trade unions given the pervasiveness of authoritarian forms of nationalism across the region. Even in South Africa, where the Congress of South African Trade Unions (COSATU) is in a formal alliance with the ruling African National Congress (ANC), there are significant limitations to its influence. It has 'evolved from an organisation that pursued wider social transformation (social movement unionism) to one that increasingly prioritises collective bargaining'.[46] South Africa does have institutional arrangements, such as the National Economic Development and Labour Council (NEDLAC) to give trade unions a formal platform in the policy-making process. However, it has been convincingly argued that on major policy decisions the ANC government has tended to ignore NEDLAC completely.[47]

Nevertheless, given the focus on decent work and the broader developmental claims made by the EU, one might expect trade unions within the SADC-Minus group to be supportive of the recent signing of the EPA. However, over the last decade the labour movement across the region has consistently remained critical of the potential impact of EPAs on workers. As a result, a recent statement by the African Regional Organisation of the International Trade Union Confederation (ITUC-Africa) continues to urge African governments not to sign EPAs. This statement encapsulates both the strength of feeling within the labour movement in the region and the central aspects of their critique of EPAs.[48] It is argued that the inequitable structure of Africa's trading relationship with Europe will only be perpetuated by the signing of EPAs. Despite the asymmetry built into the liberalisation agenda it emphasises that EPAs are ultimately free trade agreements. Contrary to the claims made by the European Commission, this statement by ITUC-Africa predicts that EPAs will result in a loss of tariff revenues, a loss of policy space which is needed to support domestic industry in the region, and an undermining of the processes of regional integration.

Similar arguments have been made by individual trade union confederations in Southern Africa in response to the SADC EPA. COSATU has been particularly vocal in their opposition to the EPA negotiations. Speaking at a policy conference discussing 'decent work' organised by the International Trade Union Confederation (ITUC) and the European Trade Union Confederation (ETUC), then General Secretary, Zwelinzima Vavi was explicit in arguing that the relationship between contemporary trade negotiations and the Decent Work Agenda was not mutually compatible. He concluded that 'trade liberalisation as proposed by the EU and the US in particular is bad news for a decent work agenda in the South'.[49] After an interim

EPA (iEPA) was agreed with SADC, COSATU put out a press release in March 2008 supportive of both the South African and Namibian governments who were refusing to sign the iEPA.[50] In 2011 in a speech to the Norwegian Confederation of Trade Unions, Vavi accused the EU of 'arm twisting-bully tactics to force African countries into an anti-development trade agreement'.[51] The case of South Africa is a rather unique one within the SADC region, as they had already signed a Trade, Development and Cooperation Agreement (TDCA) with the EU in 1999.[52] Hence, the government's aim was to resist any further opening up to European capital, whilst seeking improved access to the European market. COSATU's opposition to the final EPA was less apparent than it had been during the earlier phase of the negotiations. Their main focus was on the use of export taxes, which are more limited under the terms of the SADC EPA. Export taxes are a way to increase the value of commodity exports and COSATU argued that they 'are necessary in order to ensure that minerals are processed and jobs are created in SA'.[53]

The Botswana Federation of Trade Unions (BFTU) joined COSATU in contributing to a statement by a network of African trade unions on EPAs, which argued that the 'rapid loss of government revenue will paralyse our governments' abilities to invest in education, health and decent jobs'.[54] In responding to a Presidential State of the Nation address, BFTU were also critical of the long-term consequences of signing an EPA with the EU, suggesting that the government failed 'to place the link between diversification, economic strategy and trade policy'.[55] Similar concerns were expressed by the National Union of Namibian Workers (NUNW) who, like COSATU in South Africa, supported their own government in refusing to sign the iEPA. NUNW's then Secretary General, Evilastus Kaaronda, argued 'that the proposed tariff reductions will cut very heavily into our labour intensive sectors leaving the majority of the already languishing Namibians further trapped in poverty'.[56]

At the regional level, the impact of trade union resistance to EPAs has been significantly undermined by organisational limitations. The main platform for putting forward a regional voice, SATUCC, includes all the major national labour federations in the region. Ever since 1995 when the decision was taken within SADC to form a new sector on 'Employment and Labour', SATUCC has been formally recognised as the regional voice of labour.[57] However, SATUCC's influence is reflective of the relative strength and organisational capacity of many of the national trade union federations outside of South Africa.[58] As with other attempts at co-ordination of civil society actors in the region, SATUCC is limited by the fact that 'regional agendas are not evident to the national members and their respective constituencies'.[59] SATUCC's impact on the EPA negotiations is also reflective of the fact that different member states have been negotiating in different regional groupings. It first made a minor intervention into the debate on EPAs in 2006 when it published a brief statement outlining a number of criticisms of EPAs that were broadly in line with those made by COSATU.[60] A much more detailed publication on the broader challenges faced by the region, as a result of the dominance of neoliberalism, was produced by SATUCC together with other key representatives of the regional labour movement. Reflecting on SADC's external economic relations it was strongly argued that 'the comprehensive liberalisation agenda, the IMF, the WTO, EPA's, African Growth and Opportunity Act (AGOA), regional trade agreements etc. should be stopped'.[61]

In sum, the labour movement within the SADC region has been clear in its opposition to the negotiation of EPAs. This has been most effectively articulated within the national context, in particular by COSATU in South Africa, rather than through SATUCC at the regional level. They remain unconvinced by the claims made by the European Commission that EPAs will ensure the advancement of the Decent Work Agenda across the region. Given that the growth of PTAs has become central to the process of entrenching economic liberalisation, it is important that the international labour movement works together to resist their negotiation. In the next section, I consider the extent to which trade unions within Europe have supported the stance taken by their colleagues in the SADC region.

The SADC EPA negotiations, transnational labour solidarity and the prospects for 'decent work'

As the previous section has highlighted, African trade unions have been consistent in their resistance to the negotiation of the SADC EPA with the EU. As I argued earlier the Decent Work Agenda fits within the broader PWC global development orthodoxy. As such, it provides a framework of rights for workers that, whilst important, are often difficult to enforce. However, proponents of the PWC, such as the EU, also remain committed to comprehensive trade agreements based on reciprocal liberalisation. These seek to ensure that 'peripheral capitalist spaces become locked into new relationships of unequal exchange'.[62] The negative consequences of these agreements are often more significant for workers in the Global South and this has meant they have been more explicit in their opposition to the negotiation of free trade agreements in the first place. This contrasts with trade unions in the Global North who have tended to focus on ensuring that the agreements contain clauses that can ameliorate their overall impact on labour. As a result, this structural context makes solidarity between Northern and Southern trade unions difficult, but at the same time it is important to ensure that labour retains sufficient agency in the analysis.[63] Hence, in the rest of this section I consider the position of European trade unions in response to the EU's broader free trade agenda and the SADC EPA specifically. In doing so, I demonstrate the emergence of some more recent examples of solidarity between the labour movement in Europe and their counterparts in Africa.

Historically, however, the prospects for effective transnational labour solidarity in response to the EU's trade agenda have been limited. The trade union movement within Europe has displayed a rather ambivalent response to the EU's negotiation of free trade agreements. For example, ETUC gave rather mixed messages in response to the European Commission's 'Global Europe' strategy. On the one hand, ETUC outlined 'its disagreement with the proposed general reorientation of European trade policy in favour of an extremely aggressive liberalisation agenda in the developing countries'.[64] On the other hand, at a conference organised by the Commission to discuss the new strategy in November 2006, the General Secretary of ETUC at the time, John Monks, outlined in a speech how he was not against PTAs in principle, but that the EU should ensure that an effective social dimension (including the promotion of 'decent work') should be included in future trade agreements.[65] A similar stance was taken by the British Trades Union Congress (TUC) in 2007 when they called 'for labour standards ... to be included in all agreements with the same level of enforcement and support for their implementation as commercial clauses'.[66] Some European trade unions, particularly those representing workers in export-oriented sectors of the Germany economy, took a more overtly positive view of the 'Global Europe' trade agenda.[67] In doing so, they were reflecting the material interests of their members ahead of the broader goals of international solidarity.

In response to the particularly contentious EPA negotiations, both ETUC and ITUC jointly took the position that development should be put at the heart of the trade negotiations, and in particular they called for 'strong, effective and operational social and labour chapters'.[68] Thus, the European trade union movement took a reformist stance in arguing that the EU's normative claims to the developmental potential of EPAs were not without foundation. The key argument being made was that labour rights must be effectively enshrined with the final EPA agreements. Such positioning was clearly at odds with the much bolder approach based on resistance, taken by Southern African trade unions in response to the SADC EPA negotiations, as discussed in the previous section. In sum, Hilary convincingly concludes that the response of European trade unions to the EU's free trade agenda was 'at best to lobby for the inclusion of social conditionalities within the agreements as a means of mitigating their most damaging effects'.[69]

Partly as a result of being alerted to the more immediate dangers to workers from both the Comprehensive Economic and Trade Agreement (CETA) negotiations with Canada and the Transatlantic Trade and Investment Partnership (TTIP) negotiations between the EU and the United States, some European trade unions have recently begun to develop a more explicitly solidaristic position with their Southern colleagues. Trade unions were not at the forefront of the initial critique of these trade negotiations within Europe. However, as Dierckx argues, both TTIP and CETA, and in particular their inclusion of protections for investors, have since 2014 led to a re-think in the European labour movement.[70] Even trade unions that were previously supportive of free trade have adopted a more critical stance, such as IG Metall, which represents German metalworkers in a range of sectors including the car industry.[71] In the specific case of the SADC EPA, the TUC published a letter urging MEPs not to ratify the agreement, because it 'will restrict the policy space of governments ... cause a significant loss of revenue from tariffs and undermine fundamental labour rights'.[72] The letter also made a direct reference of support for ITUC-Africa, who in a recent statement provided a damning assessment of EPAs arguing that overall they 'will only make it harder for Africa to achieve the 2030 Sustainable Development Goals'.[73]

The recent change in the stance taken by European trade unions is also related to the realisation that there are significant limitations to the strength of the sustainable development chapters within EPAs. In its submission to the European Commission's public consultation on the future of the Cotonou Agreement, ITUC argued that the 'monitoring of efforts concerning labour rights should be conducted in a more thorough, systematic and inclusive manner'.[74] In the case of the SADC EPA specifically, the robustness of the inclusion of references to the Decent Work Agenda in the agreement was tested almost immediately after the final round of trade negotiations had ended. In October 2014, ETUC and ITUC demonstrated their solidarity with trade unions in Swaziland who had been banned by the monarchy. The ban was an explicit contravention of ILO Convention 87, which guarantees freedom of association and the right of workers to organise. ETUC sent a letter to Catherine Ashton, then the EU's High Representative for Foreign Affairs and Security Policy, which noted that the actions in Swaziland contravened the sustainable development clauses of the SADC EPA and urged the European Commission to use diplomatic pressure on the regime in Swaziland.[75] Eventually in May 2015, the Trade Union Congress of Swaziland was recognised by the regime but as a recent report suggests it is still the case that 'trade unions face massive restrictions, and workers who want to join unions or participate in union activity have frequently been intimidated and harassed'.[76]

Hence, in the case of the SADC EPA, it is only belatedly that trade union federations in both Europe and Southern Africa have begun to adopt a united position of resistance. From the European side this appears to have been driven by a realisation that the clauses in the SADC EPA, on the Decent Work Agenda, contain no provisions for effective monitoring or enforcement. This position of solidarity was encapsulated in a joint letter sent to MEPs in August 2016.[77] This urged them to vote down the agreement when it went to the European Parliament for ratification the following month. The letter expressed concern that:

> ... the EPA does not have a strong Sustainable Development chapter that would enable us to put forward social, labour and environmental concerns stemming from the implementation of the Agreement. In particular, the chapter does not explicitly establish monitoring bodies with the participation of trade unions, and satisfactory procedures for the enforcement of the sustainable development provisions are lacking.[78]

In sum, the main argument being developed here is that despite some limited recent progress in the strength of transnational labour solidarity in response to EPA negotiations by the European trade union movement, the reality is that the global development orthodoxy outlined earlier remains pervasive. This orthodoxy suggests that the inclusion of the Decent Work Agenda in trade agreements will ensure that workers across the globe will see improvements in the four central objectives identified by the ILO. This article outlines why trade unions should resist, and not legitimate EPAs with ACP states. Otherwise, they will be sanctioning a set of agreements that will ultimately ensure the 'lock-in' of a liberalisation agenda and domestic regulatory environments across Africa that serve the interests of transnational capital rather than labour.[79]

Conclusions

In conclusion, this article has highlighted some of the limitations of the Decent Work Agenda given the structural context of continuing attempts to deepen the process of trade liberalisation. Trade unions have a choice to make in the strategies they pursue in this regard. They can act as legitimators of trade policy (as has often been the case with respect to the trade union movement in the EU) or they can adopt a counter-hegemonic role by resisting EPAs and advancing a more transformative agenda.[80] As such, a set of common demands around which trade unions can unite, is a vital part of developing a more effective counter-hegemonic approach. One recent example is the 'Futures Commission' project organised by the Southern Initiative on Globalisation and Trade Union Rights. In its first publication, Bieler sketches out the central ideas that could form the basis of an alternative 'fair' trade system, whereby 'a range of joint demands may be feasible around the re-assertion of national sovereignty and against the increasing structural power of transnational capital'.[81]

If the NPE view was correct and normative interests, such as the Decent Work Agenda, were really at the heart of EPAs then why is it that African trade unions, as I have demonstrated in the case of the SADC EPA, have remained consistently opposed to them? The answer lies in the material interests and core neoliberal assumptions that are central to the EU's trade agenda. Trade unions across the Global South have refused to accept the inclusion of social clauses in free trade agreements as a sufficient mechanism for protection from the material impacts of trade liberalisation. This view is neatly encapsulated by two COSATU researchers who argue that 'core labour standards are necessary, but not sufficient, to prevent a race to the bottom as a result of more open economies'.[82]

As I have argued in this article, this is a view that the European labour movement has been slow to acknowledge. In contrast, as Hilary notes, the view of the labour movement in Africa 'is shared by European alter-globalisation organisations active on trade policy issues, as well as by social movements and the broader mass of civil society groups in the Global South'.[83] Nevertheless, as I have demonstrated, in recent years European trade unions have become more critical of the EPA negotiations. It is to be hoped these examples of European solidarity with African trade unions continue to be built upon, as the EU's desire to secure deeper trade agreements with Africa remains a part of its broader trade strategy.

Notes

1. For details, see Hughes and Haworth, *The International Labour Organisation*, 61–72.
2. Anner, "The Paradox of Labour Transnationalism," 74.
3. Van den Putte and Orbie, "EU Bilateral Trade Agreements," 265–9.
4. See International Labour Organisation, "Decent Work."
5. Ibid., 13.
6. Hughes and Haworth, *The International Labour Organisation*, 75.
7. International Labour Organisation, *ILO Declaration on Social Justice*.
8. Maupain, *The Future of the International Labour Organization*, 54–6.
9. Decent work was belatedly included in the MDGs in 2007 but it remained a goal based more on aspiration, in comparison to the other MDGs.
10. Fukuda-Parr, "From the Millennium Development Goals," 44.
11. This is one of 17 SDGs agreed at the UN Sustainable Development Summit in September 2015. Goal 8 includes an extensive list of contributory targets including 'increase Aid for Trade support for developing countries, in particular least developed countries, including through the Enhanced Integrated Framework for Trade-Related Technical Assistance to Least Developed Countries'. For further details see http://www.un.org/sustainabledevelopment/sustainable-development-goals/.
12. Teichman, *The Politics of Inclusive Development*, 14.
13. United Nations Economic Commission for Africa, *Economic Report on Africa 2013*, 61.
14. Orbie and Tortell, "From the Social Clause to the Social Dimension," 9.
15. Öniş and Şenses, "Rethinking the Emerging," 281.
16. Ryder, "Decent Work Key."
17. United Nations Development Programme, *Human Development Report 2015*, 23.
18. European Commission, *The Social Dimension of Globalisation*, 2.
19. Lamy, "Globalisation and Trade."
20. Orbie, "Work in Progress," 285.
21. European Commission, *Promoting Decent Work for All*, 8.
22. European Union, "Partnership Agreement between the Members of the African," 23.
23. Orbie, "Work in Progress," 288.
24. In the cases of the other five ACP sub-regions that are negotiating EPAs, any agreements that have been concluded so far include a commitment to continue negotiations in this area.
25. See Manners, "Normative Power Europe."
26. Ibid., 242.
27. Sjursen, "What Kind of Power?" 170.
28. Hurt, "The EU-SADC Economic Partnership Agreement Negotiations," 497.
29. European Commission, *Global Europe*.
30. Bieler, "The EU, Global Europe," 164.
31. Langan, "Normative Power Europe and the Moral Economy," 253.
32. Hurt, "The EU-SADC Economic Partnership Agreement Negotiations," 499.
33. European Commission, *Trade for All*, 24.
34. Langan and Scott, "The Aid for Trade Charade," 158.

35. Langan, "Decent Work and Indecent Trade," 23.
36. Orbie, "Promoting Labour Standards through Trade," 182.
37. Langan, "Decent Work and Indecent Trade."
38. EPA negotiations were initially launched in 2002 but during the first phase they were conducted with the ACP group of states as a whole.
39. The end of 2007 deadline was when the WTO's waiver for the non-reciprocal trade preferences enjoyed by ACP states was set to expire. At this point an interim EPA agreement covering only the trade in goods was concluded instead.
40. The SADC EPA was signed by Botswana, Lesotho, Namibia, South Africa and Swaziland (the five member states of the Southern African Customs Union) and Mozambique. Angola was directly involved in the negotiations and has the option to join the EPA in the future. The remaining eight member states of SADC have been involved in other EPA negotiating groups.
41. European Union, "Economic Partnership Agreement between the European Union," 8.
42. Ibid., 9.
43. Malmström, "EU-SADC EPA."
44. Tempest, "MEPs Approve Trade Deal."
45. Godsäter, "Civil Society and Regional Trade," 122.
46. Hurt, "What's Left of 'the Left'" 11.
47. Buhlungu, *A Paradox of Victory*, 6.
48. ITUC-Africa, "ITUC-Africa Statement on EPAs."
49. COSATU, "Zwelinzima Vavi's Speech to Policy Conference."
50. COSATU, "SA Right to Resist EU Trade Blackmail."
51. COSATU, "Zwelinzima Vavi Speech to LO Norway."
52. For a discussion of the TDCA see Hurt, "A Case of Economic Pragmatism?"
53. COSATU, "COSATU Calls on the Department of Trade and Industry."
54. Network of African Trade Unions, "African Trade Unions Statement."
55. Toka, "The Ego has Landed?"
56. Sasman, "NUNW Backs Govt."
57. Smit, "Transnational Labour Relations in SADC," 21.
58. Hurt, "The Congress of South African," 102.
59. Godsäter, "Civil Society and Regional Trade," 125.
60. Ibid., 100.
61. Alternatives to Neo-liberalism in Southern Africa, *The Search for Sustainable Human Development*, 48–9.
62. Bieler and Morton, "Uneven and Combined Development," 42.
63. Hurt, "The Congress of South African," 95.
64. European Trade Union Confederation, "On the Communication 'Global Europe'."
65. European Trade Union Confederation, "Speaking Note for John Monks."
66. Trades Union Congress, "Put Labour Standards and Development."
67. Hilary, "European Trade Unions and Free Trade," 50.
68. European Trade Union Confederation, "ITUC and ETUC Call on EU."
69. Hilary, "European Trade Unions and Free Trade," 48.
70. Dierckx, "European Unions and the Repoliticization."
71. De Ville and Siles-Brügge, "Why TTIP is a Game-changer," 5.
72. Trades Union Congress, "TUC Calls on MEPs."
73. ITUC-Africa, "ITUC-Africa Statement on EPAs."
74. International Trade Union Confederation, "Submission to the 'Towards a New Partnership,'" 14.
75. European Trade Union Confederation, "Swaziland – ETUC Letter."
76. Action for Southern Africa, "Swaziland's Downward Spiral," 4.
77. This letter was signed by ITUC-Africa, SATUCC, ETUC, ITUC and national trade union federations in Botswana, Mozambique, South Africa and Swaziland.
78. ITUC-Africa, "ITUCAf-ITUC-ETUC Letter to MEPs."
79. See Hurt, "The EU-SADC Economic Partnership Agreement Negotiations"; Nunn and Price "Managing Development."
80. For a summary of this distinction see Söderbaum, *Rethinking Regionalism*, 138–42.

81. Bieler, "From 'Free Trade' to 'Fair Trade'," 38.
82. Makgetla and van Meelis, "Trade and Development in South Africa," 111.
83. Hilary, "European Trade Unions and Free Trade," 52.

Acknowledgments

I would like to thank Mark Langan and the anonymous reviewers for their helpful comments and suggestions. Any remaining shortcomings are in no way their responsibility.

ORCID

Stephen R. Hurt http://orcid.org/0000-0002-3331-9718

Bibliography

Action for Southern Africa. 2016. "Swaziland's Downward Spiral: The International Community Must Act Now." June. http://www.actsa.org/newsroom/wp-content/uploads/2016/10/Swazilands-Downward-Spiral.pdf.

Alternatives to Neo-liberalism in Southern Africa. *The Search for Sustainable Human Development in Southern Africa*. Harare: ANSA, 2006.

Anner, Mark. "The Paradox of Labour Transnationalism: Trade Union Campaigns for Labour Standards in International Institutions." In *The Future of Organised Labour: Global Perspectives*, edited by Craig Phelan, 63–90. New York: Peter Lang, 2007.

Bieler, Andreas. "The EU, Global Europe, and Processes of Uneven and Combined Development: The Problem of Transnational Labour Solidarity." *Review of International Studies* 39, no. 1 (2013): 161–183.

Bieler, Andreas. "From 'Free Trade' to 'Fair Trade': Proposals for Joint Labour Demands towards an Alternative Trade Regime." In *Challenging Corporate Capital: Creating an Alternative to Neo-liberalism*, edited by Andreas Bieler, Robert O'Brien, and Karin Pampallis, 31–41. Johannesburg: Chris Hani Institute, 2016.

Bieler, Andreas, and Adam D. Morton. "Uneven and Combined Development and Unequal Exchange: The Second Wind of Neoliberal 'Free Trade'?" *Globalizations* 11, no. 1 (2014): 35–45.

Buhlungu, Sakhela. *A Paradox of Victory: COSATU and the Democratic Transformation in South Africa*. Scottsville: University of KwaZulu-Natal Press, 2010.

COSATU. 2007. "Zwelinzima Vavi's Speech to Policy Conference for Decent Work." October 31. https://groups.google.com/forum/?fromgroups#!topic/cosatu-press/hSWhoQSGs8Q.

COSATU. 2008. "SA Right to Resist EU Trade Blackmail." March 6. http://www.cosatu.org.za/docs/pr/2008/pr0306c.html.

COSATU. 2011. "Zwelinzima Vavi Speech to LO Norway." September 22. https://groups.google.com/forum/#!topic/cosatu-press/ZWoUsOhB81k.

COSATU. 2014. "COSATU Calls on the Department of Trade and Industry to be Firm on Export Taxes." July 22. http://www.cosatu.org.za/docs/pr/2014/pr0722b.html.

De Ville, Ferdi, and Gabriel Siles-Brügge. "Why TTIP is a Game-changer and Its Critics Have a Point." *Journal of European Public Policy* (2016): 1–15. doi:10.1080/13501763.2016.1254273.

Dierckx, Sacha. "European Unions and the Repoliticization of Transnational Capital: Labor's Stance regarding the Financial Transaction Tax (FTT), the Transatlantic Trade and Investment Partnership (TTIP), and the Comprehensive Economic and Trade Agreement (CETA)." *Labor History* 56, no. 3 (2015): 327–344.

European Commission. *The Social Dimension of Globalisation: The EU's Policy Contribution on Extending the Benefits to All*. COM (2004) 383, May 18, 2004.

European Commission. *Global Europe: Competing in the World – A Contribution to the EU's Growth and Jobs Strategy*. COM (2006) 567, October 4, 2006.

European Commission. *Promoting Decent Work for All: The EU Contribution to the Implementation of the Decent Work Agenda in the World*. COM (2006) 249, May 24, 2006.

European Commission. *Trade for All: Towards a More Responsible Trade and Investment Policy*. COM (2015) 497, October 14, 2015.

European Trade Union Confederation. "Speaking Note for John Monks" at 'Global Europe: Competing in the World. The Way Forward' Conference Organised by DG Trade, Brussels, November 13, 2006. https://www.etuc.org/speeches/dg-trade-conference-global-europe-competing-world-way-forward.

European Trade Union Confederation. "On the Communication 'Global Europe: Competing in the World'." Resolution Agreed in Brussels, December 7–8, 2006. https://www.etuc.org/documents/communication-%E2%80%9Cglobal-europe-competing-world%E2%80%9D.

European Trade Union Confederation. "ITUC and ETUC Call on EU to Root Economic Partnership in Development." Press Release, September 26, 2008. https://www.etuc.org/press/ituc-and-etuc-call-eu-root-economic-partnership-development.

European Trade Union Confederation. "Swaziland – ETUC Letter to High Representative of the Union for Foreign Affairs & Security Policy." October 10, 2014. https://www.etuc.org/swaziland-etuc-letter-high-representative-union-foreign-affairs-security-policy.

European Union. "Partnership Agreement between the Members of the African, Caribbean and Pacific Group of States of the One Part, and the European Community and Its Member States, of the Other Part, Signed in Cotonou on June 23, 2000." *Official Journal of the European Communities*, L 317, December 15, 2000: 3–353.

European Union. "Economic Partnership Agreement between the European Union and Its Member States, of the One Part, and the SADC EPA States, of the Other Part," *Official Journal of the European Union*, L 250, September 16, 2016: 3–2120.

Fukuda-Parr, Sakiko. "From the Millennium Development Goals to the Sustainable Development Goals: Shifts in Purpose, Concept, and Politics of Global Goal Setting for Development." *Gender & Development* 24, no. 1 (2016): 43–52.

Godsäter, Andréas. "Civil Society and Regional Trade Integration in Southern Africa." In *Mapping Agency: Comparing Regionalisms in Africa*, edited by Ulrike Lorenz-Carl and Martin Rempe, 115–131. Farnham: Ashgate, 2013.

Hilary, John. "European Trade Unions and Free Trade: Between International Solidarity and Perceived Self-interest." *Globalizations* 11, no. 1 (2014): 47–57.

Hughes, Steve, and Nigel Haworth. *The International Labour Organisation (ILO): Coming in from the Cold*. London: Routledge, 2011.

Hurt, Stephen R. "A Case of Economic Pragmatism? The European Union's Trade and Development Agreement with South Africa." *International Relations* 15, no. 3 (2000): 67–83.

Hurt, Stephen R. "The EU-SADC Economic Partnership Agreement Negotiations: 'Locking In' the Neoliberal Development Model in Southern Africa?" *Third World Quarterly* 33, no. 3 (2012): 495–510.

Hurt, Stephen R. "The Congress of South African Trade Unions and Free Trade: Obstacles to Transnational Solidarity." *Globalizations* 11, no. 1 (2014): 95–105.

Hurt, Stephen R. "What's Left of 'the Left' in Post-apartheid South Africa?" *Capital & Class* (2016): 1–23. doi: 10.1177/0309816816678579.

International Labour Organisation. *"Decent Work" Report of the Director-general to International Labour Conference 87th Session*. Geneva: International Labour Office, 1999.

International Labour Organisation. *ILO Declaration on Social Justice for a Fair Globalization*. Geneva: International Labour Office, 2008.

International Trade Union Confederation. 2015. "Submission to the 'Towards a New Partnership between the EU and the ACP Countries after 2020' Consultation." December 16. http://ec.europa.eu/europeaid/towards-new-partnership-between-eu-and-acp-countries-after-2020-civil-society-organisations_en.

ITUC-Africa. 2016. "ITUC-Africa Statement on EPAs." June 8. http://www.ituc-africa.org/ITUC-Africa-Statement-on-EPAs.html.

ITUC-Africa. 2016. "ITUCAf-ITUC-ETUC Letter to MEPs: Ratification of the Economic Partnership Agreement between the European Union and the Southern Africa Development Community Group." August 30. http://www.ituc-africa.org/ITUCAf-ITUC-ETUC-letter-to-MEPs-Ratification-of-the-Economic-Partnership.html.

Lamy, Pascal. 2004. "Globalisation and Trade: How to Make Sure There is Space for Development?" Tokyo, June 22. http://trade.ec.europa.eu/doclib/html/117759.htm.

Langan, Mark. "Normative Power Europe and the Moral Economy of Africa–EU Ties: A Conceptual Reorientation of 'Normative Power'." *New Political Economy* 17, no. 3 (2012): 243–270.

Langan, Mark. "Decent Work and Indecent Trade Agendas: The European Union and ACP Countries." *Contemporary Politics* 20, no. 1 (2014): 23–35.

Langan, Mark, and James Scott. "The Aid for Trade Charade." *Cooperation and Conflict* 49, no. 2 (2014): 143–161.

Makgetla, Neva S., and Tanya van Meelis. "Trade and Development in South Africa." In *Trade Union Responses to Globalization: A Review by the Global Union Research Network*, edited by Verena Schmidt, 97–112. Geneva: International Labour Office, 2007.

Malmström, Cecilia. 2016. "EU-SADC EPA – Why It Matters." Kasane, June 10. http://trade.ec.europa.eu/doclib/html/154624.htm

Manners, Ian. "Normative Power Europe: A Contradiction in Terms?" *JCMS: Journal of Common Market Studies* 40, no. 2 (2002): 235–258.

Maupain, Francis. *The Future of the International Labour Organization in the Global Economy*. Oxford: Hart, 2013.

Network of African Trade Unions. 2007. "African Trade Unions Statement on EPA." November 7. http://astm.lu/african-trade-unions-statement-on-epa.

Nunn, Alex, and Sophia Price. "Managing Development: EU and African Relations through the Evolution of the Lomé and Cotonou Agreements." *Historical Materialism* 12, no. 4 (2004): 203–230.

Öniş, Ziya, and Fikret Şenses. "Rethinking the Emerging Post-Washington Consensus." *Development and Change* 36, no. 2 (2005): 263–290.

Orbie, Jan. "Promoting Labour Standards through Trade: Normative Power or Regulatory State Europe?" In *Normative Power Europe: Empirical and Theoretical Perspectives*, edited by Richard G. Whitman, 161–184. Basingstoke: Palgrave Macmillan, 2011.

Orbie, Jan. "Work in Progress: The Social Dimension of EU-Africa Relations." In *The European Union in Africa: Incoherent Policies, Asymmetrical Partnership, Declining Relevance?* edited by Maurizio Carbone, 283–303. Manchester: Manchester University Press, 2013.

Orbie, Jan, and Lisa Tortell. "From the Social Clause to the Social Dimension of Globalization." In *The European Union and the Social Dimension of Globalization: How the EU Influences the World*, edited by Jan Orbie and Lisa Tortell, 1–26. London: Routledge, 2009.

Ryder, Guy. 2016. "Decent Work Key to Reducing Poverty and Inequality." Statement to the Development Committee of the 2016 Annual Meetings of the Boards of Governors of the World Bank and the IMF, Washington, DC, October 6. http://www.ilo.org/global/about-the-ilo/newsroom/statements-and-speeches/WCMS_531568/lang–en/index.htm.

Sasman, Catherine. 2007. "NUNW Backs Govt on IEPA" *New Era*, December 17. https://www.newera.com.na/2007/12/17/nunw-backs-govt-on-iepa/.

Sjursen, Helene. "What Kind of Power?" *Journal of European Public Policy* 13, no. 2 (2006): 169–181.

Smit, Paul A. "Transnational Labour Relations in SADC: Regional Integration or Regional Globalization?" *Journal of Globalization Studies* 6, no. 1 (2015): 14–29.

Söderbaum, Fredrik. *Rethinking Regionalism*. London: Palgrave Macmillan, 2016.

Teichman, Judith A. *The Politics of Inclusive Development: Policy, State Capacity and Coalition Building*. Basingstoke: Palgrave Macmillan, 2016.

Tempest, Matthew. 2016. "MEPs Approve Trade Deal with Six African States – Nine Years Late." *Euractiv*, September 15. https://www.euractiv.com/section/development-policy/news/meps-approve-trade-deal-with-six-african-states-nine-years-late/.

Toka, Gowenius. 2010. "The Ego has Landed?" *Sunday Standard*, November 18. http://www.sundaystandard.info/ego-has-landed.

Trades Union Congress. 2007. "Put Labour Standards and Development at the Heart of EU Trade Agreements." September 18. https://www.tuc.org.uk/international-issues/global-economic-justice-campaigns/put-labour-standards-and-development-heart-eu.

Trades Union Congress. 2016. "TUC Calls on MEPs to Reject Economic Partnership Agreement between EU and Southern African Countries." June 10. https://www.tuc.org.uk/international-issues/trade/world-tradetrade-justice/tuc-calls-meps-reject-economic-partnership.

United Nations Development Programme. *Human Development Report 2015: Work for Human Development*. New York: United Nations Development Programme, 2015.

United Nations Economic Commission for Africa. *Economic Report on Africa 2013: Making the Most of Africa's Commodities: Industrializing for Growth, Jobs and Economic Transformation*. Addis Ababa: United Nations Economic Commission for Africa, 2013.

Van den Putte, Lore, and Jan Orbie. "EU Bilateral Trade Agreements and the Surprising Rise of Labour Provisions." *The International Journal of Comparative Labour Law and Industrial Relations* 31, no. 3 (2015): 263–283.

Oil and cocoa in the political economy of Ghana-EU relations: whither sustainable development?

Mark Langan and Sophia Price

ABSTRACT
Oil and cocoa represent strategic export commodities for the Ghanaian economy, prioritised within the Ghana Shared Growth and Development Agenda. This article examines these sectors in the context of Ghana's relations with the European Union (EU). Notably, the EU constitutes the most important market for Ghanaian exports. The European Commission, moreover, has pledged to tangibly assist private sector development in Ghana, with particular reference to the UN Sustainable Development Goals (SDGs). Through its focus on oil and cocoa, the article problematises certain aspects of EU aid and trade interventions with respect to normative SDG development pledges.

Introduction

Oil and cocoa stand as strategic export sectors in Ghana's economy. The government's Ghana Shared Growth and Development Agenda (GSGDA) indicates that these sectors together represented around 40% of total merchandise exports in 2014 (see Table 1).[1] Accordingly, the GSGDA makes clear that the government prioritises oil and cocoa in terms of private sector development (PSD) conducive to employment creation and taxation generation. All efforts will be taken, according to the GSGDA, to ensure the success of PSD efforts within the oil and cocoa commodity chains. In particular, there is emphasis on need for enhanced forms of foreign direct investment (FDI) to bolster productive capacity in the sectors, and to usher in technological transformations.

Meanwhile, the GSGDA has been enthusiastically embraced by the country's main trade and development partners, including the European Union (EU). The most recent National Indicative Programme (NIP), signed between the Ghanaian government and the European Commission, indicates that the EU will provision Ghana with necessary PSD capacity building to support economic and social prosperity through export growth.[2] Moreover, the EU has promised to provide further PSD assistance to mitigate certain risks associated with a free trade deal being negotiated between Europe and the West African region – the Economic Partnership Agreement (EPA). The EU's pledge to an Economic Partnership Agreement Development Programme (EPADP) will target PSD activities in those priority sectors (such

Table 1. Cocoa and gold as strategic sites of PSD and exports in Ghana's economy (2010–13).

Share of Total Merchandise Exports (%)	2010	2011	2012	2013
Cocoa beans	20.07	15.14	16.18	11.72
Crude oil	–	21.77	21.96	28.25
Gold	29.79	23.32	19.25	22.71

Source: Government of Ghana, *GSGDA*, 15.

as oil and cocoa) identified by West African governments in their individual national development plans (such as the GSGDA). These trade and aid ties are themselves underpinned by Ghana's membership of the African, Caribbean and Pacific (ACP) bloc, which signed the ACP-EU Cotonou Agreement in 2000.

The article – in the context of the commitments made by the EU – examines the capacity of the Ghanaian oil and cocoa sectors to contribute to sustainable development. In particular, it explores whether European companies' FDI does offer a boon to job creation and economic prosperity. Moreover, it considers whether EU Aid for Trade towards PSD initiatives are likely to enhance pro-poor business growth. In so doing, the article queries certain policy rationales associated with a free market approach to sustainable development. Indeed, the article underscores certain areas in which EU trade and aid interventions in the oil and cocoa sectors may in fact undermine pro-poor SDG objectives. The conduct of European companies, in particular, is not something which may automatically lend itself to the normative objectives of sustainable development. The discussion is structured as follows. The first section provides background context in terms of the current position of the oil and cocoa sectors. The second section examines the oil sector in the context of EU companies' FDI – as well as policy initiatives led by the EU and its member states vis-à-vis sector regulation. The third section considers the condition of the Ghanaian cocoa sector in the context of EU PSD objectives. The article concludes with a summary of key lessons in terms of the EU's contribution to Ghana's sustainable development via PSD activities in oil and cocoa.

Oil and cocoa in Ghana's pursuit of sustainable development

The most recent figures from Ghana's Statistical Service indicate that cocoa bean and oil exports constitute the second and third most important commodities, respectively, in terms of export earnings (see Tables 2 and 3).[3] Both sectors' importance is also repeatedly underscored in the GSGDA, which emphasises that the government intends to support PSD objectives to augur economic development and job creation as part of sustainable development (see Table 1).[4] In particular, the government highlights the potential *of cocoa agro-processing* – combined to oil extraction – as key areas for industrial development. The GSGDA remarks that:

> For the attainment of the accelerated job creation and economic transformation ... the Industry Sector will continue to play a pivotal role, growing at an average annual rate of 13.2% over the period 2014–2017. The anticipated drivers in this sector include agro-processing, especially by increasing the share of cocoa processed locally ... [and the] development and production of oil and gas from the Jubilee, TEN and Sankofa-Gye Nyame Fields.[5]

Importantly, this outlook is maintained in other leading development plans. For instance, the Ministry of Trade's Medium Term Strategy (2014–2017) similarly focuses on value addition and industrialisation. It underscores the need to meaningfully support agro-processing

Table 2. Ghana's main export earnings in Cedis Million (2011–2015).

Commodity	2011	2012	2013	2014	2015
Gold bullion	5111.7	8.947.7	8115.8	12416.8	14605.0
Cocoa beans, superior quality raw beans	3.127.7	3530.4	2694.3	5787.4	10146.6
Petroleum oils and oils obtained from bituminous minerals, crude	4325.8	6613.7	5885.9	12807.1	9822.8

Source: Ghana's Statistical Service, *Digest*, 6.

Table 3. Ghana's cocoa exports to the EU, and tariffs under EPA or GSP arrangements (2015).

Export produce	Total value EUR million	Tariff rates under EPA (%)	Tariff rates under GSP (%)
Cocoa paste	191.8	0	6.1
Cocoa butter	101.3	0	4.2
Cocoa powder	31.4	0	2.8

Source: European Commission, *How Can*, 2.

activities in sectors such as cocoa. In addition, it emphasises the need to 'promote value addition in the extractive industry to facilitate local economic development'. It highlights the need to improve the 'development' performance of key extractive industries, including oil.[6]

In addition, the European Commission – as a leading trade and development partner under the Cotonou Agreement – recognises the importance of oil and agro-processing for Ghana's achievement of sustainable development. The most recent NIP confirms that Ghana's lower middle-income status is based largely on its 'crops such as cocoa ... and more recently [on] oil and gas'.[7] Moreover, the NIP commits the EU to the promotion of Ghana's 'sustainable and inclusive growth, with a particular focus on rural development'.[8] Interestingly, however, the EU also emphasises that Ghana's signing of an EPA free trade deal is essential for its long-term economic well-being. The European Commission points to how an EPA would secure low tariff access for Ghana's cocoa products (and other agricultural goods) into European markets (see Table 2).[9] This is in apparent contrast to the Generalised System of Preferences (GSP), to which Ghana would default if it failed to fully implement an EPA. This picture is complicated by the fact that Ghana initialled a unilateral and interim EPA with the EU at the end of 2007. It has, however, now agreed to a full regional EPA, as per the Heads of Government of the Economic Community of West African States' (ECOWAS) communication of July 2014.[10] As of December 2016, the terms of this regional EPA had gone into provisional effect in Ghana and Ivory Coast, while pending application in other West African states.[11] The lack of full regional implementation of the EPA deal (even by January 2017, the time of writing), does leave Ghana, however, in a potential legal 'limbo' with regard to sustained low tariff market access to Europe. Uncertainty with regard to the EPA is of major concern to cocoa producers, explored in the third section of the article.

Importantly, the EU has doubled down on its PSD pledges following the United Nation's (UN) agreement on the Sustainable Development Goals (SDGs). The UN SDGs under Goal 8 on *Decent Work and Economic Growth* highlights the need for donors to give additional Aid for Trade and PSD assistance to facilitate economic prosperity in developing countries. In response, the European Council emphasises the pro-poor contributions of the business community to job creation and social prosperity within the post-2015 era:

> Private sector-led economic growth is the principle creator of jobs and as such contributes to poverty reduction. The private sector should be fully engaged in the implementation of the Post-2015 Agenda ... Creating a conducive and stable business environment for the private sector and investments is key, including level playing fields for competition, as are accountable and efficient institutions.[12]

Furthermore, the European Parliament has recently endorsed a resolution on PSD (April 2016). The parliament noted the benefits of FDI, if properly regulated, in developing countries. Interestingly, however, it also sounded some alarm as to the potential impact of EPAs, and the need for sufficient Aid for Trade monies to go towards competitiveness building.[13]

In this context, it is highly relevant to now examine the capacity of the oil and cocoa sectors to contribute to sustainable development in Ghana – with the assistance (or lack thereof) of the EU. As the recent NIP states, the EU is currently Ghana's most important export market 'worth EUR 3 billion or 42.9% of total Ghanaian export ... followed by China (6.5%)'.[14] Moreover, for the reasons laid out above, the cocoa and oil sectors are particularly interesting to examine given their strategic significance. Additionally, they have received relatively sparse attention within academic discussions on PSD and sustainable development in Ghana – in stark comparison with gold.[15] The following sections therefore examine the capacity of oil and cocoa to contribute to sustainable development through export growth in Ghana. They also problematise the role of the EU as a trade and aid partner. The selection of Ghana, meanwhile, enables the article to examine a lower middle-income ACP country that has regularly been viewed as a 'donor darling'.[16] It allows us to consider the success (or lack thereof) of EU PSD interventions in an African country that has been relatively praised for its willingness to abide by donor free market rationales.

Oil extraction and sustainable development in Ghana: the EU as a pro-poor protagonist?

The discovery of oil in the Jubilee field off Ghana's coast in 2007 has heralded opportunities – and challenges – for sustainable development in this strategic ACP state. As mentioned, the government's own GSGDA now prioritises oil as a key sector for development of extractive industries. There is also much emphasis in this document that oil must not become another enclave economy (as arguably has become the case with the Ghanaian gold sector).[17] Namely, the oil sector must make linkages with other areas of the economy in order to ensure that prosperity is shared throughout Ghana. The GSGDA, in this context, has emphasised that Ghana should aspire to the processing of oil, and not merely to the export of crude oil to refineries in Europe and beyond.[18] It is clear from the initial exports of crude oil, however, that this resource alone has potential for extremely large export earnings vis-à-vis the broader Ghanaian economy. As Table 2 indicates, crude oil has grown to impressive export values from initial extraction in 2010 (after preparations which started in 2007). As emphasised in the GSGDA – as well as the EU-Ghana NIP – these revenues are expected to increase as other oil fields come online (in addition to extractive activities in the Jubilee field).

One of the most crucial policy elements in terms of aligning Ghana's oil extraction to sustainable development objectives has been the government's – and donors' – emphasis on the need for adequate regulation of the proceeds derived from this commodity. In particular there has been much focus placed upon Ghana's joining the Extractive Industries

Transparency Initiative (EITI).[19] This development platform emphasises the need to utilise oil proceeds for sustainable development:

> A country's natural resources, such as oil, gas, metals and minerals, belong to its citizens. Extraction of these resources can lead to economic growth and social development. However, poor natural resource governance has often led to corruption and conflict. More openness and public scrutiny of how wealth from a country's extractive sector is used and managed is necessary to ensure that natural resources benefit all.[20]

Notably, the EITI places expectations upon both oil companies and local governments to publish reliable statistics regarding oil production, values and sharing arrangements. This is in response to the so-called 'resource curse' in which developing countries (in particular) have been seen to experience increased corruption and civil strife after the discovery of oil deposits (for example, in Nigeria after the initial discovery of oil in the 1950s).[21]

Importantly, the Ghanaian government agreed to partake in this EITI platform, completing full validation in 2010.[22] As a result, a Ghana Extractive Industries Transparency Initiative (GEITI) was established with headquarters in the capital, Accra. The EU, meanwhile, has been a vocal advocate of such transparency commitments. Notably, the recent NIP highlights 'Governance, Public Sector Management and Accountability' as one of its two priorities for facilitating sustainable development in Ghana. The NIP thus makes clear that EUR 75 million will be made available for support to public sector management.[23] It emphasises that one of the key expected results from such aid support is that 'transparency in the management and use of revenues from natural resources, including extractive industries (mining, oil and gas) is increased'.[24] EU member states, for their part, have taken a leading role in encouraging the Ghanaian government to abide by EITI norms. The UK Department for International Development (DFID) has in fact recently pledged £14 million for an oil and gas-specific transparency initiative, known as the Ghana Oil and Gas for Inclusive Growth (GOGIG) platform. This will operate from 2015 to 2019 and aims to achieve 'enhanced policy and regulatory coherence across the oil and gas sector'; 'improved revenue management' and 'enhanced sector oversight by facilitating cooperation between government and accountability actors'.[25] The particular interest in the UK in the equitable use of Ghana's oil monies towards sustainable development owes in part to the presence of Anglo-Irish company, Tullow Oil, in the extraction of the commodity in this ACP country.

It is important to recognise, however, that the role of the EU (via the NIP), and EU member states' own development agencies (such as UK DFID), do not necessarily translate into the tangible achievement of pro-poor UN SDG objectives in Ghana. Despite European donor commitments to the principles of shared prosperity and sustainable development there are in fact certain grounds upon which to doubt whether EU trade and aid interventions are assisting (rather than jeopardising) poverty reduction. Notably, there is much concern that EITI instruments – as strongly endorsed by the EU institutions – do more to shift focus onto developing country governments, than to hold foreign corporations (often those headquartered in EU member states) to account for regressive extractive processes. Bazilian et al. emphasise here that EITI schemes do not, in practice, compel individual companies to disclose the precise details of their revenue sharing arrangements with governments such as that of Ghana.[26] Instead only aggregate corporate data is disclosed to the public domain. This undercuts transparency criteria and veils potential inconsistencies (and injustices) associated with extractive company behaviours in the Global South. More broadly, Maconachie and Hilson explain that donors such as the EU may utilise such schemes 'in deflecting criticism' from their own conduct (and that of their corporate entities) while 'shifting the focus of the resource curse debate towards developing world governments'.[27]

Meanwhile, in the specific case of Ghana, the GEITI – as well as the UK DFID sponsored GOGIG platform – have supported regressive legislation within the Ghanaian parliament. In particular, there is domestic civil society concern from groups such as Fair-Trade Oil Share Ghana that these sector bodies (with support from the EU Commission and the EU member states) have lent legitimacy to the Oil Exploration and Production (E&P) bill.[28] This act recently passed through the Ghanaian legislature and has introduced a situation in which the Energy Minister is now able to circumvent competitive tendering processes with regard to production in newly discovered oil fields.[29] Moreover, civil society groups such as the Ghana Institute of Governance and Security lament that the E&P bill has failed to remedy the lack of a formal oil Production Sharing Agreement (PSA). This is despite the fact that a PSA would do much to gain a fairer proportion of oil revenues for the Ghanaian government, rather than for foreign investors such as Tullow Oil.[30] Consequently, concerns have been raised that European aid monies have been channelled towards platforms such as the GEITI and GOGIG as a means of gaining policy influence within Ghana with respect to oil and gas production arrangements. Sceptics of the E&P bill conclude that aid monies have done more to entrench the corporate interests of European companies such as Tullow Oil than to remedy the 'resource curse' (or merely lack of equitable revenue sharing) within Ghana.[31]

Furthermore, these concerns about the contributions of the EU to sustainable development via pro-poor PSD activities in the oil sector in Ghana are amplified when attention is turned to the alleged conduct of companies such as Tullow Oil. Alarmingly, this company was implicated in high profile corruption allegations in Uganda, a state which shares many parallels to Ghana as a newly oil-rich ACP member.[32] To confuse matters, representatives of another oil company – Heritage Oil – appeared to accuse Tullow Oil of bribery in the Ugandan sector.[33] As a result, the Ugandan President, Yoweri Museveni, demanded an apology from Tullow Oil for the embarrassment caused to his government during this episode. An apology was indeed received by Museveni, although Tullow Oil have denied any wrong-doing.[34] Nevertheless, this incident does raise potentially serious concerns about the situation of European companies, such as Tullow Oil, in Ghana. This is particularly the case since – as the EU-Ghana NIP itself recognises – the Ghanaian political system remains vulnerable to graft and corruption issues. There is therefore the possibility that the aforementioned E&P law, and its loophole allowing the Energy Minister to bypass standard tendering practices, might encourage predatory behaviour on the part of oil companies. This would potentially enhance foreign corporate profits (and the wealth of individual ministers) while denying the Ghanaian people a fair share of their sovereign natural resource wealth. This is again underscored by the lack of a formal PSA in Ghana, a fact that the E&P law did not redress.

In similar terms, there is also concern that foreign companies such as Tullow Oil have successfully agreed 'stabilisation clauses' with the Ghanaian government that now compel it to compensate the company for any profit losses associated with stricter social or environmental regulations.[35] Rather than support pro-poor forms of PSD in conjunction with the UN SDGs, this EU headquartered company (at least for the time being, prior to UK Brexit) is therefore understood by certain civil society activists to lock-in regressive models of extraction in sub-Saharan Africa. Platform London, for instance, claims that:

> Tullow's website gives the impression that the company is big on transparency. Yet for five crucial years, Tullow refused to publish the contracts they signed with the Ghanaian government to

> develop the Jubilee oil field. The contracts were effectively signed in secret without meaningful public or political debate. As a result they included 'stabilization clauses' which lock-in weak social and environmental regulations at the time the contract was made. If Ghana passes new laws that set higher standards, it will have to compensate Tullow for the cost of compliance.[36]

This civil society group also points to the environmental resource repercussions of oil extraction undertaken in Ghana by Tullow Oil. Namely, that fishing has been compromised by exclusion zones that now surround the offshore oil platforms. This is seen as deleterious for local fishing livelihoods, as well as for wider food security in this lower middle-income ACP country.[37] Meanwhile – in the context of lost fishing livelihoods – there is concern that oil companies are not enabling Ghanaian citizens to benefit from skilled employment in this commodity sector. While Tullow Oil (and its US competitor Kosmos) claim that 80% of generated employment has gone to local people, this often reflects low-skilled and poorly paid forms of jobs. The Africa Europe Faith and Justice Network, for instance, states that Ghana's:

> government should be looking at the kinds of jobs the Ghanaians employed in the industry are occupying. Ghanaians should not be [only] employed providing support services like driving, controlling traffic on the roads and selling food to labourers ... the oil companies operating in the country are mainly using imported expertise and equipment.[38]

Moreover, there is broader concern that European oil companies – including the Anglo-Irish firm Tullow Oil as well as France's Total S.A. – are utilising Ghana as a de facto haven for tax evasion purposes. Due to a variety of tax treaties between these EU member states and this ACP country, oil companies can give 'loans' to their subsidiaries in Ghana as a means of reducing their overall corporate tax burden. This situation appears to be unresolved despite (or perhaps because of) the passing of the aforementioned E&P bill. The director of the African Centre for Energy Policy (ACEP) has explained the complicated practices by which this situation arises:

> if they [European oil companies] are operating in a [European] country that has double tax treaty with Ghana and the withholding tax on cross-border loans is higher [within Europe], what they do is to lend to countries where the tax is lower [thus countries such as Ghana] ... most of the companies ... Tullow Oil from the UK ... Total Oil from France ... [they will pay] rent to their subsidiaries in Ghana where the withholding tax on the interest that Ghana will pay to them is eight per cent instead of lending to corporations within France, within the UK, or in Italy [where the withholding tax is higher].

It is necessary to also note that the EU's pursuit of an EPA in West Africa will not tangibly benefit the oil sector in this ACP site of PSD activities. Given the fact that Ghana remains reliant upon the export of unrefined crude oil, it will not gain a tariff advantage in this commodity line via the signing of a free trade agreement.[39] Moreover, the EU's promised Aid for Trade monies under the transitional EPADP vehicle appears to offer Ghana less than the amount of lost tariff revenues which it will incur upon the implementation of an EPA. Therefore, the EPADP does not offer any additional 'new' monies for support to PSD and upgrading in sectors such as oil (or cocoa). It merely provides a short-term compensation for finances which will be lost to the Ghanaian treasury through tariff dismantling upon products entering this ACP country from EU member states. Overall, therefore, there are several grounds upon which to contest the EU's ostensible contributions to sustainable development through PSD activities in priority ACP sectors such as Ghanaian oil. Rather than provide opportunities for pro-poor growth, there appear to be circumstances in which European corporations gain from extractive activities while failing to equitably share revenues with host developing countries. EPAs – and the EPADP – meanwhile do not appear a boon for pro-poor UN SDG objectives.

Cocoa sector and sustainable development in Ghana: Europe as benevolent partner?

The cocoa sector stands as a significant source of employment and income revenue in Ghana, as emphasised by the government in the recent GSGDA. This is demonstrated in the quantitative data in Table 3 which indicates that cocoa produce (including beans, butter and paste) generated around EUR 324.5 million for Ghana's economy in 2015 alone.[40] This is a strong and growing Ghanaian sector. Moreover, in recent years the global market for raw cocoa and cocoa products has shown significant growth with, for example, global sales of chocolate confectionary crossing the landmark figure of $100 billion for the first time in 2011. This growth has been accompanied by predictions that consumer demand will soon outpace supply.[41] New markets for cocoa consumption in Asia are a key factor in these predictions of the ongoing strength of the sector. It is the EU, however, which remains the world's largest cocoa consuming region, with its trade with West Africa being the most significant inter-regional trade in global cocoa markets. The majority of Europe's imports of cocoa and cocoa products originate from West Africa, which has framed the importance placed on the levels of tariffs and other terms of access to the European market within the EPA negotiations.

Traditionally the trade between the EU and Ghana has been reliant on the export of raw cocoa beans for processing in Europe, predominantly in the Netherlands where the world's largest processors Cargill and ADM are located, as well as in Germany, Belgium and France. The dominant position of Cargill and ADM accounts for the Netherland's status as the biggest single processing country. This pattern of trade and production accounts for the EU's position as the world's leading importer of raw beans and exporter of processed cocoa. It is also the most important trade partner for Ghana, and the leading destination for its exports, of which raw and processed cocoa represents 43.5%.[42]

The Ghanaian cocoa sector is marked by a clear division between the types and scales of economic actors involved in production, marketing and processing within the overall value chain. Raw cocoa is predominantly produced by smallholder farmers, often operating as rural collectives. In 2008 it was estimated that there were 700,000 cocoa farmers in Ghana.[43] The Ghana Cocoa Board (Cocobod) now estimates that 'approximately 800,000 farm families spread over six of the ten regions of Ghana' are employed in the production of raw cocoa.[44] The state has retained control of the sector, in spite of an era of liberalisation in line with Washington Consensus led Structural Adjustment Policies. The government organisation, the Ghana Cocoa Board (Cocobod), plays a central role in production, research, the development of the sector, internal and external marketing and quality control. It performs these tasks alongside a number of subsidiary organisations such as the Cocoa Research Institute, the Seed Production Unit, the Quality Control Division, and the Cocoa Marketing Company (CMC) Limited.[45] The CMC, a wholly owned subsidiary of the Ghana Cocoa Board, has the sole responsibility for the sale and export of Ghanaian cocoa beans and some processed cocoa products.[46] In contrast to the state controlled market for cocoa beans, cocoa processing has mainly been undertaken by a few large-scale transnational agro-processing companies located both in Ghana and abroad.

Importantly, the dominance of Ghanaian cocoa-processing by a small number of large-scale transnational corporations (TNCs) reflects the structure of the global sector, which is characterised by high market concentration.[47] The 'big four' companies – Barry Callebault, Cargill, ADM and Blommer Chocolate Company – controlled 50% of world market grindings in 2006, with that share now standing at approximately 61%.[48] In part this structure is driven by the nature of the industry as 'capital-intensive with high sunk costs' which encourages mergers, acquisitions while deterring new entrants.[49] The Ghanaian Cocoa Processing Company, a limited company whose two major shareholders are the Ghana Cocoa Board and the Government of Ghana, is a minor operator in the Ghanaian processing sector and reported a loss of $16.3 million in the 2013–14 financial year.[50]

Significantly, the structure of production and trade of the Ghanaian cocoa sector has been recognised as posing constraints in relation to possible levels of returns to the broader economy. This has prompted an array of policy responses. Indeed, the Ghanaian government has emphasised the need to support domestic processing as a means of value addition and job creation. This seeks to promote the transition of the domestic sector from the production and export of raw cocoa beans to higher levels of industrialisation. This was evidenced in the 2012–2016 Country Strategy Paper (signed between the EU and Ghana) which identified a need to develop agricultural production and agro-processing, particularly via improved agricultural processing technology.[51] The government's GSGDA platform also underscores the need to attract enhanced FDI into processing to bolster employment opportunities, and to ensure that Ghana moves beyond the sole export of unprocessed agricultural produce. These initiatives echo the thinking of key actors in the EU. A recent European Parliament resolution in April 2016, for example, emphasised that developing countries should focus upon value addition and agro-processing activities to create skilled, decent jobs. Crucially, the European Commission also regards the EPA as providing 'incentives for new investments and job creation in Ghana',[52] as well as providing opportunities for the development of the business environment and the diversification of productive sectors.[53] However as demonstrated by the current fortunes of the Cocoa Processing Company, the potential for domestic cocoa-processing capacity in Ghana to challenge the dominance of large-scale TNCs in the processing sector is questionable.

Moreover there is much concern (particularly within the cocoa sector in Ghana itself) that the uncertainties associated with the EU's EPA in the West African region may undermine processing opportunities. For example, neighbouring Nigeria defaulted to the GSP upon its refusal to sign an interim EPA by the original deadline of December 2007. At time of writing in January 2017, the regional West African EPA is yet to be fully applied in Nigeria. This underscores pre-existing consternation in Ghana's cooca sector that the regional trade agreement may in fact be stillborn due to non-ratification in key constituent countries (despite preliminary application in Ghana itself as of December 2016).[54] Accordingly, Nigerian cocoa processors have faced higher tariffs upon entry into EU member states, effectively making them less competitive as compared to other ACP countries (such as Ghana) that had acquiesced in 2007 to the terms of EU free trade arrangements. There is currently concern in Ghana, that should the regional West African EPA collapse, then its own processors will default to the GSP and therefore face additional competitive pressures when exporting goods into the EU market.[55] Furthermore, the promises of the European Commission to furnish agricultural production, including cocoa, with Aid for Trade monies under the NIP – as well as the EPADP – is met with scepticism on the part of local business stakeholders.

This is underscored by the fact that the EPADP merely cushions the impact of lost tariff revenues (upon EPA implementation), and does not therefore represent 'new' money per se for agricultural investments.[56]

Meanwhile, Ghanaian officials' focus upon domestic cocoa processing as part of a sustainability agenda is accompanied by a focus on securing levels of supply required to meet current and future demand. As part of this long-term outlook, officials have identified the need to redress existing social and environmental concerns within the sector. Recent government policies include initiatives to tackle issues such as the ageing farming population in the rural hinterland, as well as the deterioration of existing cocoa trees, often as a result of disease. For example, the government's Ghana Strategy Support Programme (GSSP) included technical and social support to impoverished smallholders, with an eye to long-term sustainability.[57] This has been accompanied by the transnational Africa Cocoa Initiative, which has brought together the World Cocoa Foundation (WCF), the US Agency for International Development (USAID) and the Dutch Sustain Trade Initiative (IDH) in a multi-agency programme that commits to improve cocoa yields. European and US headquartered corporations have also developed their own strategies to address commercial concerns (in relation to predicted shortfalls in supply), as well as civil society critiques relating to the social and environmental costs of production. For example, Nestle's *Cocoa Procurement System*, Cargill's *Cocoa Promise Scheme* and Barry Callebaut's *Cocoa Horizons* all promote sustainable cocoa sourcing as part of a Corporate Social Responsibility (CSR) agenda aimed at environmental protection and the elimination of child labour.[58] Similarly, FairTrade programmes and sustainability certification schemes within EU countries (and beyond) have encouraged European consumers to favour cocoa produce that prioritises greater incomes for smallholder producers.[59] This has been matched by European governments, such as that of Germany and the Netherlands, actively adopting sustainable cocoa consumption initiatives.

The European Commission, for its part, has placed specific focus on the need to combat child labour within ACP-EU trade networks. This has gained particular policy resonance since the conclusion of the UN SDGs, given their emphasis on decent work objectives and child welfare. A staff working document issued by the European Commission on child labour issues highlighted the case of Ghanaian cocoa (as well as that of Ivory Coast) as being prone to forms of unjust labour in its supply chain.[60] This policy emphasis has also been adopted by the European Parliament which issued a 2011 resolution calling for the EU institutions to redress labour injustices in developing country trade links. In response to such concerns, the European Cocoa Association (ECA) and CAOBISCO (the European confectionary body) issued a joint statement which recognised ongoing problems in West African cocoa production. In the case of Ghana, in particular, these European corporate bodies noted that a 'public certification process is underway' to discourage use of children in value chains.[61]

With parallels to the oil industry, however, there are several grounds on which to question whether the EU is meaningfully supporting sustainable development via 'pro-poor' PSD activities in the cocoa sector. In relation to livelihoods and social prosperity, for example, the 2015 Cocoa Barometer warns that incomes are not sustainable for cocoa famers, who are operating in conditions of extreme poverty. Farmers earn as little as 84 cents a day and gain around 6.6% of the total proceeds of chocolate production, down from 16% in 1980.[62] Accordingly, young farmers are not replacing the old due to low pay and ongoing precarity in the system (despite the onset of the multi-stakeholder initiatives mentioned above). In addition, there are concerns that donor and government initiatives aimed at increasing cocoa

Table 4. Ghanaian cocoa production and child labour (2008/2009 and 2013/2014).

Ghana cocoa survey period	2008/2009	2013/2014
National cocoa production (tonnes)	0.66	0.90
Children, 5–17 years old, in total population (million)	2.16	2.24
Child labourers in cocoa production (million)	0.95	0.92
Children in hazardous work (million)	0.93	0.88

Source: Tulane University, *2013/2014 Survey Research*, http://www2.tulane.edu/news/releases/tulane-releases-report-on-child-labor-in-west-african-cocoa-production.cfm.

production – when combined to high rates of adult out-migration – might unwittingly exacerbate child labour.[63] While child labour in Ghana's cocoa sector fell between 2008/9 and 2013/14 (see Table 4), this could be jeopardised by increased cocoa production if donor and government authorities are not sufficiently cognisant of the issue. This is particularly worrying since the tasks in which children continue to be engaged are recognised by both the Ghanaian government and the International Labour Organisation as being among the 'worst forms of child labour'. This is made clear in a recent report by Sudwind and Global 2000 on *Bittersweet Chocolate* which details ongoing problems in the Ghanaian and Ivorian cocoa sectors:

> children can be found working on many different tasks related to cocoa farming. They use machetes and other dangerous tools to remove cocoa pods from trees and to crack them open. They carry heavy loads of cocoa beans from the field to drying racks, they are exposed to dangerous chemicals such as pesticides and fertilizers and often endure long hours in the sun. [64]

European chocolate companies and retailers continue to make large profits while child labour and low pay remain endemic within their cocoa supply chains.

Moreover, Maconachie and Fortin argue that such donor and government initiatives can possibly have negative impacts on the gendered division of labour. Namely, that they might unwittingly intensify the burden on women who remain marginalised in the sector due to social norms and structural barriers.[65] Typically it is women who often do most of the physical agricultural work, lack land rights, and combine agricultural work with caring and domestic responsibilities (while male family members sell the crops and control household financial resources).[66] This of course does not detract from the need to address the issue of cocoa supply and production demands. It does, however, call for much greater gender sensitivity as to how donor and government initiatives aimed at increasing production are felt within local communities. This point is made convincingly by Marston who states that:

> Many of the existing programs have tended towards community development in cocoa communities without understanding the links of female beneficiaries to their supply chains. Programs that focus on supporting and enabling women's contribution to the productivity, quality and sustainability of the cocoa supply chain have been fewer.[67]

Accordingly, donors such as the EU must do much more to meaningfully work with the Ghanaian government to tailor appropriate programmes to ensure genuine gender justice in cocoa supply chains (while also dealing with the problem of ongoing use of child labour).[68]

In addition, despite the current policy focus of the GSGDA and EU institutions on agro-processing for job creation and social prosperity, there has only been limited graduation from primary production to value-added processing activities within Ghana.[69] Where there has been growth in 'origin grindings', this has been dominated by European and US agro-processing companies who often import skilled labour, rather than train local citizens.[70] Meanwhile, these large-scale TNCs have benefitted from generous tax exemptions for their investments into local processing capacity, for example in the 'Free Zone' of Tema near Accra (namely, an export processing zone – EPZ). The Ghanaian government has not therefore benefited from significant taxation revenues from this FDI presence, nor have sizeable numbers of local skilled jobs been created. Moreover, there is concern that the expansion of European and US corporate activity in the Ghanaian cocoa sector has undermined the position of existing domestic processors, such as the Cocoa Processing Company. In response, public-private strategies have been developed such as a joint venture between the state-owned Cocobod and the German grinding company Host-Hammester, although these remain at an early stage of development.

It is important to note, furthermore, that the above concerns raised in the context of the Ghanaian cocoa sector are mirrored in terms of the structure of global agro-processing supply chains more broadly. Haigh succinctly characterises this as the 'corporate takeover' of African food systems as part of North-South trade networks – a takeover which he argues is facilitated by leading donor states as well as certain host African governments.[71] Often buttressed by the strategic channelling of donor aid monies to host countries, large-scale corporations (such as the 'big four' cocoa processors) have successfully accessed land resources at the expense of small-scale farmers and food security on the continent.[72] The intensification of corporate activity in sub-Saharan African, moreover, has been pursued in order to secure long-term supply – as well as companies' ongoing profitability:

> securing supplies of cash crops for export is one of the reasons multinational companies are so keen to increase their activities in Africa. For example, global cocoa traders and processors are predicting a one million ton shortage of cocoa in 2020. This is due to climate change and a shortage of cocoa farming as a result of low prices, urbanization and competition for land from alternative crops and mining.[73]

This concern about the corporate takeover of agro-processing supply chains with regard to African countries is echoed by many other actors. For instance, Elizabeth Mpofu, the General Coordinator of the international peasant movement, La via Campesina, similarly argues that TNCs are pursuing avenues in African countries for industrial farming, appropriating land and other resources while poorly remunerating workers, ignoring social issues (such as child labour and gendered injustice in cocoa production) and avoiding full taxation (often through gaining EPZ status as occurs in the Ghanaian port town of Tema).[74] Such critiques have prompted activist and advocacy networks, such as the pan-African Alliance for Food Sovereignty in Africa, to coalesce in opposition to what they regard as the corporate industrialisation of African agriculture[75]

Altogether, therefore, the Ghanaian government's and EU donor's common emphasis on the contributions of PSD, increased cocoa yields and the expansion of processing activity to pro-poor SDGs must be problematised. Rather than spurring genuine forms of pro-poor economic growth, policies aimed at enhancing production while paying inadequate attention to workers' incomes, taxation revenues and social concerns (surrounding gendered inequalities and child labour) might exacerbate ill-being in Ghana. Moreover, it appears that it is large-scale European headquartered agro-processors who have been best placed to maximise the benefits of the relationship between the EU and Ghana. While the Ghanaian state has maintained a high level of control of its cocoa sector, it faces ongoing pressures for increased liberalisation from the EU via the EU-West Africa EPA which commits Ghana to a twenty year process of free market reform. This, accompanied by a concomitant threat that Ghanaian cocoa might suffer the fallout from a default to the GSP, creates much uncertainty in relation to the future sustainable development of the sector.

Conclusion

The case studies demonstrate the centrality of two main commodities, oil and cocoa, to the Ghanaian economy. Unsurprisingly both sectors have been targeted as key drivers of future economic development and employment creation, particularly through a shift from the production of raw commodities to higher levels of value-added activities. In the context of the global sustainability agenda represented by the UN SDGs in the post-2015 consensus, the development of these key sectors is continually framed in terms of pro-poor growth and poverty alleviation (allied to environmental concerns). As such they have become central to state-led strategies, such as the GSGDA, as well as ACP countries' development partnerships with corporate investors and donor partners. This is particularly the case in relation to the EU-Ghana relationship. However, while there is a strong discursive emphasis on pro-poor growth and poverty alleviation via PSD activities in (EPA) free market conditions, the case studies reveal the potential limitations of this policy approach.

While the European Commission's policy communications – and NIP funding frameworks – emphasise the social gains of PSD in developing countries in terms of job creation and taxation revenues, the case studies demonstrate that it is often large-scale EU headquartered enterprises that have predominantly benefitted from FDI and PSD rather than local peoples. In both case studies it has been European corporations with links to key states such as the UK, the Netherlands, Germany and France, that have leveraged their positions in global supply chains and that have influenced policy decisions (such as the oil E&P bill) to generate larger surpluses. In contrast, Ghanaian citizens – especially cocoa smallholders and fishermen (denied access to resources by oil activities) – continue to face precarious conditions on very low incomes, reflecting an inequitable share of the gains within Ghana-EU trade networks. While there has been a move towards initiatives to rebalance the position of Ghanaian economic actors, for example via policy focus on redressing child labour in cocoa or creating skilled jobs in oil, there remain significant questions as to the success of these strategies. In addition the returns to the Ghanaian economy from these sectors have been severely limited by tax exemptions and opaque relationships between corporate actors (such as Tullow Oil) and domestic government.

Moreover, it is important to re-emphasise that future relations between the EU and Ghana will be conditioned by the EU-West Africa EPA. While the EPA has been provisionally applied in Ghana since December 2016, nevertheless this region-wide deal might still yet unravel due to the continuing reluctance of key ECOWAS members – Nigeria and Liberia – to implement its terms. It will be important to monitor, assuming the region-wide EPA does not collapse, how tariff dismantling and lost tariff revenues will impact the Ghanaian government amidst its attempt to achieve the GSGDA. It is notable here that EU aid monies for PSD initiatives are not 'additional' or 'new' – but rather provide a short-term cushion for monies lost through free market liberalisation and tariff reductions. It remains questionable, therefore, whether EU aid budgets will meaningfully spur enhanced forms of 'pro-poor' PSD within Ghana. Meanwhile, the economic significance of export-orientated sectors such as oil and cocoa will continue to grow – particularly as import-competing sectors struggle after liberalisation in a post-EPA environment. 'Sustainable development', in these conditions, would appear a very significant challenge, one which the Ghanaian government may well fail to attain.

Notes

1. Government of Ghana, *GSGDA*, xvi.
2. Ibid., 22–25.
3. Ghana's Statistical Service, *Digest*, 6.
4. Ibid., 15.
5. Ibid., 20.
6. Ministry of Trade, *Medium Term*, 34.
7. European Commission, *NIP*, 7.
8. Ibid., 10.
9. European Commission, *How Can*, 2.
10. European Commission, *West African*.
11. European Commission, *Trade – Countries – West Africa.*
12. Ibid.
13. European Parliament, *Resolution.*
14. See note 9 above.
15. For example, see Hilson and Garforth, "Everyone"; Hope and Kwarteng, "CSR"; Okoh, "Grievance."
16. Lawson, *Foreign Aid*, 5.
17. Government of Ghana, *GSGDA*, 74.
18. Ibid., 80.
19. See note 18 above.
20. EITI, *What the EITI.*
21. It is not within the scope of our current discussion to provide a detailed review of the literature on the resource curse. See Van der Ploeg, "Natural Resources," for an extensive introduction and overview. It is useful to note here, however, that recent contributions to the resource curse debate have emphasised that there is no element of 'predestination' or inevitability with regards to the curse unfolding in states blessed with large quantities of natural resource wealth. In particular recent examinations by the Effective States and Inclusive Development (ESID) network have explored the political economy of oil extraction in Uganda. They have found that the authoritarian, centralised negotiating style of President Yoweri Museveni has in fact helped to secure better revenue sharing arrangements than has occurred in states such as Ghana (see for instance Asante and Mohan, "Transnational Capital"; and Hickey et al., "The Political Settlement"). This focus on institutional setups is also found in Brunnschweiler and Bulte, "The Resource Curse Revisited and Revised," who argue that the concept of the 'resource curse' itself might be misguided, given the potentiality for African governments to positively utilise resource abundance for national growth strategies. This focus on the institutional setup of African regimes ties into the broader debates about the potential linkage between authoritarianism and developmental states (for instance in Rwanda, as explored by Booth and Golooba-Mutebi, "Developmental patrimonialism?"). It is important to note, therefore, that while European oil companies do push to maximise their own profits (often with the assistance of EU institutions, and the acquiescence of governments such as found in Ghana) nevertheless there is emerging debate in the literature as to how African regime structure and elite agency might overcome, or avoid altogether, the 'resource curse'.
22. EITI, *Ghana.*

23. European Commission, *NIP*, 15, 26.
24. Ibid., 16.
25. Oxford Policy Management, *Ghana*.
26. Bazilian et al., "Oil," 51.
27. Maconachie and Hilson, "Editorial," 54.
28. Lungu, *This Mahama*.
29. Segbefia, *Petroleum*.
30. Mohammed, "Oil Find"; Lungu, *This Mahama*.
31. Ibid.
32. Olanya, "Will Uganda," 50.
33. Dennys, *Tullow Oil*.
34. Ibid.
35. Phillips et al., "Sovereignty," 30–3.
36. Ibid.
37. Ibid.
38. Africa Europe Faith and Justice Network, *Oil Industries in Ghana*.
39. Sowah, *Ghana-EU*, 13.
40. See note 11 above.
41. World Cocoa Foundation, "cocoa Market."
42. See note 44 above.
43. Kolavalli and Vigneri, *Cocoa*, 1.
44. Ghana Cocoa Board, *Cocoa*.
45. Ibid.
46. Ibid.
47. UNCTAD, *Cocoa*.
48. Ibid.
49. Ibid.
50. Cocoa Processing Company LTD, "Financial."
51. African Development Bank, *Republic*.
52. See note 44 above.
53. Ibid.
54. Please see Langan and Price (forthcoming) for more detail on this consternation within the Ghanaian cocoa sector with regards to the ambiguous status of the region-wide EPA (given the refusal of states such as Nigeria to fully ratify and implement the free trade deal). This relates to the authors' own fieldwork in Ghana, and Nigeria, which explored the views of business stakeholders involved in cocoa production and processing, as well as the Ghanaian Limited Buying Companies who act as intermediaries between producers and Cocobod.
55. Business stakeholders in Ghana's import-competing sectors, meanwhile, such as poultry and tomatoes, fear that a regional EPA will perpetuate the dumping of cheap European produce onto local markets. Bagooro documents that cheap poultry imports from the EU are already destroying local livelihoods and worsening conditions of poverty, a situation which would be very difficult to ameliorate under a permanent regional EPA. See Bagooro, *West Africa*.
56. For reasons of space and remit it is not possible to expand on the interview data in this current article; again please see Langan and Price (forthcoming) for more detail.
57. Asante-Poku and Angelucci, "Analysis of Incentives and Disincentives for Cocoa in Ghana."
58. Fair Labour Association, *Improving Workers' Lives*; Cargill, *Improving Livelihoods*; Callebaut, *The Cocoa Horizons Foundation*.
59. Agritrade, *Executive*.
60. European Commission, *Commission Staff Working*, 4.
61. ECA and CAOBISCO, *Initial Response*.
62. Sudwind and Global 2000, *Bittersweet Chocolate*, 14.
63. Tulane University, *2013–14 Survey*, 2.
64. Sudwind and Global 2000, *Bittersweet Chocolate*, 18.
65. Maconachie and Fortin, "On Ghana's."

66. Parry, "Putting Women"; Maconachie et al., *Gender.*
67. Marston, *Women's Rights*, 4.
68. Maconachie and Fortin, "On Ghana's."
69. International Cocoa Organisation, *World Cocoa.*
70. Such largescale agro-processing companies are keen to develop domestic processing capacity to integrate their internal supply chain, shipping and production, reflecting the horizontal and vertical concentration that is increasingly characterising the global cocoa value chain. This has been facilitated by technological innovation and financial incentives. While traditionally high grade beans were exported for processing abroad, technological developments now allow low quality beans to be processed into an exportable value added product at origin, which is then exported for further processing abroad.
71. Haigh, "Carving."
72. Ibid.
73. Ibid.
74. Adler, *La* via.
75. AFSA, *What is ASFA.*

Bibliography

Adler, S. *La via Campesina, Building an International Movement for Food and Seed Sovereignty. An Interview with General Coordinator Elizabeth Mpofu.* Accessed January 6, 2017. https://viacampesina.org/en/index.php/main-issues-mainmenu-27/food-sovereignty-and-trade-mainmenu-38/1963-la-via-campesina-building-an-international-movement-for-food-and-seed-sovereignty

Africa Europe Faith and Justice Network. *Oil Industries in Ghana.* Brussels: AEFJN, 2013. Accessed September 16, 2016. http://www.aefjn.org/index.php/370/articles/Oil_Industry_in_Ghana.html

African Development Bank. *Republic of Ghana Country Strategy Paper 2012–2016.* 2012. Accessed September 15, 2016. http://www.afdb.org/fileadmin/uploads/afdb/Documents/Project-and-Operations/Ghana%20-%20CSP%202012%20-%202016.pdf

AFSA (Alliance for Food Sovereignty in Africa). *What is AFSA.* Accessed January 7, 2017. http://afsafrica.org/what-is-afsa/

Agritrade. *Executive Brief Update 2013: Cocoa Sector.* 2013. Accessed September 16, 2016. http://agritrade.cta.int/Agriculture/Commodities/Cocoa/Executive-Brief-Update-2013-Cocoa-sector

Asante, K., and G. Mohan. "Transnational Capital and the Political Settlement of Ghana's Oil Economy." *ESID Working Paper, No. 49*, 2015. Accessed January 7, 2017. http://www.effective-states.org/working-paper-49/

Asante-Poku, A., and F. Angelucci. *"Analysis of Incentives and Disincentives for Cocoa in Ghana." Technical Note Series.* Rome: Food and Agriculture Organisation of the United Nations, 2013.

Bazilian, M., I. Onyeji, P.-K. Aqrawi, B. Sovacool, D. Kammen, and T. Van de Graaf. "Oil, Energy Poverty, and Resource Dependence in West Africa." *Journal of Energy and Natural Resources Law* 31, no. 1 (2013): 33–53.

Bagooro, S. *West Africa and Europe Trade: Who Will Benefit More?* Al Jazeera. Accessed June 22 2014. http://www.aljazeera.com/indepth/opinion/2014/06/west-africa-europe-trade-agree-2014621155835409177.html Accessed 1st January 2017

Booth, D., and F. Golooba-Mutebi. "Developmental Patrimonialism? The Case of Rwanda." *African Affairs* 111, no. 444 (2012): 379–403.

Brunnschweiler, C., and E. Bulte. "The Resource Curse Revisited and Revised: A Tale of Paradoxes and Red Herrings." *Journal of Environmental Economics and Management* 55, no. 3 (2008): 248–264.

Callebaut, Barry. *The Cocoa Horizons Foundation: Growing Impact, Driving Change.* 2017. Accessed January 30, 2017. https://www.barry-callebaut.com/sustainability/cocoa-sustainability/cocoa-horizons-foundation

Cargill. *Improving Livelihoods For Cocoa Farmers and Their Communities: The 2015 Cargill Cocoa Promise Global Report.* Wayzata: Cargill, 2015.

Cocoa Barometer. "Looking for a Living Income." *Cocoa Barometer*, 2015. Accessed September 15, 2016. http://www.cocoabarometer.org/Download.html

Cocoa Processing Company LTD. "Financial Statement 30th September 2014." Accessed January 5, 2017. http://www.goldentreeghana.com/cpc-accounts-2014-website.pdf

Dennys, H. "Tullow Oil Apologises to Ugandan Government Over Bribery Allegations." *The Telegraph*. London, March 22, 2013. Accessed September 16, 2016. http://www.telegraph.co.uk/finance/newsbysector/energy/oilandgas/9949319/Tullow-Oil-apologises-to-Ugandan-government-over-bribery-allegations.html

ECA and CAOBISCO. *Initial Response to the European Commission Staff Document*. Brussels: CAOBISCO/ECA. Accessed September 16, 2016. http://eca2.xsite.be/public/uploads/files/Microsoft%20Word%20-%20Initial%20response%20to%20the%20EC%20staff%20working%20document%20on%20Child%20Labour-April2010%20_2_.pdf

EITI. *What the EITI Does: Building Trust Through Transparency*. Olso: EITI, 2016. Accessed September 16, 2016. http://progrep.eiti.org/2016/glance/what-eiti-does

EITI. *Ghana*. Olso: EITI, 2016. Accessed September 16, 2016. https://eiti.org/es/implementing_country/4

European Commission. *Commission Staff Working Document – Trade and Worst Forms of Child Labour*. Brussels: European Commission, 2013.

European Commission. *National Indicative Programme Ghana 2014–2020*. Brussels: European Commission, 2014.

European Commission. *West African Leaders Back Economic Partnership Agreement with the EU*. Brussels: European Commission, 2014. Accessed September 16, 2016. http://europa.eu/rapid/press-release_IP-14-827_en.htm

European Commission. *A Global Partnership for Poverty Eradication and Sustainable Development After 2015*. Brussels: European Commission, 2015.

European Commission. *How Can the EPA Help Ghana's Sustainable Development?*. Brussels: European Commission, 2016.

European Commission. *The Economic Partnership Agreement (EPA): A New Partnership for Trade and Development*. Brussels: European Commission, 2016.

European Commission. *Trade – Countries and Regions – West Africa*. Brussels: European Commission, 2017. Accessed January 7, 2017. http://ec.europa.eu/trade/policy/countries-and-regions/regions/west-africa/index_en.htm

European Council. *Council Conclusions. A Global Partnership for Poverty Eradication and Sustainable Development After 2015*. Brussels: European Council, 2015.

European Parliament. *Resolution on Child Labour in Cocoa Sector*. Brussels: European Parliament, 2011.

European Parliament. *Resolution of 14 April 2016 on the Private Sector and Development*. Brussels: European Parliament, 2016.

Fair Labor Association. *Improving Workers' Lives Worldwide*. Washington, DC: Fair Labor Association, 2012.

Ghana Cocoa Board (Cocobod). *Cocoa*. Accessed January 5, 2017. https://cocobod.gh/home_section.php?sec=1

Ghana's Statistical Service. *Gross Domestic Product, 2014*. Accra: Ghana Statistical Service, 2014.

Ghana's Statistical Service. *Digest of International Merchandise Trade Statistics (2011–2015)*. Accra: Ghana's Statistical Service, 2016.

Government of Ghana. *Ghana Shared Growth and Development Agenda (GSGDA), 2014–2017*. Accra: Government of Ghana, 2014.

Haigh, C. "Carving Up a Continent: How the UK Government is Facilitating the Corporate Takeover of African Food Systems." *Report for the World Development Movement*. 2014. Accessed September 15, 2016. http://www.globaljustice.org.uk/sites/default/files/files/resources/carving_up_a_continent_report_web.pdf

Hickey, S., B. Bukenya, A. Izama, and W. Kizito. "The Political Settlement and Oil in Uganda." *ESID Working Paper, No. 48*, 2015. Accessed January 7, 2017. http://www.effective-states.org/working-paper-48-2/

Hilson, G., and C. Garforth. "'Everyone Now is Concentrating on the Mining': Drivers and Implications of Rural Economic Transition in the Eastern Region of Ghana." *Journal of Development Studies* 49, no. 3 (2013): 348–364.

Hope, A., and A. Kwarteng. *CSR and Sustainable Development in the Mining Industry: The case of Newmont Ghana Gold*. Leeds: CRR Conference, 2014.

International Cocoa Organisation. *The World Cocoa Economy: Past and Present*. London: International Cocoa Organisation Committee, 2014.

Kolavalli, S., and M. Vigneri. *Cocoa in Ghana: Shaping the Success of an Economy*. 2008. Accessed September 1, 2016. http://siteresources.worldbank.org/AFRICAEXT/Resources/258643-1271798012256/ghana_cocoa.pdf

Langan, M. and S. Price. Forthcoming. West Africa-EU Trade and Cocoa Agro-processing: Assessing Business Stakeholders? Perspectives on "Pro-Poor" Private Sector Development.

Lawson, M. *Foreign Aid: International Donor Coordination of Development Assistance*. Washington, DC: Congressional Research Service, 2013.

Lungu, N. "This Mahama-Dagadu-Buah. E&P Bill is a Vulture Bill for Oil Companies." *The Voiceless*. Accra, 2016. Accessed September 16, 2016. http://thevoicelessonline.com/6388-2/

Maconachie, R., and E. Fortin. "On Ghana's Cocoa Farms, Fairtrade is Not Yet Working for Women." *The Guardian*. Accessed January 7, 2017. https://www.theguardian.com/global-development/2016/mar/11/ghana-cocoa-farms-fairtrade-not-yet-working-for-women

Maconachie, R., and G. Hilson. "Editorial Introduction: The Extractive Industries, Community Development and Livelihood Change in Developing Countries." *Community Development Journal* 48, no. 3 (2013): 347–359.

Maconachie, R., E. Fortin, and S. Wharfe. *Gender and Fairtrade – The Stories of Women Cocoa Farmers in Ghana*. Accessed January 7, 2017. http://www.bath.ac.uk/sps/staff/roy-maconachie/

Marston, A. *Women's Rights in the Cocoa Sector: Examples of Emerging Good Practice*. London: Oxfam, 2016.

Ministry of Trade. *Draft Sector Medium Term Development Plan, 2014–2017*. Accra: Ministry of Trade, 2014.

Mohammed, A. "Oil Find: Ghana is Losing More Than What it Gains?" *News Ghana*. Accra, September 3, 2014. Accessed September 16, 2016. https://www.newsghana.com.gh/oil-find-ghana-losing-gains/

Okoh, G. "Grievance and Conflict in Ghana's Gold Mining Industry: The Case of Obuasi." *Futures* 62 (2014): 51–57.

Olanya, D. "Will Uganda Succumb to the Resource Curse? Critical Reflections." *The Extractive Industries and Society* 2, no. 1 (2015): 46–55.

Oxford Policy Management. *Ghana Oil and Gas for Inclusive Growth (GOGIG)*. Oxford: Oxford Policy Management, 2015.

Parry, M. "Putting Women at the Centre of Cocoa Production in Ghana." *The Guardian*. Accessed January 6, 2017. https://www.theguardian.com/sustainable-business/fairtrade-partner-zone/women-centre-cocoa-production-ghana

Platform London. *Tullow Oil's Foul Play in Ghana*. London: Platform London, June 28, 2012. Accessed September 16, 2016. http://platformlondon.org/2012/06/28/tullow-oils-foul-play-in-ghana

Segbefia, L. "Petroleum Commission Rejects Claim E&P Bill Lacks Transparency." *Citi FM Online*. Accra, July 24, 2016. Accessed September 16, 2016. http://citifmonline.com/2016/07/24/petroleum-commission-rejects-claims-ep-bill-lacks-transparency/

Sowah, D. *Ghana-EU Economic Partnership Agreement*. Accra: Ministry of Trade, n.d. Accessed September 16, 2016. http://www.traqueghana.org/files/03-EPA-Presentation.pdf

Sudwind and Global 2000. *Bittersweet Chocolate: The Truth Behind the International Chocolate Industry*. Innsbruck: Sudwind, 2016. Accessed January 1, 2017. http://www.supplychainge.org/fileadmin/reporters/eu_files/Chocolate_032016_Langversion_web.pdf

Tulane University. *2013/14 Survey Research on Child Labor in West African Cocoa Growing Areas*. New Orleans, LA: Tulan University, 2013. Accessed September 16, 2016. http://www.childlaborcocoa.org/images/Payson_Reports/Tulane%20University%20-%20Two-Page%20Summary%20of%20Research%20Findings%20-%2030%20July%202015.pdf

UNCTAD (United Nations Conference on Trade and Development). *Cocoa Industry: Integrating Small Farmers into the Global Value Chain*. 2016. Accessed January 6, 2017. http://unctad.org/en/PublicationsLibrary/suc2015d4_en.pdf

Van der Ploeg, F. "Natural Resources: Curse or Blessing?" *Journal of Economic Literature* 49, no. 2 (2011): 366–420.

World Cocoa Foundation. *Cocoa Market Update*. 2012. Accessed September 14, 2016. http://www.worldcocoafoundation.org/wp-content/uploads/Cocoa-Market-Update-as-of-3.20.2012.pdf

Index